Grandmaster Jembefola Famoudou Konate and Kojo Bey at Famoudou's shrine in the
village of his birth. Mane, Guinea
Photo Credit: Mustapha Berete
Source: Kojo Bey

Copyright © 2022 by BEYKO PUBLISHING

JEMBE REVOLUTION

The Birth of the Jembe in America

ISBN: 979-8-9876068-1-0

Published by: BEYKO PUBLISHING
7926 Robinson Church Rd
Charlotte, NC 28215

Editor: Tareka Allyn Verbal
Cover art: Rajuma Bey
Cover design: Golden Box Books Publishing

JEMBE REVOLUTION

The Birth of the Jembe in America

by
Kojo Bey

CONTENTS

Foreword

African drum and dance came to America in 1929 and at that time the drum that was played was the ashiko drum. As time moved on, the art of African drumming and dance excelled into different styles and genres from the African Diaspora such as Afro Cuban, Afro Haitian, Afro Brazilian, and Afro Caribbean. In 1959, West African drum and dance arrived in the United States by way of the Les Ballets Africains company. From there the jembe became the most popular hand drum played worldwide today.

This publication will offer the reader the history of the early days of African drumming in America. Accordingly to my research, the tumbadora a/k/a the conga drum followed the ashiko drum. By the late fifties came the jembe drum. You will also learn about who introduced the jembe to America and how that changed African drumming, dancing and music here. The reader will learn through interviews and research how the traditional craft of jembe making changed forever once the drum reached the shores of America.

As drummers and dancers we are obligated to keep the African Diaspora alive for our ancestors who taught and trained us. May they rest in peace. Ashe Ashe. Modupe.

Bradley Simmons, Professor/Musical Director

Duke University

Durham, NC USA

Preface

"Everyone want to be Master Drummer."
Ladji Camara

In the spring of 2002, I met with Ladji Camara to explore the possibility of writing this book. As I entered Ladji's home in the Bronx, NY simplicity came to mind right away. His home was not filled with furniture and decorum. I could see that he was a devout Muslim committed to his prayers by the intentionally positioned prayer rug and photos in his sitting room. Ladji was in and out of his kitchen upon my arrival offering me beverages and food. His first profound statement to me was that "People don't know the history of jembe. Everyone want to be Master Drummer." Ladji, affectionately known as "Papa Ladji" also told me during our session, "I have students all over the world who I teach. They must learn more than just drumming. There are some that I even give my name to." He paused then flashed a smile at me and said, "Yes, there are Japanese students with the last name Camara!" He let out a laugh that let me know that he was fully aware of his influence over many drummers. At the same time his laugh was followed by affirmative head nods letting me know that he was very much so serious about his relationships with his students.

In addition to Ladji Camara's wit and sense of humor, he was one of Les Ballets Africains' first lead jembe drummers and the first to bring the jembe drum onstage in America. He stands out as one of the greatest jembe players whom America and possibly the globe has ever seen. He was performing with Guinea's premier performing group at a time when West African countries were reclaiming their independence and America was seeing an emergence of a civil rights and black power movement within the African American community. Ladji's students believed that he was sent on a mission to America to help fuel a movement and expand the African consciousness of blacks in America through the jembe and Manding music and dance.

Ladji Camara
Source: Bradley Simmons
~

On that spring day in 2002, Papa Ladji had me shadow his movements throughout the day. As we moved around, I observed his joy and love for life. He shared jewels of knowledge with me from my initial entrance into his space, throughout my visit, and as I was leaving him. His earlier sharing began to resonate within my spirit. He talked about working on one's character and truly loving the drum in order to be a great jembe drummer.

The sunny clear day made it possible to visit Papa Ladji's routine daily stops with ease. We moved around the Grand Concourse in the Bronx, New York and strolled by a number of his frequently visited places including the fresh vegetable and fruit market, then onto the mosque for afternoon prayer. At each destination, people greeted Papa Ladji with smiles and warmth. Papa Ladji made sure that he introduced me to all of his admirers so that I would be blessed with that good energy as well. "This is my friend Kojo," Papa Ladji would say. I did feel good. I felt renewed. I felt nurtured and included. I could not help but think about the many drummers and dancers Papa Ladji taught throughout his years in America.

After only one day with Ladji Camara, I felt motivated to approach my life and my drum with a renewed sense of commitment and love. I cannot even imagine the impact that Papa Ladji had on those other students who spent years with him. My time with Papa Ladji made it easy to see how he became the father of a cultural arts revolution in America. I believe that once Ladji arrived in America to perform with Les Ballets Africains in 1959, he was a conduit for divine orchestration. He had a master plan that would put him on a mission to spread his teachings throughout the world. He wanted people to know that there was more to the jembe and the Manding dances than just entertainment. Papa Ladji wanted the drummer, dancer, and observer to experience a deeper sense of connectiveness to the Manding culture, art, and jembe. Ladji Camara's impact on the African drum and dance genre in America was trailblazing! There were, however, a number of important drummers, dancers, events, places, and developments that took place before, during, and after Papa Ladji's arrival into New York that helped to contribute to the jembe drum explosion. JEMBE REVOLUTION: The Birth of the Jembe in America, is an attempt to highlight these people, places and events.

There have been many works written about the mysterious instrument called jembe and many recordings produced with its unique and energetic sound. Yet, for all of its years outside of Africa and into the Western world, the history of the jembe in America is largely unknown. Many recognize the jembe all over the world, however, even as the jembe continues to grow in popularity, new generations are born and the jembe has become more commercial than cultural or traditional. Today, young men and women all over the globe are unable to name the individuals who played major roles in the beginning of the jembe revolution in America. This is deplorable because to overstand today's jembe, one must overstand its history and the impact on global drumming.

This book is not meant to demystify the jembe. It is an effort to show the jembe through the lens of African drummers and dancers who were actively involved in the art form in America before, during and after the jembe became popular. From the 1930s until the late 1950s, the jembe drum had not yet arrived in America. However, African dancers were dancing to the sounds of congas, ashikos, and Haitian drums during this period. When Siguiri, Guinea born artist Fodeba Keita toured his group in America in 1959, the jembe took center stage. Subsequently, it would be events in the 1960s that would capture the attention of American born African drummers and consequently mesmerize them with the jembe drum. These events included the recording of the song "Wasalu" on Olatunji's second album called More Drums of Passion. "The World's Fair of 1964/65"; Les Ballets Africains' performance at the United Nations in 1968; and dancer/choreographer Katherine Dunham's college tour accompanied by jembe drummer Mor Thiam in the late 1960s and early 1970s.

In preparing this book, I spent thousands of hours interviewing elder drummers, dancers, and researching various archives. I believe that these artists were all honest with me and were committed to telling their truth as they lived it. I cannot possibly list all of the reviewed archived material and publications. I am, however, grateful to the many individuals listed in the Appendix who granted interviews for this publication.

Throughout this publication, a variety of opinions are expressed. I would like the reader to try and discern between fact and opinion and note that I do not necessarily agree with every quoted statement. I sought a wide variety of sources to allow for as many varied views as possible. Whenever quotations appear in the publication, I have indicated quoted source in the notes at the end of the book with the exception of those which I obtained from an interview conducted specifically for this book.

Readers may believe certain drummers and dancers should have been interviewed and quoted for this publication. Those included in this publication are those who agreed to interviews. Other drummers and dancers were contacted but declined involvement in the project. Some who were not interviewed are mentioned because of their contributions to the history of the jembe. Yet others are mentioned because they worked closely with drummers and dancers quoted in this book. There was no intention on the author's part to consciously leave any important individual or group out of this publication. Specifically, this book has set date parameters for the history of the jembe in America, principally from the 1930s to the early 1980s. A second volume of this publication would cover the 1980s to the present and would include as primary sources those younger artists who were either too young or had not yet been born during the period covered by this publication.

Currently, the jembe is played all over the world by the young and old of all skill levels. It was not always like this and the drum certainly did not always look the way it looks today. I have enjoyed many myths and stories about the mystical jembe. However, I have enjoyed learning more about my favorite instrument from the mouths of those who started the Jembe Revolution.

Kojo Bey

Charlotte, NC

Chapter 1

Jembe

"Jembe is supposed to talk. Today the jembe is very tight."
Famoudou Konate

The jembe is a rope-tuned, skin-covered, goblet-shaped drum played with bare hands, originally from West Africa. In Western music terms, the jembe is classified as a membranophone instrument which consists of a resonating chamber or body with one or two membrane heads. A jembe has one animal skin fixed to the top of the drum shell carved from a single piece of wood. Currently, goat skins are most commonly used for the jembe. Antelope and calf have been used as choice skins for the jembe as well. The Manding people traditionally used wood from the lenke trees which holds great spiritual importance for them while also lending the drum its resounding acoustic. It is normally 23-25" in height but can be smaller in many villages in Africa. The average jembe drumhead ranges from 12-15" in diameter. The weight of a jembe ranges from 11–29 lbs. depending on size and shell material. A medium-sized jembe carved from one of the traditional woods (including skin, rings, and rope) weighs around 20 lbs. The jembe is popular throughout Africa and around the globe. It is indeed the most familiar among the African percussion instruments. It was said to have been created by the Manding or Mende people. The Manding empire spanned the modern-day countries of Senegal, Gambia, Guinea, Guinea-Bissau, Ivory Coast, Mali, and Burkina Faso.

Ladji Camara's jembe with no hole tuning
"Africa, New York Drum Masterpieces" Album cover
New York, NY
Photo Credit: Daryl Solomon
Source: Kojo Bey

Up until the 1980s, the most common mounting system used twisted strips of cowhide as rope. The skin was attached with rings made of cowhide; one ring was sewn into the perimeter of the skin and a second ring placed below it, with loops holding the skin in place and securing the two rings together. A long strip of cowhide was used to lace up the drum, applying tension between the top ring and a third ring placed around the stem. The tension was increased by weaving the vertical sections of the rope into a diamond pattern that shortened the verticals. Wooden pegs wedged between the shell and the lacing could be used to increase tension still further. The pitch of these traditional jembes was much lower than it is today because the natural materials imposed a limit on the amount of tension that could be applied. Prior to playing, Jembefolas heated the skin near the flames of an open fire, which drives moisture out of the skin and causes it to shrink and increase the pitch of the drum.

The jembe can produce a wide variety of sounds, making it an extremely versatile drum. The drum is very loud, allowing it to be heard clearly as a solo instrument over a large percussion ensemble.

Historic jembe with peg tuning system
Source: Musee de l'Homme, Paris

Famoudou Konate is the oldest active Jembefola in Guinea. Mr. Konate served as lead jembe drummer and Musical Director for Les Ballets Africains from the 1960s to the 1980s. He is regarded as the Grandmaster of the jembe drum.

Famoudou Konate: "Jembe is supposed to talk. Today the jembe is very tight. Jembe should have some ring so it can speak. The sound is not aggressive. All of my children play jembe. Someone playing jembe is not supposed to be angry. Someone playing jembe is not supposed to be a jealous person. They should be about unity and happiness. You have to love the jembe before you can make people happy from playing the jembe."

* * *

Unlike many other hand percussion drums, the jembe's versatility in sound in one drum makes it more convenient for the drummer to carry around to classes and performances. Other hand percussions such as congas require the drummer to travel with several drums in an attempt to match the versatility of sound that the jembe produces.

Another type of drum, the dundun, is a double-headed, cylinder-shaped drum that is used to accompany jembe playing. In Guinea, the three sizes are the small kenkeni, medium-sized sangban, and large dundunba.

15

Chapter 2

Nummu

"The King can do nothing without getting the permission from the Nummu people" Amara Kante
~

The early history of the jembe is a mystery. Some say that drummers playing jembe and dundun drums were members of the massive caravan for Mansa Musa's famous pilgrimage to Mecca in the early 1300s. Within village life, the jembe was played by those born for the drum; those whose family members could see their destiny even before birth. Other times, the community could see the spirit of a Jembefola on a child when they were very young. A drum would be made for them by the Nummu, but the jembe would belong to the village. The jembe would be brought out for the young drummer to play for special occasions such as rituals, weddings, births, circumcisions, festivals, and other events. Originally, it was the Nummu who played the jembe and they were the ones who spread its reach out among other members of the community who were not Nummu.

Nummus, who are primarily blacksmiths, also have several important associations with music making. As sculptors, Nummus carve jembe drums and are also associated with jembe playing. Although jembe playing is not a hereditary profession, the Nummu family names such as Camara, Kante, and Dumbia are common among professional jembe drummers.

As providers of iron implements, Nummus were and still are, guardians of certain kinds of power. Nummus hands sculpt the power-laden wooden Komo masks that are emblems for the secret societies they lead and they perform the circumcisions and excisions that lift the dangerous energies of boys and girls, marking their entrance into adulthood. They also forge the hoes used for agricultural labor. Jembes are directly tied to each of these enterprises. They are played for the Komo society, for circumcision and excision ceremonies, to accompany agricultural labor, and to celebrate the harvest. Nummus are also the ones who carve the bodies of jembes, and they are often the ones who play them. Jembes are carved from a single piece of wood, the most common kinds being lenke (linge), dugur, and jala, among others. The preference for one wood over another might vary by region and availability. Lenke is particularly prized in part because of the belief that it is spiritually charged.1

I know a good number of 'jembe doctors' and even some who carve out logs to create jembes. I had not met an actual Nummu until I met with Amara Kante. We connected via phone first and the link was special from the onset of the conversation. Once Amara discerned my intentions and the purpose of this publication, he began to tear up and speak to me through the wiping of tears and the cracks in his voice. His strong Malinke accent was unable to mask the sounds of a tearful conversation. He explained that his tears were tears of joy sparked by a Black American (as West Africans like to call us), who wanted to know Nummu history. Amara shared that my research inspired him and was, from his perspective, a commitment to bring drummers together through this book. I traveled to Toronto, Canada to conduct my physical interview with Amara Kante. I was completely motivated to get this interview after experiencing the depth of Mr. Kante's knowledge about the jembe and Nummu on the phone. I had learned years ago some of the surnames that were associated with Nummu, and Kante was one of those.

When we met at my hotel, Amara asked to interview me first. I had already experienced conversations mixed with English, French, and Malinke during my research in Guinea. So Mr. Kante's occasional phrases in his native tongue, Malinke, were quite familiar. After hearing about my background and the premise of the book, he asked me to follow him outside. First, we went to his car and retrieved one of his oldest jembes that he said was very special to him. In fact, he said that while driving over to meet with me, he kept asking himself, "What does this man really want?" At some point, he heard that POP sound that we jembe drummers dread to hear when we are traveling with our drum. He said he turned around and went home with his drum to meditate on this meeting and to take a look at this drum. He decided, however, to pack up the drum and follow through with the meeting with me. At his car, he took that drum out of the drum bag and showed me the popped head. This jembe was very unique and had a mystical look to it. Amara asked me, "What do you see?" I said, "I see a broken head." He smiled and said, "What else do you see in that broken head?" I told him that I did not see anything else. I felt a bit disappointed in myself because with all of the many broken jembe heads I had repaired and handled throughout the years, I did not have any other insight to share with Mr. Kante. He pointed to the actual tear in the skin and ran his finger from one corner to the other making an arch shape in the air. I said, "A SMILE!" He smiled at me and said, "That's why I am here. The spirit of the drum gave me my answer as to why you are here and what you really want from me. The pop in the drumhead and the smile shape got my attention and told me that you are here for something very good and that I have to do something for you to help you." I was humbled by his sharing. I thanked him and stared at that smile on his drum. I thought about the many jembe heads that had popped throughout my years which I had not taken time to sit to see what THEY were telling ME.

Amara Kante asked me to follow him to our next destination. We walked to a very busy intersection in Toronto outside of my hotel. Mrs. Amara Kante was accompanying us and she became a bit uneasy with the direction we were headed. Amara stayed quiet and focused on an intersection. Once we reached the corner and the traffic slowed a bit, Mr. Kante had me follow him to the middle of the intersection. He performed a prayer and ritual which included me, fire, and gunpowder. Afterwards, while still standing in the middle of the busy intersection, he explained why he was instructed to do that for me. He told me that this book was even more important than I was aware. He had to put protection around me because I had been given a very important job by dedicating my life and time to this book. I acknowledged that I comprehended his explanation and we set off to my hotel room for the interview.

The interview with Mr. Kante offered so much more than I had anticipated. With each passing moment, the research I had done on Nummu became more and more real through my observations of Amara. He showed me his drum making tools, spiritual devices, and old items that had obviously been passed down to him from his ancestors. He even played some jembe in honor of his Nummu lineage. Nummu is not just about being a blacksmith. It is a lifestyle that I am honored to have gained insight about...firsthand.

* * *

Amara Kante: "I come from a family of Nummus. I am Nummu. The Nummu is a big history. When God made all the planets, he gave this origin history for the Nummu. Nummu is not just to learn the metal. Nummu is not just to make the jembe. Nummu is the imagination for the creation of art and industry. It is not just 'I'm born a Nummu and so I am a Nummu.' Not all Nummu have this power. You need to understand a lot before you can call yourself Nummu. The name Nummu on the

Malinke side was 'Siaki.' Why? Because we make everything. The Nummu people have a lot of magic.

The king can't do anything without getting permission from the Nummu people. The king cannot take a throne without the Nummu people giving him permission.

The Kante people are big. Anyone who knows the history of the region knows who they are. Soumaourou Kante was the king of the Malinke empire before Sundiata Keita. The Nummu people are a lot. Bamba, Fane, many Dumbia, many Cissoko, all Balo are Nummu, Fakoli, many Traore, Bagayogo, and many Camara. But all Kante are King of the Nummu.

I want to thank my masters Mamoudou Camara di Massa Camio, Issa Balo, Sekou Camara di Cobra du Mandingue, Mamady Keita Ntoma from Sakodugu. Other teachers who have influenced me greatly are Numudi Keita, Soungalo Koulibaly, and Famoudou Konate.

Teachers who have done a lot for jembe culture in the world and I have respect and gratitude for their contribution are: Bolokada Conde, Mamady Keita, Mbembe Bangoura, and Koungbana Conde.

I want to also mention those who the people might not know because they are dead. Thank you Baworo Keita, Numudy Keita, Lamin Suma Lopez, Fatabou Camara, Lauren Camara, Italo Zambo, Amidou Bangoura, Fodeba Keita, Suleman Koli, and President Ahmed Sekou Toure."

Les Percussion de Guinea's lead Jembefola throughout the mid 1990s into the early 2000s, Bolokada Conde, explained the teachings of Nummu from his native Sankaran, Guinea during our interview.

Bolokada Conde: "Traditionally when the Nummu made the drum, it was for the whole village. They would take it out for the drummer to play when there was something going on, then they took the drum back. Nummu made big knife. Nummu made hoe for the farmer. Nummu made hunting tools. Nummu made metal tools for building house.

Jembe was first important with the tree. When you see a good tree for the drum, there may be devil in that tree. Nummu has the special words; kind of praying that they would do at the tree before cutting it down to make sure it was safe for making the drum. After they cut it down,

19

everyone in the village does the praying around the wood before Nummu makes the drum.

The first jembe I played, we put skin in the water and put the skin on carved out wood and tied fabric around the skin and then put it in the sun. Other times, we put skin in water then put skin on the wood and hammer nails through skin onto wood then put in the sun. When the sun went down, we put the drum by the fire. Then, we learned how to sew the skins on and we used strips of skin to make the up and down and you couldn't pull too strong or you would rip the skin. We put it in the sun and play and as the skin cooled down, the sound would go down.

If anyone tell you that they know the first person to make the jembe you don't use it. Get away from them. No one knows the very first jembe that was made. All of the seven Mende (Manding) countries (Guinea, Senegal, Mali, Ivory Coast, Guinea Bissau, Liberia, Sierra Leonne) say that jembe come from their country first."

Lenke trees (Birthplace of Grandmaster Jembefola Famoudou Konate) Mane, Guinea
Photo credit: Kojo Bey

Founder of Tam Tam Mandingue Djembe Academy and one of the world's most famous Jembefolas, Mamady Keita, shared Nummu knowledge from the teachings of his birthplace, Balandugu, Guinea.

Mamady Keita: "The actual form of the jembe probably evolved from the mortar, at least that is what the old people and my master from Balandugu say; may he rest in peace. In the past, the drums were made by the blacksmiths (Nummu). The ceremonies accompanying the making of a jembe were still conducted as recently as twenty years ago. At that time, the jembe was built only for one's own private use. Unlike today, there was no commercial interest. Nobody would ever have thought to take money for the making of a drum. The village jembe player went to the blacksmith, gave him ten kola nuts, and asked him to make a new jembe. The blacksmith considered the making of such a drum an honor. First of all, they would go to see the tree that was to be cut. This tree most often would be a lenke tree, and they would dance, sing and drum before it. The blacksmith and his companions would bring kola nuts to the tree in order to tell the spirit of the tree that it had been chosen, and, at the same time, apologize for the cutting. After the tree had been cut, the outer rough form of the drum would be carved, then the body would be hollowed out. Another ceremony would give the jembe its voice after all the woodwork had been done and the first skin was mounted. A long time ago, this was the skin of an antelope; later goatskin was used. Finally, the jembe's skin would be stretched and tightened, and when it was played for the first time, there would be another ceremony, which would give it its voice. Even today, it is customary that jembe players give their drums kola nuts in order to be protected, for instance, from competition with drummers from different villages."[2]

Famoudou Konate: "Nummu are the blacksmiths. They know the wood. They know what the sound will be like when they work with the wood. Before, the only wood that they used to make jembe was lenke. The Nummu people used to play jembe. If you need a jembe, there was a trade instead of money; one goat for one jembe. We were not buying the skin either. The people who were slaughtering goats would give the skins to the people that play the jembe after work. All the drummers before me always gave their jembes some medicine. Jembe came from the mortar. There were four different types of jembes in the old days:

Sule jembe (mortar)

Bran jembe (small hole in the middle)

Tassa jembe (big head jembe) – sounds like metal sounds and tuning is little, but the sounds are high.

Jembe Jukudun (Cut the stem in half) – only get bass sound from this jembe, and the sound is not high and loud because that stem is cut in half."

Woman with mortar and pestle
Source: BritishMuseum.com

One of Mali's top Jembefolas, Moussa Traore, shared his understanding of Nummu from his native land of Mali, West Africa.

Moussa Traore: "Nummu are the blacksmith people. Nummu transform metal into something. They have a lot of power and do ceremonies for the community. They make the tools. They used to do circumcisions for the community. Nummu people are Dumbiya, Kante, Bangoura (Bangayugo), Cissoko, Fane, and Fakoli. Nummu people make the jembes. A lot of people make good jembes now, but the first jembes we played were made by the Nummu people."

Amara Kante: "Many people play the jembe but they don't know where it came from. The jembe is from the woman. And it is the woman who gave this gift to the Nummu people to keep safe, to develop, and to share. To know the jembe is not to just play a simple drum. You must understand and respect the history, and the root. To know the jembe is to know yourself deep. You must understand the sacred trees and elements used to make the jembe.

The original wood for jembe was lenke, jalla, iroko wood (hade or bala wood is new for business. It's not one of the original trees for jembe). Jalla is one tree for medicine. When you are sick. Take jalla, iroko, and lenke put it in a pot and boil and shower with it. Lenke wood is sacred wood to do special sacred things on the jembe.

When Nummu make the jembe the body has its own story. The jembe head is the mouth or in Malinke "Da"- mouth. Around the bowl or navel area is called "Bada" (In Malinke it's only around the navel) is the body of the jembe. "Soro" is the back or neck of the jembe. "Tole" is the bottom where everything comes out. That is a language."

* * *

While spending time in Siguiri, Guinea with my good friend Mustapha Berete who was also serving as my translator and escort, I learned about a percussion relative to the jembe, the bada drum. I was told the bada was more popular than the jembe in the Siguiri area at one time. I find it interesting when Amara Kante identified the different parts of the jembe using the Malinke language that he identified the bowl or the naval part of the jembe as "bada." When I was able to see an old bada drum up close, it looked like the bowl of a jembe with the stem part cut off. When I visited Siguiri, it was my first time hearing about and/or seeing a bada drum. I later mentioned the bada drum to Amara, and he confirmed that he knew of its history. He was very pleased to hear that I had learned about the bada drum and documented it well during my research trip.

I had heard that there was a family in Siguiri who preserved the bada drum of one of the most famous bada drummers in the region. In fact, this drummer came from a lineage whose ancestors were the original creators of the bada drum. After making inquiries in the community, we

23

found the family of the deceased Badafola, Nummu Segou. I was very surprised to see this drum looked like a twenty-inch jembe with the bottom stem cut off. It had straps on it and seke sekes all around the front. They had used kuna wood for the bada drum with a large goat skin sewn on the shell with cord that ran from the goat skin to a ring on the bottom made from skin and fabric. They put the bada in the sun to tune it, but they also used a formula to rub on the skin to help get a unique sound. The formula was a mix of kanya (honeycomb), cow hair, and black soap rubbed in the middle of skin. When tuned properly, the bada sound had a high and loud pitch. They had about five to six seke sekes around it.

We sought out Nummu Segou's relatives who knew about the history of the bada and how to play it. We traveled to another village to meet up with an eighty-year-old elder, Nouma Coulbaly. He was the most knowledgeable person to talk about the bada drum. He estimated that his ancestors created the bada drum over two hundred years ago.

Nouma Coulbaly and nephew (Descendants of Badafola, Nummu Segou)
Siguiri, Guinea
Photo credit: Kojo Bey

Bada drum (Owned by Badafola, Nummu Segou.)
Siguiri, Guinea
Photo credit: Kojo Bey

* * *

Nouma Coulbaly: "My ancestors came from Segou, Mali and migrated to Karata, Guinea. They were the original Manding. The original kuna bada drum came from Segou, Mali. Jumamusa Segou taught his younger brother Nummu Segou so he could do farming, and the younger brother became very famous. The bada drum was just kept for the family that's why it never got popular and spread out.

Bada drum was played as a lead drum for very important events like funerals, for important elders in the community, weddings, and annual spiritual rituals. When there was a wedding procession only one bada drum was played as the lead and multiple jembes as accompaniment. When dancers would begin dancing, then jembes would lead and solo."

Mustapha Berete recalls in his childhood seeing and hearing Nummu Segou play his bada in wedding processions throughout the streets of Siguiri.

Mustapha Berete: "The most famous Badafola was Nummu Segou. The 1940s was when he was playing a lot. The bada was a very special drum and had its own unique sound. When it was played you knew there was a very special event going on."

* * *

The Nummu history is very important to learn and research as a drummer and as an enthusiast of the Manding culture. According to Amara Kante, who comes from a line of Nummus, the Nummu was and still remains in Manding society. I recall stories of how various Jembefolas from West Africa received their first jembes from Nummu. Those stories were both romantic and mystical. Once the jembe arrived in America in the late 1950s and 1960s, it was virtually impossible to find a jembe to purchase. It was only the Jembefolas from the Ballets who owned the jembe drums. Thanks goes to Jembefolas Ladji Camara and Famoudou Konate for establishing relationships with Black Americans. These Jembefolas inspired drum makers in New York to embody the spirit of Nummu. I was surprised and inspired to find out about the different drummers in America who were carving, stringing up, and repairing their versions of jembes in the 1960s and 1970s.

I received my first jembe from a drum maker in Crenshaw, California named Harold Lot. Harold would travel to Humboldt County in California and cut down trees like a lumberjack. Then he would bring sections of the trees to the basement in his home in Crenshaw. He had built a turning machine to hollow out the logs. I was hooked the first time I saw his basement workshop and all the drums and skins throughout his house. I knew I wanted to be in that life. Harold offered me a selection of jembes to choose from which he had bought from a wholesaler. At that time, the popular jembes were lightweight with the long stem that flared out dramatically at the base of the drum. I had seen so many drummers playing that kind of jembe. Then he showed me a few he had made from a cedar tree he had cut down and hollowed out using his basement machine. My first jembe was the one handmade by Harold, the African American in Crenshaw, California. Harold taught me how to tune the drum using the Malian weave. I did not always remember the proper tuning pattern, so most of the time I used heat from my home stove, the sun, and portable heaters I carried around with my jembe. It was not until I began purchasing drums from wholesalers from Senegal, Guinea, and the Ivory Coast that I learned the ins and outs of stringing up the jembe. I would travel to Brooklyn and sit with Sekou Hylton. He was a Panamanian who was THE drum doctor at that time in New York. I took apart many jembes to learn how to string up those drums. I studied and studied. Both Harold and Sekou were generous with sharing information about building, tuning, and maintaining drums. Sekou was more than generous though. He showed me step by step and let me do some hands-on training in his workshop. He would always copy some blazing jembe music and gift me when I would go to his workshop for a repair. Harold also gifted me with my first audio copy and first video of Les Ballets Africains. I took what I learned from Harold and Sekou and I ran off with the drum doctor thing. From that point forward, I always maintained an inventory of jembe and dundun shells, skins, rings, rope and straps. I would always have my drums and skins available for purchase at every drum and dance class, workshop, and conference I attended.

I told this story to one of my elders and advisor to this book, Baba David Coleman, and he laughed. Baba David was a Teacher, Drummer, Yoruba Priest of Obatala, Drum maker, and Singer. When you speak about early African drumming in America, Baba David's name is always mentioned as an active participant as well as a valuable source of information. Baba schooled me on the tuning system I believed was an ancient system passed down from African drum makers to Harold and Sekou. He opened my eyes to the source of the "no hole tuning system." Baba David explained that this source is one who many jembe drummers today still do not know. Baba David Coleman spoke of none other than Chief Bey.

Not only did I feel honored to learn this information, but I felt an incredible sense of liberation. I learned that the system that called for all of the rings I had ordered and eventually welded, all of the cradles/hitches I had strung up on those rings, and the many hours I spent on each drum in pursuit of a consistent look had been created by an African American. I have seen so many jembes and dundun drums come in from West Africa throughout my years, and I was now in the jembe business. I have seen so many professional drummers from all over the globe perform with jembes strung up with the "no hole system." During my time spanning from my milestone trip to Crenshaw to purchase my first jembe from Harold Lot to my trips to Brooklyn to have my drums re-headed and repaired by Sekou Hylton, I had believed the tuning system had originated in Africa.

* * *

Baba David Coleman: "Chief told me about the time he ran into Sekou Hylton. Chief pointed to Sekou's jembe and asked whose work was that. Sekou said, "It's my work." Chief gave him an explicit gesture and said 'That's my system right there.' "

Sekou Hylton: "I bought my first drum from Abiodun McCray. He said the first time you have to fix the drum I will show you how to do it, but the next time you will have to pay. After my drum broke I did it myself and the other drummers were impressed with how I did my drum. Abiodun had an accident and ended up paying me to fix his drum when it needed to be fixed."

* * *

Abiodun McCray was one of the founders of the troupe Calabash in Brooklyn and Chief Bey was THE drum maker in Brooklyn. Like the majority of drummers in Brooklyn, Abiodun was influenced by Chief Bey. Anyone who was using rings and cradles to put heads on drums without sewing the skin on the ring was using the "no hole system."

When the question arises as to who started the "no hole system" of tuning the jembe and dunduns, a few names come to mind: Famoudou Konate, Balogun Love, Baba Yomi Yomi, and Chief Bey. When Ladji Camara, Mor Thiam, and the drummers from Les Ballets Africains came to America in the late 1950s and 1960s, all of the drumheads were either tacked on or sewn onto the drum shells. Then the drums had to be placed in the sun or by a heater to tune for classes and performances. Chief Bey had already changed the tuning system on his ashiko drum so the notes would stay consistent without heating the skin so most naturally assumed he was the one to create the "no hole system" for tuning the jembe and dunduns. I reached out to a number of elders who were there when this system was created and pushed out to the globe.

* * *

One of the founding members of the International Afrikan American Ballet, Denise Bey, spoke about the trailblazer Chief Bey.

Denise Bey: "I was a Daddy's girl. Chief James Hawthorne Bey was my Father. I know how to string my own jembe. He taught me how to string shekeres. He cut up shekeres and taught me how to string up shekeres. I learned all of my instrument making skills from the master - Chief. I watched him go from putting holes in the skin to coming up with the no hole system with the 3 rims. Watching him go through that process of not piercing the skins. When people were piercing the skins back in the day where eventually every time they tightened it the skin would rip. Even a good skin would lose its longevity because you pierced it. He figured that out. He had one of those really big drums that looked like a conga. It was a monster ashiko drum. It was tightened by strings. Yomi Yomi got the no hole system from Chief Bey. He was Chief Bey's student. I would say Yomi Yomi had some credit in it. I can see Balogun being one of the pioneers of the no hole system. I still have my first sangban made from a wine barrel that my Daddy helped me to build."

Baba David Coleman: "Chief should have named his version of the ashiko something different because it really was a different drum after he added his no hole system to it.

Neil Clarke took his jembe drum to the Ivory Coast with Randy Weston. The Ivorian drummers were impressed with the tightness of the head out of the bag. They asked him if he could do their drums like his. He said he would have to ask the man who made his drum - Chief Bey."

One of the founding members of International Afrikan American Ballet, Greg Ince, spoke about Chief Bey.

Greg Ince: "We all know that Chief James Hawthorne Bey brought the no hole system of tuning the jembe. He brought cradles around the rings."

Chief Bey with his Ashiko drum
Source: Denise Bey

One of Babatunde Olatunji's first Drum Captains and Founder of the El Shabazz Djembe Orchestra, Kehinde O'Uhuru, spoke on the early days of drum making in New York.

Kehinde O'Uhuru: "I got into changing drumheads by looking at Charles Payne's drum. Tony Robinson and Charles were the first ones to teach me how to string up the drums. I used to see Charles, Tony, and Butch Jackson working on drums. I was getting skins from Earl Edwards who used to go to New Jersey to get skins. He was a fire eater. Balogun and Yomi Yomi brought the third ring."

Amara Kante: "Important to note that it was Famoudou Konate that brought to Guinea the no hole system for tuning using rings."

Moussa Traore: "I know that after 1988 I started to see that no hole system with rings on the jembe and we started making them like that from then on in Mali. I used to tack the heads on, and I sewed them on before we started seeing the no hole jembe with rings. I heard it was Famoudou Konate who started the no hole jembe with rings."

One of the founding members of International Afrikan American Ballet and one of Ladji Camara's early lead jembe students, Walter Ince speaks about the early days of drum making in New York.

Baba Walter Ince: "Charles Payne and Butch Jackson were playing with Ladji early and got deep into jembe. They ended up carving out their own jembes. They were very smooth and slick like furniture. They may have been a bit too polished inside because the inside should have some edges for the sound to hold on to before pushing through the hole. Since theirs was so smooth the sounds flowed out quickly so you really had to be in tune with the sound to catch the notes, but they were the first one I knew that was playing strong and making their own jembes.

I had no idea how to put a head on a drum. I tried, but I didn't know what I was doing. It was a disaster. When Sam Watson came back in my life, I was living in Harlem. I was struggling; newly married and a baby on the way. Sam sent me to Nii Ayi to work on my drum. Nii Ayi was muscle bound and built. He said he had been like that from childhood. Nii Ayi fixed my drum the first time around late 1960s - early 1970s, but he required that I be there to learn. He taught me the hole technique using pegs and sewing. I was so happy Nii Ayi was showing me. Thanks to Chief Bey we have the no hole system. To the best of my knowledge, Chief Bey was the progenitor of the no hole system. The "no holes system" for the jembe didn't come into effect until about the early 1980s.

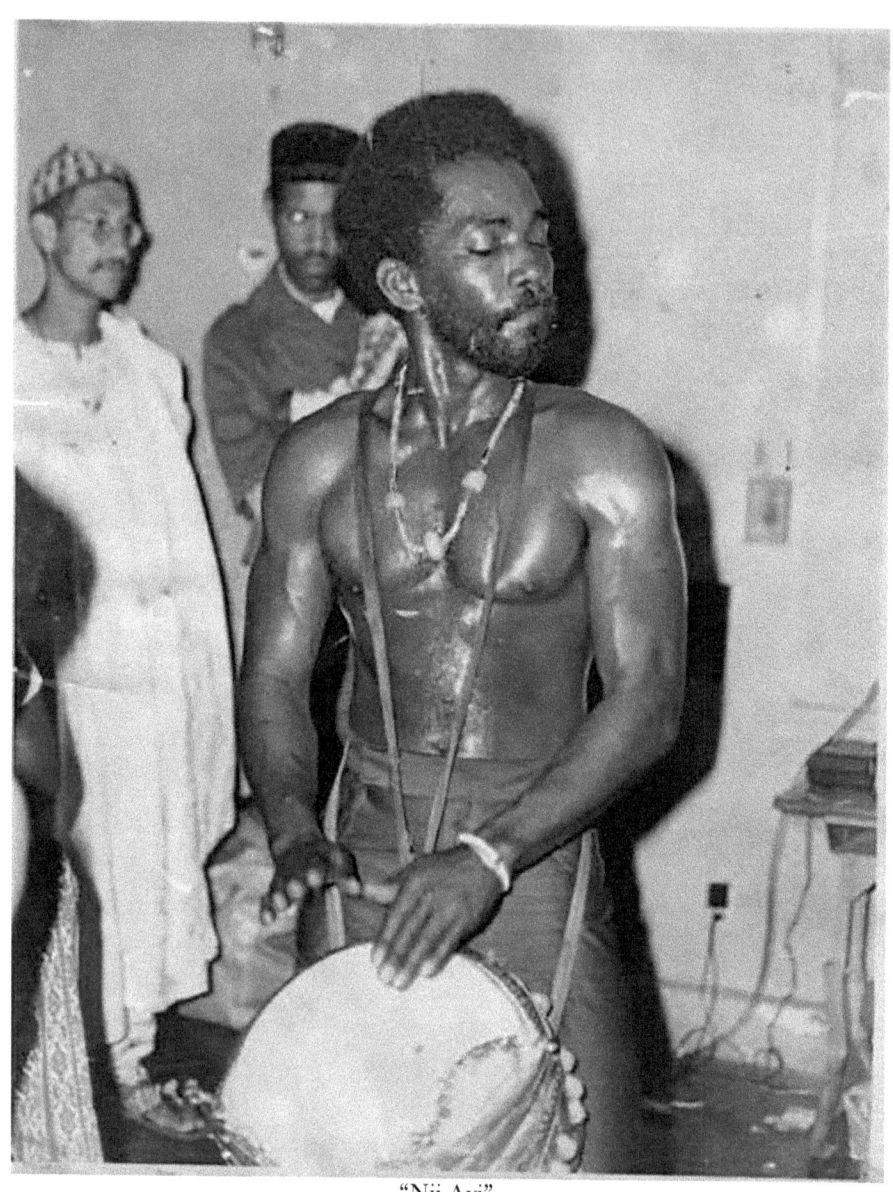

"Nii Ayi"
Source: "Nii Ayi" Nana Obrafo Yaw Wofa Asiedu

At FESTAC 1977 in Lagos, Nigeria, Famoudou Konate saw with our drums that we were using iron rings to replace the cord that was used inside the skin, but we were still using the hole system. The iron ring allowed for the head to be even because the ring couldn't be bent. Before that, we used a cord on the inside. That cord had to be thin and when you pulled it, it had to be TIGHT. There were two strings, the one inside, you pulled that one very tight and then you braided it around. Then, from that one, you got another string and you made one hole going out of the skin. Then you made a slip knot and put the other one on, so now you had one sitting on top of the inside ring and that was a second ring. Then you began measuring exactly the amount of holes you were going to make and the distance between the holes. When you make it exact, it reduced the possibility that the pull down would be uneven. Then, later I decided to make a third ring that sits on top. The third ring was what you utilized with the holes instead of the second ring. It went through two layers of the same skin which then allowed for the pull to be more even and tighter, but then again it trapped all of that wet skin in between. We weren't using a bottom ring yet. Once you made all of the holes, you used the excess cord and wrapped it around making it tighter and tighter. When you were going to string it to the bottom ring, we used coat hangers. We wrapped the coat hangers around, and then taped it with the sticky side on the outside and we went around and around until the ring was tight. When the cord was wrapped around that tape it stuck to it and helped you to make it very tight.

Balogun had the ring on his drum and I'm not sure where the ring came from initially, but I know Chief Bey started that no hole system. That did not start in Africa. The environment in West Africa was hot and dry. The skins can stay high by just putting them in sun. Here in America, it's colder and more damp so those same drums here did not stay as tight. We had to use hot plates and heaters to keep those drums dry and tuned high. So, the no hole system changed everything; that drum stayed high and tight. It came out of the bag ready to go."

Famoudou Konate: "The start of putting drumheads together with the rings and rope was invented by Black Americans. When the Ballets went to America, we were putting heads on traditionally. We nailed the heads or sewed the heads on. We weren't putting heads on the jembes that way the Black Americans were doing it. I went to a festival in Lagos in 1977 (FESTAC) and I met some Black American drummers like Balogun, and I saw their drums and I was IMPRESSED. After the festival, I looked at their drums and saw that it was put together really great. I tried to do it the same way for about a month and I couldn't get it. But then I finally got it after about one month. It was the Black Americans from New York that invented this system of putting the jembe together."

One of Chuck Davis' original jembe drummers and one of the eldest active African American drummers in America, Yomi Yomi, spoke about the early days of jembe drum making in New York.

Baba Yomi Yomi Awolowo: "There's a lot of controversy about who started the no holes system. To me it don't matter. It's a system that a lot of people are doing now. When we were doing it Billy Bungo, myself and Richard Byrd used to go out to Jersey to get skins. We would bring them back to wash and stretch them. When they dried we scraped the hair off. To make the lacing we used to strip the skin then twist it with a stick. Many days I stayed home making lacing to string the jembe. A lot of people claim to have started the "no holes system" but back in 1964/65 I worked for transit. I was doing welding. I used to make the rings for transit at the job. I made the metal rings. I was the only one that had access to a welding machine. They can say what they want but I still have rings I made back then. Before that they used to take coat hangers and wrap material around it, then the tape, then they used that to roll the skin on. But when the metal ring came it took on a new direction. That eliminated a lot of hot plate heating and all that. Cause that's what we did in the early days. We used the hot plates.

I can remember making drums with my buddy Skip. He came up with this idea to use a vacuum cleaner and put charcoal inside the drum and put it on the blow setting and use it as a blow torch to burn the hole then chip it out then blow more. The wood was cracking man. (Baba Yomi Yomi busted out into laughter). It was good days, man.

When Famoudou Konate came in 1968, we exchanged ideas about stringing the drum. He was the first person I saw throw the skin on the floor and walk on it to loosen it up. Then he sewed it on to the drum. He would wash his skin until it became like a washcloth. He would throw it on the floor and walk on it and roll it roll it over and over. And when he put it on . . .DING DING, without any heat without anything.

Chief Bey used to lace his heads after putting holes in the skins. I made a tool just for that. He was one of the first to string up the drums. His drum was the ashiko drum. Chief was about the stick and hand. That was our sound back then. That stick and hand. That comes out of the Congo.

In between 1962-1964 I was learning how to make drums that looked like jembes. I was listening to UNESCO music so I was listening to Les Ballets.

There were other brothers that were drum making also. Sonny Morgan, Stacy Adams, Babafemi, Richard "Pablo" Landrum. These were band drummers. They could play jembe but they played it like it was a conga. They were mostly making bata drums. Butch, Charles, Spanky those guys were the early jembe players.

I grew up in Harlem. I went to visit my friend in Queens and when I got to his house he had drummers there, Wendel Hayes, Tony Robinson, Nathaniel Bettis, Chief Bey, Lawrence Tweet, Olukose Wiles, Clarence. Egbe Ife - Chief Bey's organization."

Another of the eldest active African American jembe drummers and longtime student of Ladji Camara, Kehinde Donaldson, recalled the early days of drum making in New York.

Kehinde Donaldson: "In 1972, I started putting heads on drums after Yomi Yomi, Balogun and Chief Bey. Chief Bey was the first I saw do it. Yomi Yomi and Balogun showed me how to do it. Yomi Yomi showed me how to sew the skin on. He was also the one that came out with the metal rims. Yomi worked at Metropolitan Transportation Authority (MTA) back at that time so he was working with steel and welding."

Drummer, Artist, Priest of Ifa, and Founder of the Bungo's Hilife Band, Billy Bungo spoke about the early days of drum making in New York.

Baba Billy Bungo: "Chief James Hawthorne Bey was one of the first cats to make the no holes jembe; the same style that everyone is using now. Baba Yomi Yomi figured out how to put the jembe together without the holes in the skin. Chief Bey inspired me to repair and make drums.

We used to sew on the skins, so I know when it all changed over to the no holes system.

In Pablo Landrum's lifetime, he made one million drums and died broke. I met Pablo in 1967/1968, and he was messing around with making drums then. He made slap drums; made the cone shape. He made a lot of us a lot of drums. Then one session Me, Pablo, and Olatunji, we made one hundred drums in two days. Then we had to figure out how to put the heads on. We just followed Pablo's lead. I'm telling you, these cats were top shelf."

Yoruba Priest of Obatala and Drummer, Richard Byrd, spoke on the early days of drum making in New York.

Baba Richard Byrd: "I went from 125th St and Madison Ave., the Olatunji Center, to the Church of the Mass, Chuck Davis Dance Company. Balogun, Yomi Yomi, Kweyao and Spanky were there. They were the drummers. I was introduced to Balogun and Yomi and they took me in like fresh money. I had a black conga that I carried. I used to tune it up as high as I could. It had a very thin conga head. I wanted it to sound like a jembe. There was a brother named "Skip" Floyd Taylor that was making drums with Balogun and Yomi. There was Charles, Butch, Black (Black atlas type of dude). They could play. This dude Skip used to take a log and make a hole in it then burn the inside then make drums from it. He was the one that taught me how to string sangban drums with holes in the skin. I didn't learn how to string sangbans with no holes in the skin until I got with Chief Bey. Balogun said "Man, you need a jembe man. I went to Chief' Bey's house. It was ON after that. His wife Barbara, my Godmother, gave me a hard time. LOL. When I went to Chief's house with Bungo for the 2nd time, Olukose and Neil were there. I said I have to get a jembe. Chief was always working on something. He was stringing something together when I went there. I said, "Man, I can do that!" Neil and especially Olukose laughed at me. Balogun, Yomi Yomi and them laughs was different. But these cats' laughs was like 'you ain't and you never going to be'. I told them in 2 weeks I would be back with a drum. I went home and got a log and pulled out a mallet and a chisel and started carving me a drum. I got to a point in the log the hole in the log was so deep this gouge wasn't long enough. My father, a fantastic man, and ultimate carpenter found a 2¼ pipe and cut half of the pipe and filed the pipe sharp to make a gouge so I could finish carving it. My Father said take a picture of this because he couldn't believe that I was working on this night and day. I was finished in 1 week. That following week I was back at Chief's house with that drum and Olukose's and Neil's mouths were WIDE open. Chief was like "Yea man, you my horse if you never win another race...Let's go!" He gave me a skin and we started stringing it up right there.

Billy Bungo was the first one to get goat skins. He took me to Green Village Packing House in New Jersey. Goat skins were $2. We got Murphy's Oil Soap and Pine Sol and cleaned them up. Yomi Yomi needed skins, so we picked up Billy Bungo and went to get some skins.

After that point that was Billy Bungo's claim to fame. He was one of the first skin men. Don't get it twisted. The real skins for us over here was live from the slaughterhouse. Olukose was getting skins from Senegal. Neil Clarke was getting skins and putting lime on the skins."

One of Chuck Davis' early lead jembe drummers, Jalal Sharriff, shared about drum making.

Jalal Sharriff: "Ngoma was carving jembes, and he taught me how to make my homemade jembe in 1981. Ngoma was from Durham, North Carolina and was with Chuck Davis' group.

I remember when Chuck and I went to Portland, Oregon to do a residency at an art school. The drummer there never saw a jembe. He used to play with this band called "Pleasure". When he heard jembe and started learning it, he went home to his basement and cut his conga to make a dundun; that's what I'm talking about, "madness." Two months later, from the day I left, he was in Africa. He never had any intentions to go to Africa. His name was Bruce Smith."

Jalal Sharriff carving out a log to make a jembe.
Source: Jalal Sharriff

Jalal Sharriff and Phillip "Spanky" Williamson making Jalal's jembe.
Source: Jalal Sharriff

Yoruba Priest, Drummer, Artist, and longtime Drum Maker, Baba Baile, spoke on Nummu and the early days of jembe drum making in America.

Baba Baile McKnight: "Jembe is a player in the Kingdom." Jerry Workman (Reggie Workman's brother) and I carved drums together in early 1970s. Jerry learned ashiko making from Chief Bey.

Jembe is not at the place of the king or the Kortejuga. Jembe was brought to the place of the Nummu; the Smythe. The Farmer goes to the Smythe or Smith or Nummu for a hoe. The Wife of the Smith goes to the Smith for a razor blade to cut a portion of the clitoris off of the daughter. The butcher goes to the Smith for a cleaver. The Nummu is the foremost powerful personage in the kingdom.

1971 was the beginning with the hand drum for me. We didn't have jembe at this time. Barnett "Duck" Williams had the first jembe drum in the Washington, DC area.

The making of the drum started for me when I was learning how to weld.

I carved a drum for Sun Drummer Mosheh. Atu is the founder of Sun Drummer. He came from Birmingham, Alabama. Atu taught, when you learn the drum, you learn the bell first. The old school percussion orchestra for us in Washington, DC was centered around the conga drum. We took hardware off of the conga drums. We laced the skins and created what we called the "bush" drum or "earth" drum. In 1971/1972 in DC and Baltimore, we cut the conga drums in half and used the top bowl to make a jembe and the bottom half we used to make a miniature conga and stick that in the bottom of the tumbao and tacked heads on. I didn't know about Sun Drummer at this time. I was amazed at the continuity of Sun Drummer.

I carved a jembe for Baba Aidoo and his brother in 1976. I went to the hardware store and bought a chainsaw and went to the park and cut a couple of logs from a fallen tree.

Taiwo DuVall has one of the ashikos given to him from Moses Miannes. I made an ashiko drum for Taiwo in 1976."

One of the members of the Ohio chapter of The Sun Drummer, Jubal Harris, spoke on drum making in the early days in America.

Jubal Harris: "Mosheh Milon Sr. was the first person I met who made and played a jembe drum. He was out of Chicago. African drum making technique was brought to Chicago by Harlod Atu Murray and Musa Lalu Mosley, founders of Sun Drummer.

In 1975 a dancer from Melvin Deal African Heritage Drummers and Dancers Washington D.C. taught an African dance class at the Cincinnati Art Consortium. She invited me to come to DC to study. I did just that. I stayed with a friend and walked to Melvin Deal's studio. He gave me an audition. "Oh you want to be a drummer?" He took two sticks and played a series of rhythms then had me repeat his rhythm. I told him I really want to learn how to make my own drum. Melvin gave me Baile McKnight's information. Melvin told me, "Go over there and he can show you how to make a drum." I went to find Baile the next day. Baba Baile established the African Cultural Center after returning from receiving initiation in Nigeria.

Baba Baile occupied an old drug store building on Park Rd in D.C. He had a wood burning stove downstairs and we would find logs to carve. Upstairs the sisters created a market to sell food and African merchandise. It was at this center that I met Baba Ishangi. Baba Ishangi rolled up in a bus with his family. He had 2 wives and several children. I was so impressed. He taught Yoruba language, drumming, dance, etiquette, proper diet, exercise, and African spirituality.

Musa Lalu Mosley was a drum maker for Muntu Dance Theater of Chicago. He also taught me drum making techniques.

Chief Bey invented the "no hole iron ring system." That is now used throughout the world to head African drums. As a member of Sun Drummer, we learned how to tack on heads like the Cubans did.

Then we learned how to sew the skin on the traditional African way. The last thing we learned was the no hole system which was Chief Bey's invention."

One of the members of The Sun Drummer in Chicago and a founding member of the Muntu Dance Theater of Chicago, Mosheh Milon spoke about the early days of drum making in America.

Baba Mosheh Milon: "Atu made the "earth drum." When I finally got invited to come into the Sun Drummer, I had to find me an "earth drum." But I didn't have one. I found a conga. We would take all of the hardware off of the conga, closed the hole, then we would rope it, like a traditional drum. We used a can to make our dunduns. Atu was the first one that showed us anything about drum maintenance, making, and lacing. Our understanding is that he learned his drum making in New York from Chief Bey, drumming with Big Black, Olatunji and whoever was around. Then Atu went back to Chicago and created The Sun Drummer."

Sun Drummer Jubal Harris' ashiko drum he made with Chief Bey
Photo credit: Steven Cutri
Source: Jubal Harris

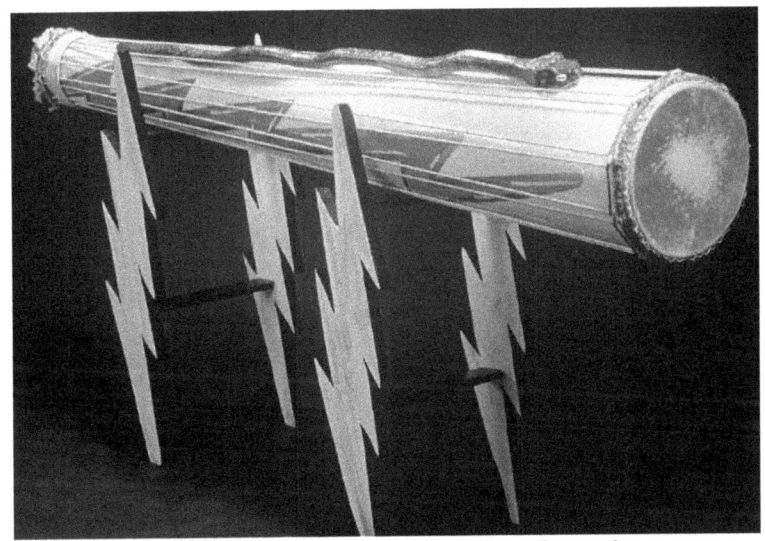

Sun Drummer Jubal Harris' log drum he made
Photo credit: Larry Allen McBee
Source: Jubal Harris

One of the members of The Sun Drummer in Chicago and a founding member of the Muntu Dance Theater of Chicago, Babu Atiba Walker, spoke about the early days of drum making.

Babu Atiba Walker: "We had conga drums that we would convert to what we called "earth drums." We would take all of the metal and all hardware off and fill up all of the holes, then put a tack head system on at that time until we moved into the rope system.

I didn't get deep into the drum making, I wanted to play. I made it because in order to be a Sun Drummer, it was a requirement to make a drum. I made a log drum, then I made an earth drum out of an old pickle barrel. We broke the slats down on the pickle barrel, then had to plane down the wood so that they could fit into a smaller circle. We had to make a band to put around the drum to hold it together; that was the earth drum that I made. I made that in 1975 with Atu directly at his house. Moussa was our drum maker. He used to make the log telegraph drum. I sat down with Moussa to carve out my log drum together."

One of the founding members of The Sun Drummer in Chicago and a founding member of the Muntu Dance Theater of Chicago, Enoch Williamson spoke about the early days of drum making in America.

Enoch Williamson: "We had our first Sun Drummer class with Atu Harold Murray at the old Moorish Science Temple on 75th street right off Cottage Grove [Chicago]. Kalen Phil Koran was offering classes from various guest artists at the Temple. This is where we met Atu. There he was standing there powerfully built, with robes over one shoulder the rest exposed, rings in his ears and nose; and no shoes on - just sandals in January. It was bitter cold outside. My first impression was who is this cat?! My first question was WHERE ARE YOUR SHOES? He said he didn't want to cover up his "understanding" which was in his feet. I was intrigued immediately. So his first words were that a drum is a hand bell and that we needed to play bell to understand the high frequencies that were in the bell. That the constant hum of the drum was key to understanding the spirit of the notes being played. The hum was vibration which was one of the laws of the universe which meant that we were lawful in our playing of the instruments. This was a DIVINE undertaking. WOW, one hell of a first day. There were 7 of us. Moosa Richard Mosley, Kewo Saba, Selah Gary Allen, Sura Ramses, Eusi Tim Holly, Oye Bisi, Enoch Williamson.

Atu came up with the name SUN DRUMMER, one universal drummer. Our goal was to sound like one drummer. Derf Reklaw (Fred Walker) came in after a minute because he was playing with Kelan Phil Koran and saw what we were doing and wanted to be a part of it. Chief Bey was Atu's teacher. He talked about Chief Bey.

There were other cats in the group that could play as good as Atu and sound better. But he had another thing going. He was playing what he called an "earth drum." He got an old pickle barrel he took the slats down then redid it. At first we would tack the heads on and sit them in the sun to bring the pitch up. Then we started with rope. He taught us about these different drums. He had us taking hardware off of congas then redo it by pulling rope through the holes in the skins. Atu had a jembe and called that an "air drum" because you stood up and played it off the ground. Earth drum you played sitting down with the drum on the earth. Moussa made these big drums called "council drums." Big drums that looked like kettle drums and we played those with 2 big sticks. He taught us how to play bells, shekeres and these small branches of a tree with sticks along with the drums. Atu's style was making up proverbs and creating rhythms to go along with them. He wanted our style to be different and not like anyone else's. I had the opportunity to see Les Ballets in the 70's and met Famoudou Konate. After that I asked Atu why don't we call the air drums jembe because that's what they are called. Atu said that we didn't want to copy anyone's style. We wanted to be original.

When Atu went to Ghana I got into the jembe more. I cut down a tree and made my first jembe. At that time you couldn't get jembes anywhere. Right down from the Moor's house, there was an empty lot with these huge trees in the lot. I had a Priestess ask permission if I could cut the tree down and we got permission. Moussa and I cut down the tree which took a while. I was in my early 20s at this time. I took 2 nice size pieces 14" across and 40 inches tall. We took these logs in a truck to Moussa's house. Moussa taught me how to take care of the logs so that the wood wouldn't split. Moussa gave me tips now and then but he wasn't well versed in drum making because he was still learning. I got me different size gauges and a hammer and worked on it during my free time. 6-8 hours a day working on it. I finally got through it and made 2 of them. I still have the jembes that I made. After we would finish we would put it in plastic and paper inside to catch the moisture. And we would carve out a little at a time because if you do too much too fast the wood would crack. At the end I let the drum dry out in the plastic for 7 days. 3 times each day we would change the paper inside and it didn't crack. We put some linseed oil on it which I learned I should not have done. I finished it and at that time we were putting holes in the skin and I roped the skin onto the shell.

By now I told them that we need to learn how to tune these drums. Atu went up to New York and came back with this no hole system. This was about 1975/1976. When I saw it I said this could revolutionize everything. I said this could change everything. When he came back he was living with me. He lived in my basement. I went downstairs and said you have to show me how to do this! He said, "No, you have to wait 21 days and something. I have to take you through the thing." I was really upset. I said, "Man what are you talking about, show me how to do this!" He said, "No!" He wouldn't do it. So I was really upset with him. I was sitting trying to figure how I could get through these 21 days so I could learn how to rope the drum.

I was sitting looking at my quinto and had an epiphany. Atu said I could have one last look at the roping for no more than 3 minutes then give it back and leave the room. I was looking at the conga and realized that's all it was. The braids were the rope. I did it and was so happy I couldn't believe it. When I looked at him, he was SHOCKED. I started doing everyone's drum. Because now we could keep the pitch.

The African drummers and the Ballets weren't stringing their drums with the no hole system at that time. They learned that from here from African Americans then brought that back to Africa. I was the only one in the Chicago area at that time doing the no hole system on the jembes. I was doing everyone's drums and the more I did it, the better I got at it."

Founder of The Sun Drummer in Chicago, Atu Murray, spoke about Chief Bey and drum making.

Atu (Harold) Murray: "If you are going to have a village, the first thing you have to have is a blacksmith (Nummu). I got into drum making in New York with Chief Bey around 1969.

When the drum was tuned to sound like a hand bell then you know you have the right sound.

My first drum I ever made was called mamo, a pickle barrel drum. Baba Chief Bey showed me how to make it with no nails, tar, and bands from the barrel. Chief Bey was my inspiration. Anything he said do, I did it."

Enoch Williamson: "I met Chief James Hawthorne Bey while on one of my trips to St Louis for the festival. He was teaching at the festival. He was the teacher of Atu Harold Murray who was our teacher in Chicago. When I met him I could understand my teacher Atu Harold Murray better. They had slight philosophical differences in applications of interpreting the drum in our culture. Afro-Americans had no knowledge of hand drumming even though it was prevalent in the Caribbean, Central & South America. It was totally forbidden in North America. You were threatened with getting your hands cut off if you did. Chief Bey became my Godfather in the Yoruba religion."

One of Arthur Hall's lead drummers and one of Ladji Camara's first drum students, Nana Nii Ayi, spoke on the early days of drum making.

"Nii Ayi" Nana Obrafo Yaw Wofa Asiedu: "When I didn't have a jembe I cut a conga drum in half and used the bottom half as my so called jembe drum. I didn't know the Malinke style of stringing. I knew how to use the peg system, like the Ghanaian drums. I got my first real jembe drum from an elder African American drummer in New York City who was bringing drums in from Senegal. Then I brought that jembe back to

Philly. It was a Ballets' jembe. It was very big like Mali drums. It was strung with all skin from the cradles to the weave and diamonds. It was loud, like two people playing sound. I was using the peg style until I went to New York and was hanging out with Yomi Yomi and them. They were sewing heads on and using the Malinke tuning style. I can remember hanging out with the Ballets when they came. They were showing me their technique of stringing, tuning, and repairing their drums. For example, when their drums would break at a show, they would take a skin and put it in water for about fifteen minutes. They would put that skin back on the drum and that drum would be ready to play by the matinee. I was like "now how the hell...?" You know how we put the skins in water and let it sit overnight and put it on the next day? They soaked their skin for maybe fifteen to twenty minutes then put the skin back on the drum. Using less water would help the skin to contract and dry faster. These were small things I was learning that not too many people were getting, but I shared with others. I was the one teaching the jembe drummers in Philly. How to string up their drums from what I learned from the New York drummers. Ishangi was the first one to teach me about the peg system of putting heads on and tuning. While I was in Ghana, I learned that the peg system history was that the peg was supposed to be the penis and the hole was supposed to be the vagina. If you look at the string hoops that go into the hole, it looks like a vagina. The brothers in Ghana were very serious about how they strung up their drums because of that."

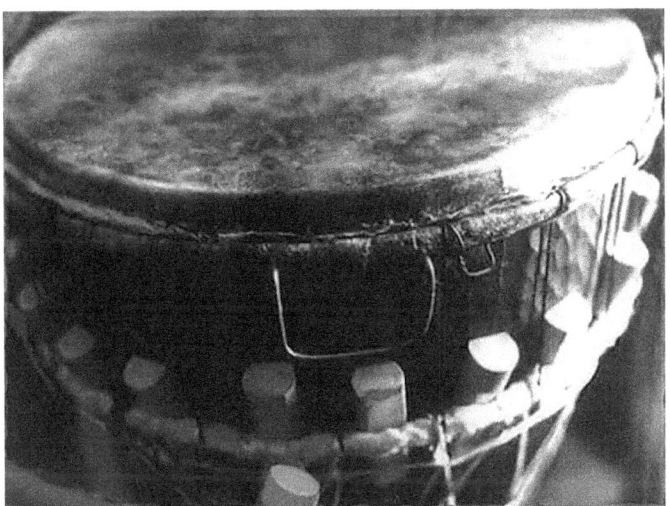

Nii Ayi's jembe with the peg and sewing system.circa:1970s
Photo credit: Jon Young
Source: "Nii Ayi" Nana Obrafo Yaw Wofa Asiedu

One of the foremost scholars on African drumming in America, Drummer, Teacher, and one of the LaRocque Bey's first drummers, Bradley Simmons, spoke on Chief Bey and drum making.

Bradley Simmons: "I was sitting in Chief Bey's house one day in the mid to late 70s. He took the conga drum and the jembe drum in front of him and said, "I can turn this jembe into that conga." I said, huh? Chief said, "We won't have to worry about heating the drum anymore. We can do this the same way as the conga drum is set up with the no hole system. I can put two rims on top or three rims on top and rims on the bottom and lace it up, then pull the rope to the pitch you want it and lock it in place where you want it."

He did his ashiko that way first. He turned his drum (ashiko) into the no hole system first before he did the jembe drum. When people saw that they started putting their drums together the way he was doing it. He showed us how to do it and once he showed us how to do it that's when it caught on and from that day on we never sewed a skin on a drum again. We were using metal hangers and tape wrapped around the hanger and formed them into rings at first.

When skin on skin opened up we asked Jay Barret to make rings for the jembes. And he did it. He was making the rings for us to put skins on with the no hole system. Baba Yomi Yomi brought the ring in first. Balogun and Yomi Yomi were working closely together making drums. Yomi Yomi was one of the first to perfect that no hole system with the rings. We used to bring our jembes to Yomi Yomi. Then James Cherry figured it out then we started bringing them to James. We were either going to Brooklyn to James Cherry or to the Bronx to Yomi Yomi."

Chief Bey: "Most drummers when I was coming up didn't know how to fix their drums. Ismay Andrews told me "if you can't fix your own drum then you ain't shit."

Chapter 3

Jembe Manding

"A lot of truth you know you shouldn't speak about, there are a lot of older people who may be able to speak more about what you want to speak about."
Moussa Traore

It was three o'clock in the morning in Conakry, Guinea, and I was getting into a vehicle with my good friend and translator, Mustapha Berete, and his driver. The night air had a West African warmth to it. It is amazing how much activity goes on in the middle of the night and early morning in West African cities. I could hear the cars and people moving around and the faint odor of city life. I was suffering from a sinus condition due to having the fan on me all night. I had my roots and herbs, but I didn't want to make frequent bathroom stops on the road so I went without drinking my teas. I decided to chew on one of my favorite roots, kanto (the mucus eliminator), to heal my sore throat. I was surprised at the many cars that were on the road already by the time we set off for the Hamanah region of Guinea. This driver was bobbing and weaving through the city traffic like he was a professional obstacle course driver. He even backed up for about three city blocks after running into some standstill traffic. I do not know how he orchestrated reverse driving with all of the traffic. However, he pulled it off, and we were on our way again. So, I thought to myself, "This guy can drive! We got the right driver!" Since the roots were healing my sore throat fairly quickly, I was able to settle into the ride a bit. This allowed me to think about this nearly twenty-hour ride to Siguiri which would include a stop in Kouroussa to see the Grandmaster Jembefola, Famoudou Konate.

From the first time I heard Famoudou Konate play his drum, he instantly became my favorite jembe drummer. He reigns as the Grandmaster of the jembe in my humble eyes. Aside from Quincy Jones and Stevie Wonder, there have not been many musicians whom I felt so strongly about meeting. I first heard his drumming on a cassette tape a drummer shared with me during my early years as an enthusiast of jembe music. His notes on his drum were so clean and clear, and his orchestration was so warm and simple. I would play that tape everyday like a ritual to ready me for my day or whenever I was working on my drums in my early years studying the jembe. Like many other jembe students, I listened to the jembe legends such as Ladji Camara, Mamady Keita, Percussions De Guinea, Mor Thiam and Les Ballets Africains. I learned so much from all of them, and they were playing on heavy rotation in my home. To me, however, Famoudou's sound and energy was more inviting and completely resonated within my whole being. Adding to my fascination with Mr. Konate, I was gifted at that time with a copy of a video recording of the Les Ballets Africains performance at the United Nations in New York in 1968. Famoudou Konate was the lead jembe in that performance and he was the epitome of ENERGY. JEMBEFOLA (jembe drummer who makes the jembe speak) for REAL! Here I was on a twenty-hour car ride to the interior of Guinea. I am a student of the jembe who is headed to meet the Grandmaster Jembefola and my favorite of all time, Famoudou Konate!

Famoudou Konate with Les Ballets Africains
Source: Famoudou Konate

The ride became calmer as we approached Kouroussa. There were so many mango trees and so much vacant land! There were not many vehicles on the road in this region and this resulted in a smoother trip. When we arrived at Famoudou's compound, I was enthralled with the peace I immediately experienced. I could feel his energy just by looking at the architecture of the buildings and the landscape on his property. We were deep in Manding territory and I could feel the Manding culture all around me. We were invited to sit in his courtyard outside of his main home while we waited for him to arrive as he had been attending a wedding in a neighboring village. As I looked around at the different buildings and rooms within his private fence, I could see how his vision and dreams for his compound had manifested. One of his plans had included housing for visitors traveling to see him to learn more about jembe drumming; it was important that these visitors reside in the area where he grew up while they learned. I could see purpose everywhere my eyes wandered-the fire pit in the middle of the courtyard and the room with the cut logs, carving tools, metal rings and skins. Not only did I feel honored to be invited to Mr. Konate's compound, I also felt at home.

When he arrived home, Famoudou was excited to meet us. He spoke little English but made full eye contact when engaging with us. He knew Mustapha well and was happy to welcome him at his home for the first time. He was accustomed to performing and conducting workshops at Mustapha's home in Conakry where students travel to study African drumming and dance throughout the year. I believe Mustapha was even more excited than I was to be at Famoudou's home. Famoudou Konate is a living legend and a global icon and as such is one of the most revered drummers for jembe enthusiasts in Guinea. Once he and I were formally introduced, his humility humbled me. I felt as if I had known him all of my life. I felt like he could 'overstand' all of what I thought and shared despite the language barrier between us. As it is customary in most traditional African villages, the host requests the mission of the visitor. We obliged and explained our mission to Famoudou expanding on what we had previously discussed with him about this book via telephone. I further explained that I wanted him to share his wisdom and the history of the jembe and its migration to America.

* * *

Famoudou Konate: "Right now the jembe has been modernized. The jembe has been successful now with drummers coming from all over.

They mixed up all of the rhythms. They don't know what they are doing. I'm very happy that you come all the way from America to my village where I was born. I'm very happy about this story. A lot of black people are getting into the jembe but don't know about the jembe history. You have come all this way to learn the history so I have to tell you some secrets about the jembe. I built a jembe school in Conakry and no blacks come to learn jembe from me. It's only the white people that come to learn about the jembe from me. If many blacks come the way that you come, I will be very happy."

Then Mr. Konate spoke about his childhood and how long ago only farmers were the Jembefolas (jembe drummer). He spoke of their relationship with their jembe drums.

Famoudou Konate: "I was born in 1940 in the village of Mane. I am the oldest Jembefola in Guinea. I grew up farming and drumming in Mane. My father was a farmer, hunter, and Jembefola. He was born in Mane. All of my children play jembe. When I was young, the jembe drummer would sleep together in the same room with the jembe drum. Sometimes while you are asleep, the jembe talks to you. The things that the jembe would say, only the drummer sleeping will know the meaning of that. In the morning when he gets up, he will give the proper offering to the jembe. You talk to the jembe about success. When you play the jembe you want many people to come and for the people that come to be good."

World renown Jembefola, Mamady Keita, also spoke about the dual roles of the farmer and Jembefola.

Mamady Keita: "If I was still in the village, I would be a farmer and a little Jembéfola. My master spent his whole life in the village as a farmer and Jembéfola. But, as a Jembéfola you don't earn anything, you don't make any money – nothing. You do all the ceremonies and festivals the people ask you to do – for free. You do receive gifts. You cannot live from only these gifts. You cannot survive on these gifts."[1]

One of Les Ballets Africains youngest lead jembe drummers and Les Merveilles first lead jembe drummer, Yamoussa Camara, shared ancient teachings passed on to him from his teacher, Kemoko Sano. Sano was the great choreographer for Les Ballets Africains, Ballet Djoliba, and Les Merveilles.

Yamoussa Camara: "No one was born with jembe. You have to go to someone to learn. When I was growing up the drummers didn't drum just to drum. They always played for a reason. My Mother didn't want me to play drum. She wanted me to go to school and learn. I had to run away from home and find a teacher. I found the Choreographer for Ballets Africains, Mohammed Kemoko Sano. He took me into his home. He taught me about the drum and helped me become a professional drummer. My teacher used to make me sit and put my hands on the drum and just sit and listen. He said, "It will talk to you. Your ancestors will talk to you." Sometimes you just sit in front of this little instrument and listen to what it has to tell you. It will speak to you. You have to have love in your heart and for the drum. The drum has a spirit."

Famoudou Konate continued to discuss his mentors and traditions within jembe life.

Famoudou Konate: "You know one jembe player way back who used to live in New York, Ladji Camara? Dugufana, a jembe player from Mali? Fadouba Oulare? Sidiman Konate, one of my brothers, Jembefola Alamanako, that was a Nummu. Jembefola Mamady Kouyate. Bankan Mamady (Sangbanfola). He never married. His Sangban was his Wife. Nunkuma Dama, Sangbanfola - the devil came for him. All of these people played before me. When I was young, I saw all of them. All of those drummers had herbs and special things in their drums. Before they were only using lenke to make jembes.

Because you have come all the way here to my village from the United States to learn about this history, I am going to bring you to my village where I was born to show you some secrets of the jembe. I have never brought anyone from outside there. I have three lenke trees in three different villages that no one can cut them. I'm going to show you what I do there with the one in my Father's village where I was born. No one has ever seen this lenke tree. You will be the first to see this. I want you to know these secrets."

The ride to Famoudou's birthplace, Mane, was about 40 minutes away from Famoudou's compound in Kouroussa, Guinea. The road was a good road until we turned onto a dirt road which was a typical village dirt road lined with bushes and trees. The rain and automobiles are not kind to dirt roads like this, and we had to dodge potholes, bumps, and massive puddles. As we drove, a familiar cloud of dust hovered behind us while we forged forward toward our destination. Once we arrived, Famoudou walked us around to see different projects he has worked on through the years. These projects had been funded by his supporters and students from all over the world. It was even more serene and peaceful in Mane than at his compound in Kouroussa. However, since the distant clouds were showing signs of possible rain, we had to quickly start on the journey by foot to his special place – the lenke tree. We walked at least two miles to the Grandmaster's sacred space where he has been the custodian of a long tradition his father had passed on to him.

Famoudou Konate: "Every Monday I give the kola to the lenke. This (tradition) was from my Father. When Islam came they didn't want these things to be happening, but I continued because my Father did it and it was our tradition. It's very rare to see three lenkes together like this. It's very special. I have been coming to these trees since I was very young. These lenkes are about 150 years old."

Famoudou said a prayer between the towering three lenke trees and performed a special ritual closing for me. His Malinke prayer requested that the jinn of the lenke grant me success. I thanked him. "I ni ke." ("thank you" in Malinke).

Famoudou Konate: "Before, the only wood that they used to make jembe with was lenke. Lenke is the wood that Jembefolas play to make spiritual things happen. Each lenke tree has its own jinn. The jinn is a special spirit that can work for you in a good way. It can do bad too. It can even take you.

The Nummu people used to play jembe. They were the original Jembefola. Nummus are the blacksmiths. They know the wood. They know the lenke. They know what the sound will be like when they work with the wood."

It's not only in Guinea where the spirit of the drum is highly respected. Moussa Traore is one of Mali's prominent Jembefolas. He is known for his love for the old traditional ways of the jembe, drumming and dance.

Moussa Traore: "You have to respect and learn the whole of the drum to really master the drum. You can be a jembe player and you can be hurt. As long as you believe in the power. You can be killed. Famoudou and Bolokada know this. What we say in Africa, a lot of truth you know you shouldn't speak about, there are a lot of older people that may be able to speak more about what you want to speak about."

Mamady Keita: "There are very few of us that are dedicated to preserving these traditional rhythms. Above all my mission today is to teach the culture and the history so that you don't lose it, so that it is not lost. We can accept that we are born and we will die, but we shouldn't accept that history die. History must remain, we cannot turn back the pages of history but let's put it somewhere where it can still be conserved. That is very important.

If you were asking a question to Famoudou, "what is the name of that rhythm?" he tells you quickly without scratching his head. If you ask him, "what ethnic group plays it?" He'll tell you quickly without scratching his head. "Why is this rhythm played?" Again, he answers without scratching his head. All of the questions, what region, what ethnic group, he'll answer all of them without scratching his head. He's not even going to take time to think about it. That is a master!"2

Some say the name of the "jembe" came from the Bamana in Mali, who said "Anke je, anke be" to call their people together, as the saying translates as "everyone gather together." "je" means gather and "be" means everyone.

There have been several spellings for jembe; the most popular being "D'Jembe." I am comfortable with the spelling "jembe" because my research indicates it is closer to the traditional spelling from the Manding nation. The "D'Jembe" spelling was given to that instrument by the French.

Kehinde O'Uhuru, one of Babatunde Olatunji's early Drum Captains is from Harlem, New York and had this to say about the name 'jembe':

Kehinde O'Uhuru: "I remember Yaya Diallo leading a drum workshop and taught that the word 'jembe' means Unity and Harmony."

Bolokada Conde is from Sankara, Guinea and had this to say about the name 'jembe'.

Bolokada Conde: "We speak about three to four different dialects of Malinke and from where I come from our dialect jembe is called "djiben". Conakry they say "jimbe". Susu people call it "sanbani". French word "tam tam". Lily people called it "jembe"."

Yamoussa Camara from Conakry, Guinea said this about 'jembe':

Yamoussa Camara: "Susu people call jembe "yimbe.""

Mousa Traore is from Bamako, Mali and had this to say about 'jembe':

Mousa Traore: "Jembe means Union and Together 'Je'- Together; 'Mbe' - Get along. Jembe comes from stick and mortar. You can take capital D and apostrophe off which is French and that's what I knew growing up, 'jembe'. I think because of the Ballets they brought the spelling 'D'Jembe'."

Famoudou Konate from the Hamanah region of Upper Guinea, grew up with another story about the origin of the name 'jembe.'

Famoudou Konate: "This drum carving tool is called jenne (Jin NAY). The carvers were carving out drum with the jenne and the jenne fell. So, the boss said "give me back my jenne." 'Be' means fall. So the boss said jennebe. "My tool fell give it back to me." "jenbe." "

Jalal Sharriff: "Papa Ladji told me this is the way they said it, "dimbe"."

The jembe originated from the Mande-speaking societies of West Africa such as the Malinké (Maninka) and Ouassoulounké (Wasulunka) located in northeastern Guinea and southern Mali. Early in the thirteenth century, the West African Mande (or Mali) empire was established by the legendary warrior and hero, Sunjata, and his allies. The Mande homeland (also called Manden or Manding), situated along the Upper Niger River roughly between Bamako in southwestern Mali and Kouroussa in northeastern Guinea, gradually became the center of one of the largest and wealthiest empires in West Africa.

As Mande people dispersed throughout the West African savanna, they assimilated to various local cultures and shared their own culture. Today, their descendants account for significant parts of the population of many West African countries. In Mali and Guinea, they are known as Maninka (or Malinke in French writing). In Senegal, Gambia, and Guinea Bissau, they are known as Mandinka (or Mandingo in British writing).3

Bolokada Conde: "Sunjata was a very important story. My dad told me how he became a king. He was a special person."

Mousa Traore: "When you say Manding, we talk about Sunjata. Manding was really big. It was Mali, Ivory Coast, Senegal, Guinea, Guinea Bissau, Part of Mauritania, Gambia. 'Manding' means 'Ma'- Human being and 'Ding'- Child."

* * *

The stage presentations of jembe drumming and dancing more than likely started in the late 1940s or early 1950s with Fodeba Keita who was based in Paris. Fodéba Keita had been born in 1921 in the town of Siguiri in the far northeast region of what was then the colony of French Guinea. His efforts eventually led to the formation of Les Ballets Africains. The original company was founded not in Guinea but in Paris in 1952. The company was called Les Ballets Africains de Keita Fodeba which was a variation of an earlier name, Le Theatre Africain de Keita Fodeba. Under the former name, they toured cities in France and Switzerland from 1949 through 1951.

The original company did not entirely consist of artists native to Guinea. The company consisted of ex-patriots from Guinea, Senegal, Mali, and the French Caribbean, all of whom were living in Paris. In September 1958, when Guinea voted to become the first French West African territory to gain independence, Ahmed Sekou Toure became the first President of the Independent Republic of Guinea. Subsequently, Fodeba Keita returned to Guinea to serve as Minister of the Interior. This revolutionary move would make Guinea the second African country to attain its independence, Ghana being the first. In his new government position, Fodeba left the Ballets in the hands of his long-time collaborator, Facelli Kanté. The Ballets retained Keita's name during this period. It was not until the end of the 1959 tour that the company switched its base of operations to Conakry, Guinea, disbanding and then re-forming in the spring of 1960 under the government's auspices as Les Ballets Africains de la République de Guinée (Les Ballets Africains).

Each year, competitions or repetitions were held from the village or district communities. This was the first stage in a largescale mobilization of the people in the service of the arts. Each of these arts companies presents a play, choral work, a ballet, and some instrumental folk music.

The best productions go into the second stage of the competition, which is also held annually. At the end of these competitions, the winning companies take part in a two-week arts festival. The best productions are selected for the national festival, which is held every two years.

Les Ballets Africains began this new competitive process through which top artists from around the country were chosen by government appointed juries. President Touré's government also had a strong say in the development of artistic content, particularly at the level of the national ensembles. Of the country's thousands of new performing arts companies,

Les Ballets Africains, and the other national ensembles were the only ones permitted to tour internationally as cultural ambassadors presenting highly polished renditions of Guinean arts, culture, and history.3

Fodeba Keita
"Chants et Danses d'Afrique Guinee-Casamance" Album by Keita Fodeba et Son Ensembe Africain
Source: Mangue Music Blog

Les Ballets Africains de Keita Fodeba (Before Les Ballet Africains de Guinee was formed)
Les Ballets Africains De Keita Fodeba Vol 2 album cover
Photo credit: E. Petraroli

Famoudou Konate: "I was a farmer and a drummer. I never went to school. In 1959, I left the farming and came to Kouroussa and started playing for Ballets around there. In 1960, through repetitions (competitions) they brought me to Conakry to play with Les Ballets Africains. In 1960, 1961, and 1962, I went to Conakry and went to Kassa and did three more repetitions (competitions). In 1962, I went to the United States and went all over Europe and to Japan. What Sekou Toure did for me - He gave me life. Because of Sekou Toure, I was able to know five continents. Jembe taught me a lot. Jembe taught me how to live in this world. I never went to school. I got my education through the jembe. When Sekou Toure died, I left the Ballets because I knew that things would not be good without him. I used to sit down with President Sekou Toure. He wanted black people to do for themselves. He wanted Africa to go beyond where the nations of the West was."

Mamady Keita: "As long as I can remember, I have been told that I was born to be a drummer. Before my birth, a soothsayer had announced to my mother that her son would be well known all over the world. When I was five years old, my parents took me to the Jembefola of the village for instruction and training. My master, Karinka Djan Conde, was not a famous musician. He lived as a simple farmer in our village. But he was a true master who had practiced the tradition and the magic of this instrument for many years. This man, Balanka Sidki, was charged with selecting the musicians for a music festival in Conakry, and so he came to Balandugu to look for me. He talked with my older brother, my family and the village chief. The family did not want to let me go, but even so I had to get ready. It was like a calling. At first, I went for one year to the province capital, Siguiri, where we prepared ourselves for the big national festival in Conakry. In 1964, I went to the capital and was chosen from five hundred other musicians and dancers to join the National Ballet. We all were brought to the Isle of Loos and stayed there for nine months of training and rehearsal. Every day, we played many hours. During this time, I learned the rhythms of other regions of Guinea. We all played before a cultural commission, and after the festival the Minister of Culture, Sports, and Youth, Fodeba Keita, announced the names of the selected artists. In addition to me, there were forty-five other artists from all over Guinea; five of them percussionists for the jembe and the dundun. Fodeba Keita gave the group the name "Djoliba," which is the name of the Niger River in Upper Guinea. Our first concert tours were to Ghana, Liberia and Egypt."4

Bolokada Conde: "All of my life in Guinea that I see presidents the first was Sekou Toure. All artists all of my life everybody says that Sekou Toure was the best president because he loved artists and culture. When the first ballet was started in France with artists from different parts of Africa, Sekou Toure saw this and said that he wanted to see this in Guinea. Sekou Toure gave the National Ballet concept the power. All those artists from different parts of Africa went back to their countries and started their own Ballets. If you were in the Ballets, the artists didn't pay taxes, they didn't have to pay for housing, they got the best medical care."

Yamoussa Camara: "Sekou Toure didn't want his people to study any European languages. He wanted everyone to study the languages of Guinea so everyone could communicate with each other."

For Sékou Touré, a staged performance constituted a highly effective means of broadcasting nationalist messages. As Touré himself phrased it, performance acts not only rely upon the intellect, but also upon sensation; by the physical presence of the actors, the materiality of the decors, the comportment of the characters on stage, it delivers an expression more complete than that of the literary work.5

President Sekou Toure: "While we insist, ever again, on the necessity for our artistic and cultural performances to be integrated into our popular revolution and to serve educational purpose, this does not apply to the National Ballet, whose task does not consist in educating foreign spectators, but in acquainting them with our cultural values and artistic riches. The National Ballet should present Africa, make her known and esteemed. Its programmes are not chosen in view of their educational and mobilizing qualities, but rather of the artistic representativeness of Africa and of the life of African peoples."6

President Sekou Toure (First President of Independent Guinea)
Soure: Britannica.com
* * *

With the independence of Guinea, the national ballet became a showcase directed to foreign audiences. In a curious charge from the new president, a distinction was made between educating audiences (the role of domestic troupes) and acquainting them with African culture (the role of the touring ballet).7

Fodeba Keita, of Siguiri, Guinea, brought a tour of Les Ballets Africains around the world. The jembe appeared on stages first in Europe then in North America. It became more popular in the U.S..8

One of Fodéba's main goals for the Ballet was to dispel many of the ideas about Africa that Europeans developed through films and lectures.

Fodéba was concerned that Europeans had developed a too narrow view of Africa, a continent with as much or more cultural diversity than Europe. For this reason, he decided to create a dance-based theatre company.9

* * *

Fodeba Keita: "To make Africa and all its variety known, we have chosen dance, not only as an excellent means of universal expression but also because, with us, it is connected with all the other arts . . . A characteristic phenomenon of our life, it can become ritual, magic, witchcraft, exorcism, an expression of freedom, morals and sundry sentiments . . . for dance is able to reach into a man's instincts, and his subconscious powers and express him completely."10

Les Ballets Africans de Keita Fodéba received funding from the French government through Malraux, which enabled the troupe to tour Europe and North America in 1959.11

Within a short time, the "Ballets Africains de Keita Fodeba" had been enthusiastically welcomed in Eastern and Western Europe, the British Isles, South America, and even at home on the African continent. Fodeba explained his work in the following terms:

Fodeba Keita: "In preparing our programs it has been our constant care to avoid leading the audience into error in presenting to them a picture of a fictitious Africa. It is because our songs and dances belong as much to the traditional and precolonial Africa of our ancestors as to the Africa of today, which little by little is becoming tinged by Western civilization. To us authenticity is synonymous with reality. To the extent that folklore is a mixture of traditions, poems, songs, dances and legends of the people, it can be no other than the reflection of the life of the country and if that country develops, there is no reason why the folklore which is the living expression, should not develop as well. That is why modern folklore in present Africa is as authentic as the Africa of old, because both are a real expression of the life of our country lived in different times of our history."12

* * *

Significantly, not only was Guinea the birthplace of Les Ballets Africains' two principal organizers, Fodéba Keita and Facelli Kanté, it also became a magnet for Black radicals and artists, including Julian Bond, Fanny Lou Hamer, John Lewis, Kwame Toure (aka Stokely Carmichael), Miriam Makeba, and Harry Belafonte. The latter, in particular, played an important role in the development of Guinean post-independence performing arts. Inspired by Les Ballets Africains' U.S. performances and by his South African collaborator Makeba, who had moved to Guinea under invitation from President Sékou Touré, Belafonte visited Conakry, where he met Touré and was offered artistic directorship of a new national company, the Ballet Djoliba, founded in 1964.13

Longtime Director for Ballet Djoliba, Ansoumane Conde, shared his perspective on the role Harry Belafonte played in the establishment of the Guinea based Ballets.

Ansoumane Conde: "Harry Belafonte realized the incredible cultural treasures Guinea had to offer after seeing the Les Ballets Africains directed by Guinean Fodeba Keita on tour in the U.S.. In 1959, Belafonte and the South African diva Miriam Makeba won a prestigious Grammy Award for the album "An Evening with Harry Belafonte." At the time, the young singer was banned from her homeland and had moved to Guinea after Sékou Touré personally invited her to do so. Belafonte went to visit Makeba one day, met President Sékou Touré in person and as a result of this encounter found himself offered the position of artistic director at the Djoliba National Ballet."14

Harry Belafonte and Miriam Makeba (Grammy award winning album. Chief Bey played percussions on this album)
"An Evening with Belafonte/Makeba" Album cover
Source: Discogs.com

Mamady Keita spoke about his journey from a youth to becoming a member of the newly formed Ballet Djoliba.

Mamady Keita: "I was a little boy born into the Keita family, descendants of the Sundiata family. I was not able to drum. The Keita family is not a caste into the Nummu. I was drumming on everything as a young boy. The family took me to Karinkadjan Konde, Jembefola in the village for my Rite of Passage. Between the age of 10-12, I was taken to Siguiri with a small group of children for playing drums for festivals. During that time, the focus was on the small group Ballet in that area of Siguiri. Not knowing that Harry Belafonte and President Sekou Toure's friendship brought on an idea of traveling throughout the Manding of Guinea to find the best of the best artists to formalize a group for Harry Belafonte to bring to America. Once this tour happened, I was 13/14 and was chosen to leave Siguiri and go to Conakry to start practicing for this Ballet. I had Keita family members in Conakry to watch over me.

Me and other artists were on the island of Kassa to practice for this Ballet. There were American artists there as well as artists from Guinea. The numbers started out with hundreds of people and scaled down to about 45 people for the Ballet. I remember one day we got up to practice and noticed that Harry Belafonte and the American artists were packing up and was being shipped to the palace in Conakry. Next thing we find out that Mr. Belafonte and the American artists we were rehearsing with left Guinea and didn't return.

This Ballet on the island of Kassa became President Sekou Toure's private Ballet called Ballets Djoliba. We were all freedom fighters."15

Singer, Civil Rights Activist, Songwriter, and Actor, Harry Belafonte, shared with me his role in the establishment of one of Guinea's premier Ballets, Ballet Djoliba.

Harry Belafonte: "In the 1960s, I had the opportunity to go on a trip with President Sekou Toure to all the cities and towns in Guinea. My purpose being to see all the different tribes' environ and the different dances associated with each and to select from those groups the core which we organized into Ballet Djoliba. After I helped to create Djoliba, it became a part of the national identity and was integrated into a permanent part of the culture. At its core were the Guinean drummers who were considered to be the finest in West Africa."

After interviewing Harry Belafonte, it became evident to me that Africans from America not only played important and significate roles in the development of the jembe as we know it today, but also in the development of the early Ballets coming out of Guinea with revolutionary messages that would play out on stages throughout the world. Harry Belafonte is not only accomplished as a musician and actor but also as an activist for the Civil Rights Movement and other important social justice causes for Black people in America. I knew that Mr. Belafonte had a close relationship with President Sekou Toure, but I was pleasantly surprised to learn about his active involvement in selecting, developing, and promoting jembe music and dance from Guinea for the world to experience.

* * *

With Les Ballets Africains now serving as cultural and political ambassadors of the African independence and resistance movement of West Africa, the jembe took center stage and would become the new vehicle for revolution in the American artistic community. In Les Ballets Africains, the jembe soloist has the drum strapped on and thus becomes another dancer. In this context, the jembe functions, not only as a musical instrument, but a dramatic prop through which the player challenges the other dancers to a rhythmic bout.

The first and only African American to perform with Les Ballets Africains on stage, Sam Watson, shares about his first encounter with Les Ballets.

Sam Watson: "Raymond McKeithan took me to the Ballets Africains and I met them in 1967. This was after I got out the army. They performed at Brooks Atkinson Theater in New York City. When I sat in the theater and I saw the Ballets for the first time, I said, this is me. I couldn't sit down. I got up and I ran around the back of the theater. I said, this is what I have been looking for all of my life and it hit me right in the face. At that time black people didn't go to the ballet. The people who went to the ballet were rich white people throughout the world. Elombe Brath brought Les Ballets to the Apollo theater. That's when Les Ballets was introduced to black America. I was on the bus on opening day of the Ballets at the Apollo theater. I was at the hotel where they stayed and I was on the bus. I had to be there. After Les Ballets appeared at the Apollo, people started naming their kids Sekou and things like that."

One of Dinizulu African Dance Company's early drummers, Mensa, spoke on the West African Ballets' early performances in America.

Kobla Mensa Dente: "There weren't many jembes here until the Guinea National and National Ballets from Senegal came in the late 60s/early 70s. That's when the jembe started to explode because no one had seen anything like that before. The jembe attracted so many people and you see that even until today."

One of International Afrikan American Ballets' dancers, Amaniyea Payne, recalls her first time seeing Les Ballets Africains.

Amaniyea Payne: "In 1972, Les Ballets Africains appeared in Baltimore at the Morris Mechanic Theatre. That was my real introduction to the jembe orchestra for that was one of the main instruments being played at that time. I remember sitting in the back of the theatre not sitting in the seat but on top of the seat. I recognized that these people were "FLYING". Consciously, I had never seen anything like that before that captured me like that, so at that point, the search was ON."

The jembe became popular in the United States when Ladji Camara, the lead drummer with Les Ballets Africains, relocated to America in the early 1960s to teach. By the mid 1960s, the jembe had drummers, dancers, and enthusiasts in a trance. This was the beginning of the Jembe Revolution in America.

Chapter 4

Jembe Jewels

"You can never play the Jembe without the Sangban! That is tradition."
Mamady Keita

I was born with the gift of listening. People have a tendency to tell me all about themselves and their aspirations because it is not often one gets the opportunity to speak to a genuine, sincere and bona fide listener. Many people engage in dialogue just to get their thoughts out. They listen to the speaker but are not focused on details. They are listening for the break in the conversation for their turn to unload. I know plenty of people throughout my travels who consider me a very close friend. I know it is because of my listening skills. I, on the other hand, have very few close friends. Those I do call my close friends are the ones who I recognize as listeners for me; they offer reciprocal relationships. I believe that I learned to appreciate my listening skills more as I developed my self-awareness. I consider myself an eternal student, so listening is crucial to learning all that I can while I navigate through this vast sea of experiences called life.

I am fully engaged when listening to others, especially elders. I pay close attention to what others feel is important for them to share. I asked clear questions during my interviews with the many drummers and dancers in this book. It was very interesting to hear what they wanted to share with me in those moments. Their sharing were not necessarily the topics I had asked during the interview.

* * *

Here are some jewels from Jembefolas who have dedicated their lives to playing and teaching jembe music at a very high level all over the world:

Ladji Camara: "The key to mastering your jembe is to love your drum and love playing it. Really love it from here. You heart."

Famoudou Konate: "Someone playing jembe is not supposed to be angry. Someone playing jembe is not supposed to be a jealous person. Unity. Happiness. So many people got healed at our performances from the jembe. The vibrations heal.

Performers got sick and the jembe healed them. You have to love the jembe before you can make people happy from playing the jembe. Jembe is supposed to talk. Today the jembe is very tight. Jembe should have some ring so it can speak. The traditional sound is not aggressive.

When I left the Ballet, I started teaching and conducting workshops for people. All of the places that I went with the Ballet, the people from those places came to me in Guinea to learn how to play jembe. I went to Switzerland to perform, and the owner of the hotel where we stayed gave his son to me to teach him the jembe for one hour. He paid me a lot of money for one hour. That was the start of me teaching and doing workshops."

Moussa Traore: "I met Famoudou and we speak about jembe and we always share the same experience because jembe is made for African people especially (those from) Mali and Guinea. We own jembe. But at some point jembe used to be for everybody but because of religion and western influence the jembe player became the lowest person in the society. Until the western people come back and try to be interested in jembe again, it changed the entire dynamic. I discussed some of this stuff with Famoudou. If you wanted to be a jembe player, you would have all the problems you want. The family would say man can you go do something better than playing jembe. People say man you have a lot of energy you are smart how about you go to school and be a political guy or be in military be a general. You couldn't marry anybody. You make a deal with a woman and say you want to get married and you go to the family to perform rites, the family would say hey are you crazy? You want to marry jembe player. Famoudou said they experienced the same thing at some point but at least the community still respected the culture.

How did the jembe get so big? Because of the Ballets. We all grew up with the teaching style from the Ballets. They brought to us the phrases to play. The rhythms, the dances, songs, the repertoire. Our job was to learn all of that then perform. But we weren't taught to take those studies to another level to teach people another way of playing a specific rhythm and dance. I think because of the Ballets they brought the spelling 'D'Jembe.'

Sega is my Teacher. He is ninety-six now. My dad fight him asking him why you want to make my son a jembe player. He's supposed to go to school and be someone. I told him that I'm going to do something with this. I'm good at it. He said who is going to pay you to go to Europe and those places to play and do things. He gave me a hard time. You jembe player, you sleep with other men's women, do drugs, stealing, and stuff. I went to Europe for ninety days and didn't tell him I was going, and he was worrying my teacher and my mother. I came back, and he argued with me and I told him where I was and he couldn't believe me. A few months later, he saw a bunch of Europeans come to Mali looking for me to learn. He said, "Oh this boy was telling me something."

Mamady Keita: "A master, especially a master of the jembe, must master all rhythms and know exactly when each is played and why. There are also some sounds of the jembe that a master transmits to only one student, who is devoted, body and soul, to the jembe. One must also know the virtues of the jembe, which is to say how to achieve strength and precision in playing the drum, and certain magical practices, such as protection against bad influences. Of course, here in the Western world, one has to be very careful with these things since people are not initiated in this tradition."1

Moussa Traore: "What makes a jembe player a master. If people call themselves master then they need to make it specific and clear to where they are a master at. Like I am the master jembe drummer from Guinea or from three-fourths of the country. But if I choose to speak for everybody then that means that you are trying to make the jembe speak one way. But if you can't find one language for all of Africa, then you can't be a master jembe player for all of Africa. No one can be a master jembe player. You don't understand the language from all of the different places where these rhythms come from. Too many languages to speak. If you know all of those different languages then I will call you Grand Master Drummer. We play jembe now for Western favor. We speak everyone's language on jembe because people are trying to making a living. Everything is mixed up.

Mamady had his own technique and playing style. He played very well and his technique was very good. But that doesn't mean he knew jembe more than everybody. It doesn't mean that he was a better player than all other jembe players. It's taking people a long time to learn this. We are from different areas and speak different languages and have different cultures. I don't know much about Guinea jembe drumming. I know Mali. The only rhythm I feel I really know from Guinea is dununba because the area dununba comes from is really close to Mali. That area of Mali speaks Malinke so we have a lot in common in that area."

In the 1960s, jembe music and dance entered the programs of state-sponsored folkloric ensembles and became a national symbol in both Guinea and Mali. At the same time, jembe music and dance became part of the urban popular culture in these countries as well as, in the following decades, in neighboring Senegal, Ivory Coast and Burkina Faso.2

One of the first professional jembe drummers in America, Mor Thiam, spoke on the jembe language.

Mor Thiam: "The drum speaks the language." With the comment, Mr. Thiam spoke a phrase and then played the same phrase on his jembe. "If the drummer is playing and someone walks in, he (the drummer) can tell you who the person is and what the person has been doing (with phrases played on the jembe.)"3

Bolokada Conde: "My mom told people when I was two years old that I was going to be a drummer. She took me to see all of the Jembefola teachers. She take me to see all Jembefola performers. After performances, my mom would take me to those performers to have a talk and tell them my name. At eight years old, one woman saw me teaching my friends how to play parts for rhythms that I heard Jembefolas playing. She said we want him to perform for us today. My mom took me to Malinke Bara where they do performance. When I play, everybody changed. Asked who is that and they say "Bolokada, Oh my God!" Then my village people asked about me and if I could play for them. My dad learned about this and said "No, I work with Bolokada in my fields. If Bolokada keeps playing for the village, then who is going to work in my fields?" My mother said you have to let him play for them. The village said why isn't it good for Bolokada to play for us? If Bolokada play for us isn't it good for village. My Dad said "no! if he plays jembe for the village then it's going to be very hard for me. I want to work with Bolokada in the fields." The village said "now Bolokada will play for us and we will work in your fields." My Dad said yes and everyone loved my Dad after that."

Mamady Keita: "In general, rhythms are usually composed of two accompaniment parts, or three accompaniment parts if there are more jembés in the village. There is always one sangban, one kenkeni, and a dundunba, or sometimes just the sangban, or just the sangban and the kenkeni, or just the sangban and the dundunba. But you can never play the jembe without the sangban! That is tradition."4

Famoudou Konaté and Mamady Keita standardized the repertoire of drumming pieces and invented methods of formally teaching jembe

68

music. For instance, while simple break phrases served as calls in the Ballets and marked the ending of individual dance solos in traditional celebration music, in the teaching context, these breaks were reinterpreted as interfaces between cyclic drumming patterns to work around the difficulty of creating musical form through more flexible changes between phrases and variations.5

Mamady Keita: "The rhythms of the Ballets have been mostly traditional rhythms which are modified, even radically changed, for presentation on the stage; for instance, in regard to the tempo, the jembe accompaniments or the dundunba voices. But we also create entirely new rhythms. In a manner of speaking, the Ballets transforms tradition into a kind of folkloric presentation, and, in doing so, loses some depth and authenticity. In working with the Ballets, a traditional drummer has to revise his playing completely. They play much faster; and one does not know the arrangements. The performances are full of breaks and compositions."6

Chapter 5

Before Jembe in America

"Dunham Technique has given the black dancer a vehicle in which he could express another way." Arthur Hall

~

I was about to walk into a historic hotel in New York City right off of Broadway for an interview with the oldest African American African drummer at the time, Eugene Osborne (Oz) Smith. It was a typical summer day in New York City. However, as I looked around through the sea of people and vehicles and the waves of heat rising from the asphalt, I realized I was not too far from the venue where Ladji Camara and Les Ballets Africains performed in America for the first time in 1959. Their performance set off a spark that would ignite a fire in many drummers, dancers, and the artist community. I walked into this hotel that had converted rooms into condominiums and felt as if I had taken a step back into the roaring 1950s era. It was a fitting backdrop for the pending interview. Mr. Eugene Osborne Smith took me back in time to help me 'overstand' the beginnings of this African drumming and dance consciousness in America before the jembe arrived.

Eugene Osborne Smith ("Oz" or "Osborne"): "I was born in 1927 in Miami, Florida. I started playing the drums when I was a little boy in Florida. I left Miami in 1934/35 at nine years old with my younger brother headed alone to New York to be with our mother. My background is Seminole, Creek, and African American. The first time I got into drumming seriously was with Moses Miannes, and he was drumming for Pearl Primus. I knew Pearl from grade school. So, we knew each other for a long time. Asadata Dafora had the first African drum and dance group in America. I was thirteen/fourteen when I met Asadata and was playing with his group. Asadata Dafora gave me my first drum; an ashiko."

* * *

Before Mr. Osborne Smith's interview, I had only read and heard about Asadata Dafora's legacy. I certainly never met anyone who actually knew him, never mind played and/or danced with him and his group.

Asadata Dafora was a multi-talented singer, dancer, choreographer from Sierra Leone. Dafora arrived in the United States after serving in the British army during WW II. Although he had initially chosen to stay in

Europe after his tour of duty and had begun to study voice with the hope of becoming an opera singer, he was unable to achieve this goal. Instead, Dafora achieved a fluency in Italian, German, and French as well as a firm grounding in European classical music. Ironically, when he arrived in the United States in 1929, he quickly became an ambassador of West African culture. In fact, he was the first African dancer to present African dance in concert form within the United States (Walser 1999: 163). With a small group of African men of various cultural backgrounds, The National African Union (a social club) with all members all living in Harlem, Dafora formed his first performing dance ensemble called "Sholonga Oloba." In 1933, this group staged scenes from Dafora's first African 'opera,' entitled Zoonga, at Madison Square Garden (Long 1989: 48). After the success of this first performance, Dafora augmented his group through the addition of African American women. Within the year, this expanded troupe put on the first full-length African dance-opera ever staged in the United States, Kykunkor (1934), which opened to rave reviews. Given that most of the African American women added to the troupe had no stage experience or knowledge of African culture, Dafora (by necessity) became a teacher not only of dance, but of African music and culture. He was also the choreographer and drummer in a 1936 stage success, Orson Welles's all-Black Macbeth performed in Harlem on Broadway and on national tour. With his collaborator, Abdul Assen, he helped create the unique sound and feel of the Haitian "voodoo" sections of the performance. Over the span of his career, Dafora taught most of the African American dancers who would later become leading teachers and choreographers. Ismay Andrews, Alice Dinizulu, Katherine Dunham, Pearl Primus, Esther Rolle, and Charles Moore were all dancers who initially trained under Dafora. In addition, Dafora taught Babatunde Olatunji, a Nigerian drummer who would later lead a revival of African drumming in New York. Dafora's student, Ismay Andrews, was responsible for training James Hawthorne (Chief Bey) who became one of the most sought after drummers in the American scene in the 1960s and 1970s.1

Asadata Dafora
Source: Schomburg Center for Research in Black Culture
* * *

Eugene Osborne Smith ("Oz" or "Osborne"): "Moses Miannes was playing with Pearl Primus and I was playing the ashiko drum. Moses was from Nigeria and played the ashiko drum with Asadata and taught Taiwo DuVall and a bunch of other drummers at that time. I was supposed to be in the original Porgy and Bess production on Broadway, but I took the opportunity to be with the traveling production of Porgy and Bess. I believe that Chief Bey took my spot in the Broadway production. In the early 1950s the production went all over America then spent a lot of time in Europe. I toured with Porgy and Bess for about one and a half years. I drummed in Porgy and Bess playing the ashiko drum."

I had the distinct privilege of interviewing Mr. Taiwo DuVall regarding his legacy and contributions to African drumming in America. He made me realize how important it is to acknowledge and teach about these pioneers of the African drumming and dance world such as Moses Miannes, Asadata Dafora, Babatunde Olatunji, and others. Taiwo DuVall, in the early 1950s, became a member of Asadata Dafora's entourage through an introduction by Montego Joe and traveled for many years with Baba Moses Miannes as his obafun drummer. Moses Miannes' ashiko drum was passed on to Taiwo after Miannes was killed after being hit by a cab in front of the Apollo Theater in 1964.

Taiwo spoke about his first encounter with Baba "Machine Gun" Moses Miannes.

Taiwo DuVall: "Showing up late for a rehearsal was a good way to get fired, so I hopped in a cab and rushed to the studio. When I got there, I heard all these drums playing, and I thought, they must have already found a replacement for me. I opened the door, and it was just the old man playing - he sounded like three drummers."

During one of my sessions with Taiwo, he apologized for his loss of memory and requested for the sake of accuracy that I reference his publications for information regarding his early drumming days, particularly with Moses Miannes. I learned that Taiwo was the epitome of the Harlem Renaissance. He was a Visual Artist, Drummer, Teacher, and a Writer.

Taiwo DuVall: "While standing on the southeast corner of 127th Street and Lenox Avenue one day [Harlem, New York], I saw an elderly black man standing there. He was wearing a gray gabardine trench coat and a wide brimmed fedora-looking hat cocked on the side of his head. He was a proud looking soul. In his hand he carried an army duffel bag that I could see contained some kind of drum! He went up the steps and entered an auditorium. There were other people waiting for him. There were two or three male dancers there. Mickey Newby, Zebede Collins, and a big guy named Joe Commodore. The female dancers there were Esther Rolle and her cousins, as well as Joan (Akwasiba) and Merle (Afida) Derby. The leader of the group was a guy named Asadata Dafora. They were mesmerizing! The other drummers there were Montego Joe and Chief Bey. I couldn't believe all of this was going on within a few hundred feet from my place on 127th Street! The elderly man and his two cousins had my undivided attention. I had never heard any drumming like that before! I was told his name was Moses Miannes, but he was called "Machine Gun Moses" by the people of Harlem. They said his hands were so fast when he played that his drum sounded like the rapid fire of a machine gun! I also met up with another up-and-coming drummer who was doing the same thing I was doing (digging the drumming scene). We started talking, and he said his name was Al Humphrey. He is known as "Babafemi." Getting together with these guys became a weekly event and was my first introduction to real African dancing and drumming.

Baba Moses Miannes was a member of the Ijaw people of Nigeria, who lived on the delta of the river Niger. They were great seafarers. So, it would only stand to reason that he would have become a merchant seaman. However, he fell ill in England on a voyage there and the ship had to sail on without him. In the meantime, another ship came into port looking for another hand. They were sailing for New York City Harbor, Manhattan.

Baba Moses jumped at the opportunity to come to New York. He had two Ijaw cousins there who lived up in Harlem, and he was about to surprise them by knocking on their door. Baba Moses had heard so much about Harlem growing up as a boy. Now his dream was about to come true! He arrived in America in 1933. He did not come with a drum, because he felt it was not needed. Nobody was playing African drums in America. It was only a short time later that he decided to stay in Harlem and would need employment. Mr. Miannes had no marketable skills required for big city living.

Moses Miannes and his two cousins were standing on the corner of 125th Street and Lenox Avenue one day trying to help him find a job. All of a sudden, a Cadillac limousine swerved over to the curb, and this white guy, with a big cigar in his mouth, jumped out of the car, walked up to them, gave out his card, and said, "if any of you guys know of any 'African looking' Negroes who can beat some drums, give me a call. I got some work for 'em at the Chicago World's Fair." As the man was walking back to his car, one of the cousins wanted to confront him, but Moses stopped his cousin and said to the man, "Okay we will be there!"

As fate would have it, that was a talent scout in the area looking for some "African-type" Negroes to perform as drummers at the Chicago

World's Fair in 1934. He had to restrain his cousins because they felt the white guy was making a racist remark.

Baba Moses convinced his two cousins to forget their anger and join up with him in a search for some drums in New York City that they could purchase to audition for this job. They had no luck finding any African drums in New York. He now wished he had brought his drums. One of the neighbors suggested he go talk to the neighborhood carpenter. The carpenter was a Trinidadian who was familiar with the type of drums he needed. Baba Moses gave the Trinidadian carpenter the proper dimensions and specifications, and he went right to work.

The carpenter made three drum shells. The first and largest shell was called "Iya Ilu" (mother drum), the second, smaller in stature, was called "Omele," or "Obafun" (father drum). The third drum, smaller still, was called "Kekere" (child drum).

Now, they had to find a slaughterhouse in New York City where they could purchase three freshly killed calf skins. They were told about a slaughterhouse in Brooklyn operated by some Jewish Rabbis. They went there, picked out three skins, and were off to the hardware store to buy several hundred feet of rope. They cured the skins with lime and, several days later, went about skinning the three drums.

The ashiko drums were finished in time for the three men to make it to the audition. They also found out they had absolutely no competition, because they were the only drummers in New York State. The audition officials approved them, and they were on their way to "The 1934 Chicago World's Fair" and the debut of America's First Ashiko Drum Family. Incidentally, it was also the year Thomas Taiwo DuVall was born; destined, it seems, to be the inheritor of Baba Moses's Drum.

The job at the World's Fair launched their career, to say the least. Baba Moses became known in the Harlem area as "Machine Gun Moses and Family." The people of Harlem gave his two cousins American Indian names because of their features. They were called "Geronimo" and "Cherokee." They later teamed up with a man named Asadata Dafora, a dancer and choreographer from Sierra Leone. This marked the beginning of America's first African Dance Company. The names of some of the members were: Esther Rolle as the Dance Captain; her sister Martha and cousins were among the dancers, Zebedee Collins, Charles Moore, Curtis James, Mickey Newby, Aquasiba and Afida Darby, Ida Capps, Joe Commodore, and Tommy Johnson, to name a few, were among the dancers. Ismay Andrews was the Lead Singer. The Drummers were Montego Joe and Chief Bey (Singer and Drummer). In the early sixties, one of Baba Moses's cousins died and the other took the obafun ashiko and went back to Africa, where he later died."2

Baba Moses Miannes with his Ashiko
Source: Taiwo DuVall

While listening to stories from Mr. Taiwo DuVall and Eugene Osborne Smith, it became clear to me that the ashiko was setting the tone for the arrival of the jembe. These drummers like Moses Miannes, Chief Bey, Montego Joe, and Taiwo DuVall were creating the African drum culture of that time and paving the way for West African Jembefolas. However, that drum culture could not have risen to the heights that it did without the dance culture. The pioneers of African dance like Asadata Dafora, Katherine Dunham, Pearl Primus, Ismay Andrews, Aquasiba and Afida Darby, Joe Commodore, Charles Moore and others. While all of these dancers paved the way for many African dancers after them, Katherine Dunham's name has been mentioned more than any other with regards to spreading the jembe throughout America in the 1960s. She is credited with promoting Ladji Camara outside of New York in the early sixties in California and St. Louis. Some even believe that while performing in Paris together in 1952, Dunham was the one who convinced Ladji to stay in the United States once he arrived in New York. She also brought Mor Thiam to the United States in 1968 and toured many universities throughout the United States. Those tours may have been the start of the jembe attraction by colleges and universities all over the United States.

* * *

I had the privilege to interview the great Mor Thiam, a very youthful elder who explained to me that his parents did not keep records of his birth so he goes with a birth year of 1948. His name is known all over the world for his jembe drumming. Many publications have cited Mor Thiam as a one time Director of the Ballets de Senegal.

Mor Thiam: "I have always been solo and was never a part of the Ballet de Senegal. I played with them and performed at the same events but was not a member of the Ballet."

It was not easy to get Mor Thiam's interview. Many do not know that he is the father of recording artist Akon who has experienced major global success in the hip hop and pop industry. Mr. Thiam was not easy to catch up within the music industry because he left the music scene after making his Hajj (a Muslim's holy pilgrimage to Mecca). He is now a spiritual teacher with a school in Senegal teaching the ways of Islam.

Mor Thiam spoke with authority and confidence. I acknowledged how proud he must have been of his son Akon's success and accomplishments. He responded with "Of course, but I'm also very proud of you for your work." That set the tone for the periodic check-ins that he and I now offer one another whether in Africa or the United States. Based on our conversations, he is very aware of his impact in the music industry, particularly African drumming. Not only did he make it clear how important a role he played in making the jembe popular all over the world, but also the role Katherine Dunham played in promoting jembe drumming in America in the 1960s.

Mor Thiam: "I don't drum anymore. I only teach about Islam now. The jembe history is important for people to know so that is why I want to tell you about my story."

I asked about Katherine Dunham and the first drummers to play and teach jembe when the jembe first arrived in America. Dunham had been invited to Senegal by President Léopold Senghor to train the National Ballet of Senegal in 1967. President Senghor appointed her to the position of adviser for the first World Black and African Festival of Arts and Culture, also known as the World Festival of Negro Arts (Festival des Arts NŹgre), held in Dakar. The U.S. State Department gave Dunham official status in naming her the U.S. representative to the 1967/68 Festival in Dakar.

Mor Thiam: "Katherine Dunham and Miles Davis came to the World Festival of Negro Arts (Festival des Arts NŹgre), held in Dakar, Senegal in 1968. I was a solo drummer who welcomed them at the airport when they entered into Senegal. From that meeting Katherine brought me into the United States in 1968. I traveled with Katherine Dunham to universities all over the United States teaching and performing. I traveled to Senegal every year after traveling to the United States in 1968. I was about 20 years old."

Mor Thiam
The First World Festival of Negro Arts (FESMAN)
1966, Dakar, Senegal
Source: Library of Congress

Mor Thiam
Photos: The African History/Facebook: @akon
Source: Instagram

Greg Ince: "Mor Thiam was the man from Senegal. He was the Master jembe teacher in St. Louis and Chicago area for years."

Baba Mosheh Milon: "Mor Thiam was big too and I studied under him in St. Louis. You could damn near walk to Chicago from St. Louis. My first understanding of the jembe could have been through Mor Thiam."

Enoch Williamson: "Ms. Katherine Dunham brought Mor Thiam to St Louis. He was from Senegal. After a while they began these huge drum and dance festivals in St. Louis and they'd bring in artists from all over the country and around the world to host African drum and dance classes. These became a big hit for Black People who were a part of the Cultural Renaissance movement in the Black community. I would attend these festivals.

Thiam began to teach me the high value that he placed on his art. I was going to the University of Missouri doing graduate work in music for Ethnic Musicology. I was a director of a music program that brought artists to the University for the students. I wanted to bring Mor Thiam in but he cost more than the University could afford. I went to his office in St. Louis thinking I could change his mind. While there, he got a call from Japan, they wanted him to come there. He told me to take the call and negotiate for him. I took the phone and they were offering him a sizable amount of money, I thought. I told him the amount and he refused. So I hung up. He said don't worry they'll call back and they did. They then offered a 10% increase and he said "refuse and then hang up." I said, "man that's a lotta money, don't you think you should take it?" He said, "don't worry they'll call back." Which they did and offered another 15% increase. He took the phone and accepted the deal. He told me, "never sell yourself short and understand your value and your value increases the harder you work."

Katherine Dunham toured many colleges and venues in the United States. She also traveled throughout West Africa, South America, and the Caribbean, not only as a dancer/choreographer, but also as an anthropologist. Her studies in these destinations would eventually aid her in developing a dance style which we know today as the "Dunham Technique." She documented her journey while in Accompong Town in the Cockpit Country in the mountains of Jamaica. Her Accompong memoirs would eventually be published under the title Katherine Dunham's Journey to Accompong. She traveled to Martinique and Trinidad, but it was her travels to Haiti that would give Dunham a renewed purpose in her craft and in her life.

One of Papa Ladji's first dance students and Theatre Director, Akin Babatunde, spoke about Katherine Dunham.

Baba Akin Babatunde: "Kathrine Dunham's legacy is that she was a spiritual giant. Not only was she an anthropologist but she became a high priestess in Voodoo. She was a celebrated Mambo. Harold Pearson choreographer said about Katherine Dunham that Charles Moore told the story where they were in a boat and she got possessed by a water deity and put a cake in the water. Charles said "Oh I thought we were going to eat that!"

Eugene Osborne Smith ("Oz" or "Osborne"): "Katherine Dunham was a very intelligent person. The last time we saw each other was in Paris. We were both in Paris. Her show was struggling in Paris so she asked me to help her out with her show. She said "Brother, go out there and show them your stuff." I agreed and played drums in her production and she was so happy. We had a great relationship. It was easy to help Katherine because she was a generous person. She helped so many people become successful artists. People like Pearl Primus, Harry Belafonte, Ladji Camara, Eartha Kitt, and so many others. I just can't remember them all."

Katherine Dunham
Source: lustnspace.tumblr.com

It is interesting to note that Eugene Osborne Smith shared that Dunham assisted Harry Belafonte. Belafonte recalled Dunham teaching him about Haitian music and culture. He recorded several successful songs because of her Haitian teachings. In keeping with the theme regarding the jembe and its birth in America, Mr. Belafonte would go on to co-found one of Guinea's premier African drum and dance troupes, Ballet Djoliba. Ballet Djoliba would eventually launch one of the world's most famous Jembefolas to ever play the drum, Mamady Keita. It is also noteworthy that one of the first African Americans to be initiated into the Yoruba Religion back in 1959, Walter Eugene King (Oba Efuntola

Oseijeman Adelabu Adefunmi), was a part of the Katherine Dunham's Dance Company. Oba Adefunmi is also credited as the founder and developer of the Oyotunji Yoruba village in South Carolina. He traveled with Dunham's company to Haiti in 1954 and to Europe and North Africa in 1955. Undoubtedly, Katherine Dunham's direct and indirect influence on the spread of jembe music in the West was unprecedented and unparalleled.

Harry Belafonte: "I think what Katherine Dunham brought to America and indeed all of Europe was a sense of depth of culture that resonated within the world of the peoples of color. Not just Africans and African Americans and African Caribbeans, but also the dance and the music of the people of Latin America. And I think until the advent of her breaking into the world of dance, very little regard had been paid to the art form of the dance for the people from those regions."[3]

Katherine Dunham won fellowships from the Guggenheim and Rosenwald Foundations in 1935 and 1936 to pursue anthropological fieldwork in the Caribbean. She traveled through Jamaica, Martinique, Trinidad, and Haiti where she underwent the first level of initiation into voodoo.

The influence of Haiti and the folk dances of the Haitian people on choreography and teaching in the dance world today is due chiefly to the work of Katherine Dunham. The dance career of Jean Leon Destine, who was later to be the preeminent exponent of Haitian dance in the United States, was fostered by Katherine Dunham when Destine first came to the United States.

Dunham's Caribbean itinerary began in Jamaica, where she stayed in the Maroon village of Accompong, deep in the Cockpit Country. This had served as a place of settlement for escaped slaves who had been able to conserve their African cultural elements to a greater extent than was possible in the plantation life. She then went to Martinique and to Trinidad for brief stays before arriving in Haiti in 1936.

She would eventually, give up a scholarly career in order to pursue a life in dance; becoming famous for her innovative and immensely popular choreography that fused balletic within the vernacular of folk traditions. Through a rigorous practice and daunting performance schedule, she spent decades of her life traveling with her dance company. Dunham gave audiences around the globe an experience of the dances of the African Diaspora.

When Dunham returned from the Caribbean in January 1938, she premiered a ballet that was set in a fishing village in Martinique called L'Ag'Ya, a fantastical blend of martial arts and Afro-Caribbean movement, danced to the music of drums and sticks. Dunham would eventually formalize many of the movements in L'Ag'Ya as she codified the "Dunham Technique," a method and practice that helped to take black dance out of the burlesque. L'Ag'Ya became a staple of Dunham's repertoire for the next decade as she built her touring company, established a school in New York, and soared to international fame.

Long time dancer with Dinizulu Dance and Drum group and a dancer at the Dunham School, Ajaibo Waldrond, talked about his experience with Katherine Dunham.

Ajaibo Waldrond: "I was part of the Katherine Dunham school around 1951. I was fourteen and dancing around Harlem but I was eighteen when I started formal training. Kathrine Dunham's style was mostly Caribbean. During the 1951-1953 time period, when I first went to the Dunham school, the second or third person I met was Floretta Donald (Akosua Panyin). She was my dance partner for a couple of years. We were in a group together called "Caribeana". This was one of the experimental groups made up of students from the Kathrine Dunham school. Akosua and I became good friends and were in other experimental groups at the Dunham school. We would do performances and raise money for the school along with Montego Joe and Lance Haven who were singers and drummers for Caribeana."

Akan Priest, Dancer, Artist, Choreographer, and Producer known as the Father of African dance and drumming in Philadelphia, Arthur Hall, spoke about Katherine Dunham.

Arthur Hall: "The technique that I use again is tied into the philosophy of the group, black awareness. Maintaining of images of Black people. Katherine Dunham is an anthropologist and she was the first black woman to create a dance technique. I was brought up in the traditions of this technique. This is what I used. It wouldn't have been feasible for me to use this technique for the last twenty years that I would not add a little me. The Dunham Technique was based on Haiti and I have done a lot from the African tradition. Dunham used the snake and vertebrae of the snake for the development of her technique, to free the entire body. She used Haiti and the spirit of the ancestors in Dunbala; you trace that mythology back to Dahomey, Benin. Looking at the movement of the snake is fluidity. Fluidity of movement is what she developed her technique around. The goal is to get every part of the body in tune with the rhythm. If you could not move your shoulders and pelvic areas, then you could not do African dance properly. Katherine Dunham had a method to her madness. The Dunham Technique has given the black dancer a vehicle in which he could express another way."4

The legend, Katherine Dunham, spoke about the "Dunham Technique."

Katherine Dunham: "I was exposed to some modern as well as ballet. In my early days in Chicago I had some oriental dance and Spanish dance as well. I went to all the concerts I could manage to go to. I mean I went to as many financially possible. As I began to teach more and more in the black neighborhood, I realized that I wasn't getting across what I wanted to. Without being able to verbalize it. I had been awakened through studies in Anthropology to the fact that there was a whole field of performing arts that was more or less black and had not been explored in this country to its fullest and to its best. There certainly had been black shows and artists but it was not on a scale it would have needed to be for a whole movement and understanding to what dance is to black people and its origins in Africa; its remnants in the West Indes, South America and North America. So this became a passion for me to learn more about these origins to understand primitive dance of other people and to try and distill from this a vocabulary - a technique that would be serviceable for expressing the culture of black and third world people and for developing into a technique of performance and instruction which gradually became known as "Dunham Technique.""5

Katherine Dunham with drummers 1940 Broadway hit production of Cabin in the Sky
Source: Katherine Dunham Collection
Photo credit: The Library of Congress
* * *

On her return to Chicago, Dunham reassembled her dance group, composing for them exercises and dances based on her Caribbean experience, particularly that in Haiti. In March 1937, she journeyed with her group to New York to take part in the Negro Dance Evening at the YMCA organized by Edna Guy. It was at this time that she met the young dancer, Archie Savage, and the Haitian drummer, Augustin, both of whom she would share an extended artistic association with.

In 1941, she returned to New York where she remained until 1945. She continued her studies and adopting the stage name La Belle Rosette, made a number of theater and nightclub appearances. She also resumed teaching at the New Dance Group where in 1942, the young Pearl Primus was one of her students.6

From the beginning of her career as a modern dancer, Primus manifested a great interest in African themes and subjects. After her first visit to Africa in 1948, she was to devote herself almost exclusively to African dance.

In 1948, Primus received a Rosenwald grant which enabled her to make her first trip to Africa. Remaining there nine months, she had an overwhelming experience, and shared some of it with her public by way of a letter to John Martin, which he later published. In Nigeria, the Oni of the Ife conferred upon her the title Omowale – child who has returned home. Among the compositions inspired by her African experience were Fanga and Prayer of Thanksgiving, both in 1949.

The existence of a traditional African dance tradition in New York going back to Asadata Dafora and Shologa Oloba in the early 1930s, and considerably enhanced by the work of Pearl Primus in the 1940s, provided a frame of reference for the professional dance companies. On their return from Africa in 1961, Pearl Primus and Percival Borde organized an African Carnival, which was held for a weekend in November at the 69th Regiment Armory in New York. Special performers were Babatunde Olatunji from Nigeria, Jean Leon Destine from Haiti, Mongo Santeria from Cuba, and, naturally, Percival Borde representing Trinidad.7

Eugene Osborne Smith ("Oz" or "Osborne"): "Pearl Primas was a great artist. I should have married her. I really admired her, and we had a great relationship. She spent a lot of time in Liberia and Ghana."

Ayishah Shabazz is the ex-wife of Taiwo DuVall . She recalled her years with Dr. Pearl Primus as a dance student and eventually a member of her performing group.

Ayishah Vivian Lewis Shabazz: "Pearl Primus would say that Katherine Dunham got more recognition because she was dancing with more revealing costumes. And her movements were more sensuous. Joan Akwasiba Derby and Merle Afida Derby were sisters and were Pearl Primus' earliest dancers. Other dancers were Edith Bascombe, Mary

Waithe, Benjamin "Bobo" Sterlin, Noble Ewje, John Destine, Pearl Reynolds (close friend of Nina Simone), Ida "BB" Capps, and Charles Moore. Charles Moore did the Bird dance and only he could do that. Drummers were playing Haitian drums; Alphonce Cimber, Montego Joe, Bean Robert, and Taiwo DuVall. Levidia Williams was another well-known dancer and amazing. Charles Moore's wife Ella Thompson was excellent. Geoffrey Holder and his wife Carmen Delavalant were excellent dancers that also danced with Pearl Primus."

Pearl Primus: "The subject matter of African dance is all inclusive of every activity between birth and death. The seed which trembles to be born, the first breath of life, the growth, the struggle for existence, the reaching beyond the everyday into the realm of the soul, the glimpsing of the Great Divine, the ecstasy and sorrow which is life, and then the path back to the earth-this is the dance."8

Pearl Primus with Moses Miannes and Alphonse Cimber on drums
Source: Taiwo DuVall

Ayishah Vivian Lewis Shabazz: "I was nineteen years old (1963) when I first discovered Pearl Primus' dance studio. She had her company since the 1950s though. She was at 17 West 24th street in NYC. She had just returned from Africa and she had all of this fresh energy. She had a lot of energy anyway. Her love and devotion to dance were her greatest attributes. I was in awe of the movements she was giving me, I wanted to be in her company. After a few classes she told me that I was IN.

Dr. Pearl Primus was attending NYU majoring in Anthropology. She was allowed to do her dissertation on African Dance. When Pearl Primus went to Liberia, she came back with Fanga/Funga Dance (Welcome Dance). Apparently, in 1943 Asadata Dafora brought Fanga Dance back as well. When the Derby dancers went to Olatunji they changed the Fanga movements which are the moves that we know today. But we did Fanga much different with Dr. Pearl Primus.

One thing about Pearl Primus, she didn't demonstrate her dances like so many other teachers did. She would actually tell you how to move your foot. So, she had like four different positions of your feet. For instance, one of the foot positions was first neutral. She would sit there with her staff in her hand and would say put your feet in first neutral and take your right foot and lift it sharply then put it back down. So, you do that. Now do the same with your left foot. Now continue with your right foot then the left foot; you are walking along lifting your foot and putting it back down, and you got the step. They don't do the Fanga the way she did because there's a lot of undulating in your back when you are coming out low; because it's about the earth. The earth is welcoming. You are using the earth and sky to welcome your guests. And that's what Fanga is about. She would say put your hands on my back then she would do the back movements. Then tell us that's what you do. She was an amazing teacher. I have been telling people for years that Fanga is our (African Americans) folk dance."

It was intriguing to learn that research about the dance Fanga (Funga) in the United States reveals that Asadata Dafora was, in fact, the first to perform a version of Fanga in 1943. Dr. Pearl Primus' version of Fanga was not created/choreographed until 1959. Fanga was further popularized by Primus' students, sisters Merle Afida Derby and Joan Akwasiba Derby. When the Derby sisters joined Babatunde Olatunji, they brought Pearl Primus' version of Fanga with them. Olatunji described Fanga as a dance of welcome from Liberia and he with many others used a song created by LaRocque Bey to go with the rhythm and dance. They were assisted by some of the students in his Harlem studio, during the early sixties. LaRocque combined the original Fanga word with Yoruba language to create the popular song for Fanga that we know today; "Funga Alafia Ase Ase." The song that Primus and her students sang for Fanga can be heard on Olatunji's Drums of Passion at the beginning of "Baba Jinde" (Baba-Gee-Un-Day).

* * *

Since I was very young, I can remember seeing my father jump up and off the drum when the rhythms and energy elevated in the room. Whether it was a dance class or a performance, he would go into his ritual dance. He would dance in a circle moving his arms and hands in a forward circular fashion in front of his body. Then he would go into a side-to-side movement with alternating left and right kicks. Years later, I would recognize his movements from Akoms (Akan religious ceremonies which included chanting, drumming, and dancing) in which I had participated at Dinizulu's spiritual services in Queens, New York. My father attended Akoms in his younger years as a guest of his African dance teacher, Akosua Nsia Oparebeah Panyin (Floretta Donald). Akosua was initiated as a Priestess under Nana Yao Opare Dinizulu I. Akosua would eventually establish one of Westchester, New York's first African dance and drum troupes in which my Father, Abishai Ben Reuben, was one of the original drummers. My Aunt, Tanya Jackson-Smith, was also a member of Akosua's troupe as a principal dancer.

Akosua's daughter, Yaa Serwaa, reflected on her mom's relationship with Nana Dinizulu:

Yaa Serwaa Oparebeah Pintora (Janet Rush): "She did not dance with Nana Dinizulu's performing group as far as I remember. Ajaibo was his right hand and was very close to him with the performing group. Nana Dinizulu used to publicly introduce my mother (Akosua Panyin) as his oldest and dearest friend."

Nana Akosua Panyin
Source: Abdur Rahman Wheeler

Akosua studied at the Katherine Dunham School of Dance in New York City alongside her longtime dance partner, Ajaibo Waldrond. The two of them studied and eventually taught the "Dunham Technique" as a result of their dance studies and performances in Katherine Dunham's experimental groups. Both Akosua and Ajaibo would find themselves connected to Nana Dinizulu as well - Akosua as a Priest in training, attending, and leading Akoms, festivals, rituals, and ceremonies on a regular basis and Ajaibo as one of Nana's main dancers for his drum and dance group.

Ajaibo Waldrond: "I danced with Nana Dinizulu for about thirty to forty years on and off. Joe Commodore, Chief Bey, Ralph Dorsey, and

Jonny Eshun from Ghana were Nana Dinizulu's main drummers in the beginning."

Akosua and Ajaibo would prove instrumental in training dancers and drummers in Westchester, New York to form the Akosua African Dance and Drum Troupe out of Mount Vernon, New York. Akosua African Dance and Drum Troupe utilized the Dunham Technique as a template in developing its dance and drum repertoire. The group's high-spirited energy and ceremonial feel was influenced by the founder's connection with the Dinizulu spiritual system. When I began to take an interest in the African drum and dance world as a youth, I was more drawn to the parts of Akosua's repertoire that reminded me of the Dinizulu Akoms. It is no surprise then, when I decided to undergo a name change, that I went to the Dinizulu order for the reading and the naming ceremony. The ceremony was conducted like an Akom. All in attendance danced in a circle. All in attendance performed the side to side move with the alternating left and right kicks. Interestingly, even though the drummers were playing all Akan drums at my ceremony, some of those young drummers would eventually make up one of America's hottest jembe groups, Asase Yaa Entertainment Group. This was Nana Dinizulu's legacy. He had a vision and that included living an African cultural and spiritual tradition right here in America.

Ajaibo spoke about Dinizulu's legacy.

Ajaibo Waldrond: "I was fourteen dancing around Harlem, but I was eighteen when I started formal training. I didn't do any drumming until I joined Dinizulu in 1954/55. I was about twenty-one and that's when I started playing shekere and the bell. Alice Dinizulu, Nana Dinizulu's wife, studied and danced with Asadata Dafora. Mickie Newby was taught the Ostrich dance and she danced with him. Joe Commodore played for Asadata Dafora. Ismay Andrews danced with Asadata. Ismay Andrews taught in the 1940s and I remember taking classes with her. Chief Bey and Nana Dinizulu studied with Ismay Andrews and Joe Commodore played for her classes. When Nana Dinizulu started his group, it was a combination of Caribbean and African. After he returned from Ghana, he changed the style to mainly Ghanaian."

Nana Yao Opare Dinizulu I, Nana Adzua Opare, Kobla Mensa Dente, Nana Kwesi
Agyeman Circa 1978/79
Bosum-Dzemawodzi Temple, Long Island City, Queens, NY
Photo credit: Nana Kwame Amartey Dente
Source: Kobla Mensa Dente

Long time Dinizulu drum and dance group drummer, Kobla Mensa Dente, spoke about Nana Dinizulu's legacy:

Kobla Mensa Dente: "Dinizulu was the first African American African drum and dance group. Dinizulu started as a professional group in 1947. When they first started it was Nana Dinizulu, his cousin named Mattie and her husband named Joe Commodore who were the original drummers. It started with 2 drummers and 2-3 dancers. Ralph Dorsey (Drummer; famous jazz drummer as well) was like Nana's right-hand man, Amate Dente (my older brother who actually brought me in), Jonny Eshun, Lante Lante, Ajaibo Walrond, Chief Bey, Russell Robinson who had the Liberation House in Queens. I believe Russel Robinson played jembe with Nana Dinizulu. Later, as a teenager, his son, Kamati Dinizulu joined the company and the rest is history. Nana used the format structure of the Ghanaian orchestra of drums. When I started playing with the company in the mid-seventies, we used conga drums. We would wrap them with cloth and played them like that. As time went on the main drums Nana used were the fontomfrom drums which are drums used from the chieftaincy. He would play them standing. Nana would play the fontomfrom with his hands and the drummers on either side of him would play hand carved akyene drums with sticks.

There was a Gumboot dance from the early 60s that the vocalist Ayodele Beaner had taught the company. Then we had other folks from South Africa that worked with Dinizulu. A choreographer from Ipotombe worked with Nana after the play was shut down due to protesting. He taught a second version of Gumboot dance that we learned. We worked with cast members of the play Umabatha. Welcome Nsomi and his wife vocalist, Thule Dumakuta taught us a Zulu war dance. With these dances were all new styles of drumming that we had to learn. In addition, Master drummer and dancer Kwesi Mante from Ghana, taught us a vast array of traditional dances from all over Ghana.

Oseijeman (Oba Adefunmi) was the first narrator for Dinizulu. He introduced each segment of the performance. He became the Chief Priest in the Yoruba religion in America and started Oyotunji village. Oseijeman is also the author of "The Ancestors", which is a chronicle of the Asantehenes of the Asante nation in Ghana.

Kamati Dinizulu started with the company around early 70s. He traveled to Ghana in 1976 to study and returned in 1978. He brought back with him the Ga gome drum, the Ga social drumming called kpanlogo and the Fanti asafo drums. We performed the gome at Dance Africa and blew everyone's minds. It was one of those moments that stayed with you for the rest of your life. It was just him on the stage and KweYao playing the bell behind him. Reckless Abandonment."

When one thinks about the beginnings of African drum and dance in Philadelphia, there is one name that usually rings out, and that is Arthur Hall. There is no doubt that Mr. Hall left a very important legacy for generations to come. In 1951, at the age of seventeen, Arthur moved to Philadelphia with his mother, studying dance under Marion Cuyjet, Joe Nash, and John Hines among others. During this period, he found early inspiration for the standard of costume design which was to become his hallmark in the work of Katherine Dunham, Josephine Baker, and Uday Shankar of India. Particularly influential was his close association with the Ghanian artist, Olympic athlete, and Ghana's Cultural Minister, Saka

Acquaye, in Philadelphia from 1952 to 1959. Acquaye was a pioneer in his own right, infusing West African art forms into United States culture. Saka Acquaye saw so many African Americans with no traces of African culture and decided to start a dance troupe that would embody authentic African art forms. From 1952 to 1953, Arthur Hall was a part of Saka Acquaye's Black Beats Band, and he went on to become a principal dancer in the West African Cultural Society of Saka Acquaye. From 1954 to 1958, he also participated in Saka Acquaye's African Ensemble in America. Hall cited Saka Acquaye as the most influential person in his dance career:

Arthur Hall: "I studied with him (Saka Acquaye) three years, and during this time I decided to dedicate myself to keeping this lore in America. After all, there are 20 million black people here, and I think we must know something of our culture. Our people are not aware of their culture and heritage. I saw in the dances a chance to bring grandeur back into blackness."9

One of Saka Acquaye's first dancers in his American based group, Ione Nash, spoke on her experience with Saka Acquaye:

Ione Nash (Ione Shirley Osborne Nash): "I was born in Philadelphia on October 1, 1923. I went through elementary school in New Jersey and all other grades in Philly [Philadelphia]. In 1950, they had arts around in the parks two to three times during the summer. I saw a picture of a dancer lacing up her dance shoes and I said to my five-year-old daughter, "that's what I would like to do." Later on, a gentleman came up to me and said he heard what I had said about wanting to dance. He said he knew a woman that teaches dance in West Philly and he gave me her card. Her name was Olive Bowser, she was my first dance teacher; ballet, jazz, and little bit of tap. I was with her for about three years. I studied ballet at Marion Sujack's dance school on Chestnut Street. There were so many black students attending, the school had to leave [move] because there was really only whites on Chestnut street. After about three to four years, Marion asked me to choreograph a number for a group of girls. After that, I went to Joe Nash. He had a school below Marion's school in the same building. Joe Nash came in from New York. He taught more modern jazz dance.

An African came into Philly and was holding African dance auditions. I went to audition. Arthur Hall went to audition too. Karen Steptoe auditioned. We passed the auditions. His name was Saka Acquaye. Out of all of the people that auditioned, he only took ten and we were part of the ten. He formed a dance group. A lot of people think that Arthur Hall started African dance in Philly. But no, it was Saka Acquaye. Arthur was IN Saka Acquaye's group. Saka Acquaye stayed in Philly for about three to four years then he left."10

Daryl Kwasi Burgee: "Ione Nash and Arthur were like any two of the most proficient dance partners you can think of, that was them. Ms. Nash was an incredible ballet and modern dancer along with African [dance], but she also had a black belt in martial arts. She danced up until she was ninety something. And could still kick her leg up high.

Saka Acquaye taught Bobby Crowder, Arthur Hall, Ione Nash, and a lot of other people. He was probably one of the first to teach about African culture as a direct source. Saka Acquaye had a company. Bobby Crowder, Arthur Hall, Ione Nash, and Ishangi were all part of his company. Saka Acquaye came before Olatunji. When Arthur taught us, he taught us that Saka Acquaye had an impact on his life."

John Wilkie: "In the 1950s, Saka Acquaye came here from Ghana and started a group. That group consisted mostly of African Americans. They had drummers Sonny Morgan, Bobby Crowder, and Garvin Masseaux, and the dancers were Arthur Hall and Ione Nash. They put out an album called Gold Coast Saturday Night; Hilife Ghana with a little traditional in there."

"Nii Ayi" Nana Obrafo Yaw Wofa Asiedu: "When I went to the Saka Acquaye's center in Accra, there was a statue of Bobby Crowder there. We had a show to do at Saka's center in Accra. Before you walk inside the gate on the righthand side there is the statue of Bobby Crowder playing the talking drum with his name on the bottom and Saka Acquaye's name.

Saka Acquaye told me in 1975 while we were in Ghana "I like your spirit on the drum." Saka Acquaye loved the Philly drummers because the drummers in Philly were culturally aware and easy to work with. It was easy to teach them. He just loved Bobby Crowder. Bobby would play anything you gave him and remembered whatever he played."

Bobby Crowder: "It clarified and helped me become more alert to what I was about. Saka was a big influence on my drumming because he was a historian also and studying with him started opening up things."11

I can still remember the day Baba Doc Gibbs shared Saka Acquaye's album titled Gold Coast Saturday Night with me. It was hard for me to believe that this album was not big during the 1960s. Baba Doc talked about Saka Acquaye's impact on the Philly drummers and dancers. He also talked about how Acquaye's teachings would eventually affect the New York African drum, dance, and music scene.

Saka Acquaye's Gold Coast Saturday Night album cover Released: 1959
Source: Baba Doc Gibbs

~

Baba Doc Gibbs: "Bobby Crowder, Sonny Morgan, and Garvin Masseaux; those three were like a battery. They were the ones that started the African drum thing in Philadelphia. They studied with Saka Acquaye. Saka Acquaye was from Ghana and was coming to study at the Pennsylvania Academy for the Fine Arts. Somehow, they found out that he was coming to study at the Academy. So, they knew that he was a drummer and started preparing for his arrival. Saka took the three of them on as students because he saw that they were already experienced drummers. They worked on a record with Saka and the drumming on it was far superior than what was being played on Olatunji's Drums of Passion. At the same time that they were recording the record in Philly with Saka Acquaye, Olatunji was recording his record Drums of Passion with Chief Bey. Olatunji had the lyrics or the poetry and Chief and them had the rhythms. So, they put the rhythms together with his lyrics. That's where those songs came from. All of those rhythms on that album were nothing but Rhumba and Samba the way African Americans heard it back then. The shit that they were doing in Philly had that Ghanaian shit all in it. They weren't able to finish the album with Saka because his father had passed away and he had to go back to Ghana. And by the time he came back, Olatunji's record came out and it was big. Upon completion, Saka's album didn't have much of an impact because the industry was like we already have an African record. And also Saka moved to California to try to get it going out there but it never really took off. So, he eventually went back to Ghana. He became a Statesman - a political figure. When he went back to Ghana, he took a statue that he made while studying at the Academy in Philly. Saka was studying at the Academy to learn fine arts and he made a sculpture of Bobby Crowder called the "Unknown Drummer". He took that sculpture with him when he moved back to Ghana and installed outside of his cultural center in Accra. Years later Bobby Crowder had received some grant money and they sent him to Ghana. He visited Saka in Ghana and took a photo standing by that sculpture of himself."

Bobby Crowder statue made by Saka Acquaye Accra, Ghana
Source: Acquaye Family

* * *

While I was in college, I remember attending a house party at the home of one our cultural community mothers. We had great food, drinks, and conversation. At some point towards the end of the evening, we played Babatunde Olatunji's Drums of Passion album, and we danced hard and sang for hours as we repeated selected songs. I know I listened to that album many times when I was young. For some reason, the sounds of Baba's chants along with the drums were the perfect accompaniment to the vibe we had created in that house. Ever since I was young and up to the moment when I decided to study percussions, I was under the impression that Olatunji was the master drummer from Nigeria who brought his Nigerian drummers into the studio and recorded that epic Drums of Passion album. I later learned from elder drummers and dancers that Babatunde was actually a singer and had a variety of Yoruba songs in his repertoire and that the drumming vibe to which we were grooving was created by African American drummers. Babatunde Olatunji explains his beginnings in America leading up to the recording of his legendary Drums of Passion album.

Babatunde Olatunji: "Luckily, by divine right, both of us (his brother also) won the Rotary Educational Scholarship in 1950. That's how we came to the United States, to go to Morehouse College in Atlanta, Georgia. We went to school in the South. At our arrival at Morehouse campus, which is a black college, we saw some people who looked like people we knew at home. They would tell us "No, we're not from Africa." I'd tell them" you look just like my cousin" and they'd say "no way!" We went through all that whole period of trying to educate our brothers and sisters about their African heritage. That's how the whole thing started with me as a lecturer. The way the whole situation started was that I had been in a situation where before I left Morehouse college, I had established myself in a way of letting it be known that this is a cultural basis for our unity. I did this by presenting African music and dance while at Morehouse. I wanted to create the true image of African-not Tarzan or the Hollywood image.

In 1956, I contributed to the first UNICEF recording for children. I had a sponsor who was teaching history in Boston and we recorded it when he returned. The UN Choir was singing at a party for New Year's Eve, which I went to. I was asked to do a chant and the choir director said 'Ooh, that voice!'

I was introduced to a man at Radio City (Music Hall), Raymond White, the arranger for their Symphony Orchestra. I went there and met him and (we) collaborated- we did a twelve minute piece called "African Drum Fantasy" in 1958. That was my biggest break.

It was then that Al Han, artist's representative of Columbia Records, came to me and said 'We'll put you in the studio.' That was the recording of Drums of Passion. It was number thirteen on the Billboard charts. It was the first African recording that really demonstrated the impact of percussion in music.

The first one was actually a signature to let people know what African percussion is all about. We put it together to make music. It really speaks for itself. You know, for twenty-eight years, I didn't collect any royalties. I was so excited when I signed the contract. I didn't read it! (laughs) I didn't cross the T's and dot the I's!

At that appearance at Radio City in 1958, I had been here [United States] eight years and in 1957, Ghana became independent. I was getting five hundred dollars a week, so I was able to save money. I was invited to a very important meeting in Ghana- the All African Peoples Conference held by President Kwame Nkrumah in 1958. So, I was able to go to Ghana- that's when I was elected President of the Student's Union (at Morehouse). I was very political in those days. I had a degree in diplomacy, and I had to organize African students from all over.

I went to that meeting and read a paper at the conference. I was a non-voting member because I was a student. In essence, I said that there should be a cultural center in every major city in America so as to disseminate information about the rich cultural heritage of Africa to correct the ugly image of Africa in the mind of Americans. The President applauded the speech and the next day, he called me and my wife to his castle. He said 'that was a great thing- why don't you just pursue that (drumming)? We will be able to help you.' So, the first drum set I had for Drums Of Passion actually came from Ghana. I didn't have money to buy drums in those days. I was just leeching around, using a few conga drums that I rented. I didn't get that set until years after I graduated from college in New York in 1954. This was four years later!

Drums Of Passion was the first album. I didn't know that I would get a contract but we would rehearse every day, Monday through Sunday. Those who say they were gonna charge us, they say 'when you're finished, you come over here.' This group was mainly African Americans, some from the islands. We came together and we were a very unique group-they were interested and eager. That was the beginning of it. From there, it became a necessary way of life with me to pursue and look for support from abroad and from here. That led to the establishment of the Olatunji Center of African Culture."12

Ayishah Vivian Lewis Shabazz: "The Derby sisters, Mary Waithe, Edith Bascombe, Ida "BB", and myself all danced together with Pearl Primus. But not for very long. They were on their way out to dance with Olatunji when I came in. I was young and new so I was enthralled with Pearl so I stayed. Olatunji was doing more. They wanted to dance and Primus was stifling everyone. She didn't want you to go too far away. I did eventually start dancing with Olatunji. Taiwo DuVall was the one that got Olatunji going with playing the drums."

Left to Right: Taiwo DuVall, Ralph Dorsey, Babatunde Olatunji, "Beans"
Source: Taiwo DuVall
~

Taiwo DuVall: "There was a restaurant called The Shadow Box, and several times a week, I would see the same African guy there ordering his lunch. One day we had to share a table, so I introduced myself, and he said his name was Michael Olatunji. During our lunch hour one day, he told me he was the President of the African Students Union here in America. He said they had asked him to speak at a convention in New

York City at the Manhattan Center on Thirty-Fourth and Eighth Avenue. He also said he had told the Students Union he wanted to play drums as part of his presentation, and they were trying to discourage him, and he said the students were embarrassed by the idea! Some even said it was "savage" and that he should avoid anything that would make them look "uncivilized." I asked him what he wanted to do, and he said if he got his drums in time, he would play them. I asked him where his drums were.

He said, "They have not arrived from Africa." Well, you can borrow mine, if you want to, until they arrive, I said. He was shocked when I said that. "You play drums?" he asked. Yes, I play drums, I said. I showed him some handmade tack heads drums from Cuba. He was surprised and amazed by my knowledge of Yoruba music and wanted to know more about the history of drumming in the Caribbean. He wanted to know how it could be, and I told him my friends from Cuba, Haiti, Trinidad, and Jamaica had been instrumental in teaching me the fundamentals of their culture.

One day while on our lunch hour, Olatunji expressed his desire to quit his job and take his drums on the road. He wanted to know if I would join him. I said, what would we be known as...'Mike and Tom,' the African Drummers? He laughed and said, "My African name is Babatunde Olatunji. They call me 'Tunji.'" Well, my name, 'Thomas,' means 'the first born of twins.' What would that the 'first born of twins' be in Yoruba? He said, "It would be 'Taiwo.'" So I said, hey, 'Tunji and Taiwo'...that might work! Tunji had two singers/dancers with him. They were the Derby sisters, Joan (Akwasiba) Derby and Merle (Afida) Derby. They definitely added life and luster to our drumming and singing.

It was about this time that a few of the drummers began leaving the Asadata Dafora Company for various reasons. Montego Joe tried to interest me in working with Baba Moses, but I was a bit overwhelmed by the man's drumming and felt too inadequate to face Baba Moses Miannes. One day there was a knock at my door, and it was Montego Joe. He said he was there to take me to meet Baba Moses. After working with Baba Moses awhile, I tried to talk him into hooking up with Olatunji, but Baba Moses said Tunji was going commercial, so for a long time I was torn between the two. Julito Collazo was hired to work with Baba Moses, and I was thrilled to have Julito there. He was a master drummer from Cuba. But Baba Moses was having trouble with Julito being there. He said that Julito was always singing. I said, "That's the way those Cubans are.

They sing and drum at the same time!" So, Baba Moses said, "Oh, OK." From then on everything was smooth sailing."13

I recall one year contacting one of my elders, Jimmy Cruz, to pull together Spirit Ensemble to perform with my group at our annual Extravaganza in Connecticut. We had new costumes, new choreography, stilt walkers, and good ticket sales. I had been a fan of Spirit Ensemble ever since I saw them performing with all African instruments. Once they recorded their album, I had that on repeat for months. Jimmy Cruz and Brother Zeleka were like uncles. They knew me and my family well. So, when Jimmy agreed to bring Spirit Ensemble to Connecticut, I was extremely honored, but things changed with The Spirit Ensemble the day of the Extravaganza. Jimmy Cruz was not going to make it, nor were most of the members I knew. He told me that he was sending us a gift, and that the artists will still represent Spirit Ensemble well. Jimmy sent their steel pan player, Baba David Coleman on congas and Chief Bey on ashiko. I knew Baba David Coleman and had only heard of Chief Bey. I asked Baba David, "Where is the rest of the group?" He told me, "We are IT." I tried to hide my disappointment, but he saw it right away and said, "Man, do you know who you got here?? You got Chief Bey!" I always liked Baba David so that made me feel more at ease, but I still did not know what to expect. For their first set, they placed Chief center stage with warm lights behind and a spotlight on him and his ashiko. I believe Baba David played a bell as accompaniment from the side of the stage. Chief took us on a journey with that ashiko. He transformed the place, and I instantly understood Baba David's affirmation about Chief. Baba David urged me to get some time in with Chief during intermission and after the show was finished. I did not realize what a gift Jimmy Cruz sent our way that day until I finished my session and walked Chief and his drum out to their car. Chief Bey was truly a gift to the world of drummers and dancers.

Chief Bey: "Ismay Andrews was my first drum teacher. Me and Joe Commodore was attending class with Ismay together. She told me that I was going to be a drummer. I said "No I'm not, I'm a singer." She said "You don't believe it, jump Nigga, I'll kick your ass." She was probably the first African American woman to play and teach traditional African drumming.14

Ismay Andrews had a kettle drum and Chinese tam tams. She played with her hands and stick. She came from Philadelphia. She taught at Michael Studios on 8th Ave between 46th and 47th. Her company used to rehearse there. Olatunji learned how to play from us at Michael's Studio. She also taught at Abyssinia Church community. Ismay met great opposition with regards to her teaching African dance in Harlem. When asked why she was teaching that "African mess" by a member of the Abyssinian Baptist Church, Andrews replied, "do you know why you call yourself Abyssinian? As long as you call this place Abyssinian, I'm going to play my drums.15

Chief Bey with Ismay Andrews' Dance Group Circa: 1950
Source: Photographs and Prints Division, Schomburg Center for Research in Black Culture

Ismay Andrews and her dance company Circa: 1950
Source: Photographs and Prints Division, Schomburg Center for Research in Black
Culture
~

The people there [Abyssinian church] were somewhat black minded but they were the bourgeoisie. Adam Clayton Powell, Sr. was in charge at first, and he really ran that church, but then the son, Adam Clayton Powell, Jr. took over [officially in 1937], and he said "no," when they wanted to get rid of Ismay. He said, "as long as I'm pastor here, she can teach dance here." You see, most of the congregation didn't live in Harlem, they lived in the areas around Harlem. And a lot of them were Black conscious but they were real uppity with it. It was funny, but they were the very people who didn't want to be around Whites, but they wanted to live like them and they didn't want to have anything to do with Africa."16

"She believed in presenting the material authentically." Bey recalled sometimes having rehearsal in the basement of the Schomburg Library, after they had read, talked, and discussed music and art. The accounts given say she explained everything she did to her students: what the songs meant, what the movements meant, the history behind something."17

Chief Bey was born James Hawthorn on April 17, 1913 in Yemassee, South Carolina. As a boy, he moved to Brooklyn then Harlem where he played drums and sang in church choirs. He actually trained as an opera singer. In the 1950s, Chief Bey performed in "Porgy and Bess" starring Leontyne Price and Cab Calloway.

Bey studied the ashiko drum with Moses Miannes, Taiwo DuVall, Ismay Andrews, and played for dancers like Pearl Primus, Dinizulu, and Olatunji. Olatunji hired Chief Bey as one of the principal drummers to record the legendary "Drums of Passion" in 1959.

James Hawthorn Chief Bey founded three dance companies; Royal Household, in the early 1950s; Egbe, in the late 1950s; and Chief Bey and the Five Men in the 1970s.18

Chief Bey: "Gus Dinizulu (Nana Opare Dinzulu) gave me my first ashiko. We (African Americans) were able to listen to music from all over so we learned how to play everything. Indigenous people only know what they know. African Americans were the only ones that could jump on top of the different rhythms from all over. Other drummers couldn't do that."

Left to Right: Babatunde Olatunji, Nana Kimati Dinizulu, Chief Bey
Source: Denise Bey

Chapter 6

1959

"The exhilaration after seeing Les Ballets lasted me hours and hours after leaving the theatre." Kehinde Donaldson

What happened in the year 1959? Fidel Castro came to power in Cuba after a revolution. The Dalai Lama was forced to flee Tibet. Alaska became the 49th and Hawaii became the 50th state in the United States. NASA introduced America's first astronauts to the world. A loaf of bread cost twenty cents and a gallon of gas was twenty-five cents. The average cost of a new house was $12,400. In 1959, Chris Oliana and Walter "Serg" King were the first African Americans to be initiated as Priests in the Lucumi religion in Cuba. Motown Records was founded in 1959. "A Raisin in the Sun" play opened on Broadway.

Legendary jazz trumpeter, Miles Davis finished recording "Kind of Blue" and it became the best-selling jazz album in history. Ghana's Saka Acquaye released his "Gold Coast Saturday Night" album with Elektra Records with mostly all African American artists. Nigerian Babatunde Olatunji finished recording "Drums of Passion" in 1959 for Columbia with all African American artists. Guinea celebrated its first-year anniversary of independence from France. Guinea's Les Ballets Africains, the world's first professional and internationally touring African performance company, arrived in New York in January of 1959 under the name "Les Ballets Africains de Keita Fodéba" – and the jembe drum entered America taking center stage. The latter would turn out to be a major 1959 event and a catalyst for the beginning of the jembe revolution.

Miles Davis: "I had gotten into the model thing by watching the Ballets Africains from Guinea. We went to this performance by the Ballets Africains and it just f'd me up what they was doing, the steps and all them flying leaps and shit. And when I first heard them play the finger piano that night and sing this song with this other guy dancing, man, that was some powerful stuff. It was beautiful. And their rhythm! The rhythm of the dancers was something. I was counting off while I was watching them. They were so acrobatic. They had this one drummer watching them dance, doing their flips and shit, and when they jumped he would play DA DA DA DA POW! in this bad rhythm."[1]

Harry Belafonte: I attended the Les Ballets Africains performance in 1959. All I can say is that it was absolutely WONDERFUL!

"Performing throughout numerous cities in the United States, the several-month tour of Les Ballets Africains would prove quite revealing, propelling artistic and politically symbolic ties between African and African American independence and the American Civil Rights movement. Although few aspects of Les Ballets Africains' history have been addressed in scholarship, the company's early showings in the United States—first in 1959 as a private, Paris-based company, then in 1960 as the National Ballet of the newly independent Republic of Guinea—are significant not only for the convergences they effected between performing arts practices and liberation struggles in Africa and America, but also for what they reveal of the transformations sweeping traditional West African arts in the twentieth century.

The highly charged political and racial climate in America during the late 1950s and early 1960s has provided grounds for scholar Angela Watson (2008) to offer the following statement on the Guinean ballets' early U.S. tours: "With the Civil Rights Movement and the Black Power Movement taking place at the same time that the independence movement was giving birth to Les Ballets Africains and the Djoliba National Ballet, black youth and practitioners of the arts made connection with the African dance that these companies presented as a part of reclaiming their heritage and rights to an African identity and sense of self. When Les Ballets Africains first came to the United States, it was immediately received with great enthusiasm by its African American counterparts. Strong connections across cultural and linguistic barriers were made with the first appearances of the national ballets of Guinea."2

Les Ballets Africans de Keita Fodéba received funding from the French government which enabled the troupe to tour Europe and North America in 1959. The initial troupe consisted of ex-patriots from Guinea, Senegal, Mali, and the French Caribbean, all of whom were living in Paris. During his first American tour with Les Ballets Africains de Keita Fodéba in 1959, Ladji Camara had already begun establishing connections with important African American artists with whom he would collaborate for the rest of his career. In January 1959, Ladji met the legendary drummer Chief Bey. Chief Bey was his first African-American brother.

During Les Ballets Africains first tour of the United States, Fodéba was the director with Ladji Camara and Italo Zambo among the all-star cast. The company did a run of forty-eight performances on Broadway from February 16 until March 28, 1959 to glowing reviews. According to Camara the ballet troupe remained in the United States from early 1959 until May 1960. Camara stated that it was only after their return to Africa in May of 1960 that they became Les Ballets Africains de la Republique de Guinée, the official national ballet of Guinea.3 "

Kehinde Donaldson: "In 1959 at the Majestic Theatre off Broadway, I saw Les Ballets Africains. Ladji didn't play the Ballets. He would just come out to play the solos. The exhilaration after seeing the Ballets lasted me hours and hours after leaving the Theatre. After the performance, I immediately purchased tickets to see them again."

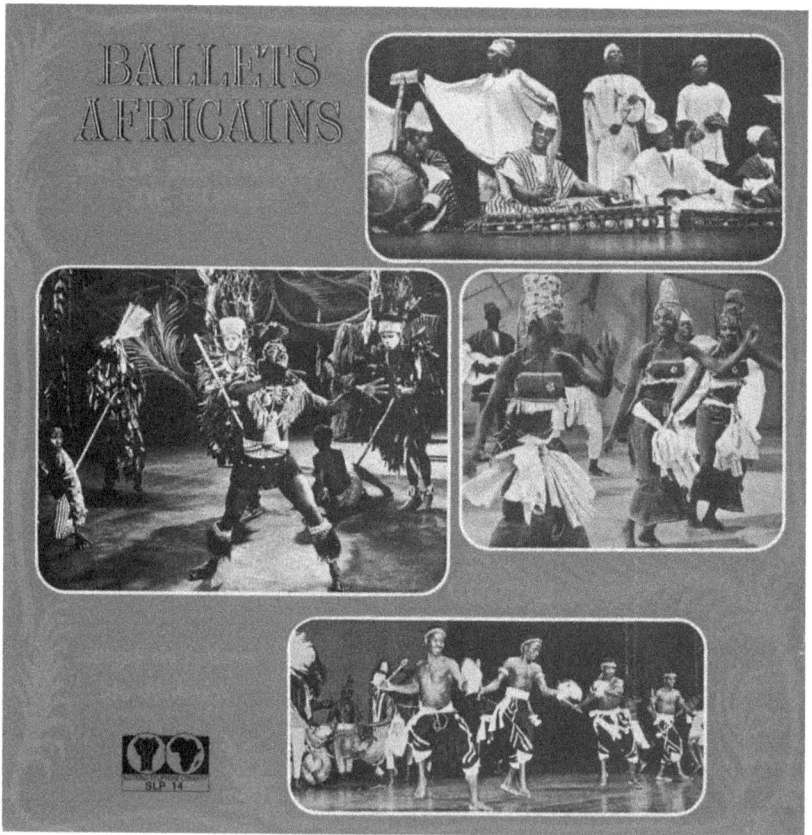

Les Ballets Africains De La Republique De Guinee album cover Released: 1970
Label: Syliphone Conakry
Source: Discogs.com
~

Ajaibo Waldrond: "The jembe first came into play with my dance when the Ballets Africains performed in NY for the first time in 1959. I

108

was studying dance at the Phillips Ford school run by Buddy Phillips and Sevilla Ford. Sevilla Ford was the Director of the Dunham school and Buddy Phillips was her husband; he was a jazz and tap teacher. They left the school and got their own school on 44th street right off of Broadway. The Ballets Africains lived in a hotel on 44th street near the theatre where they were performing which was also on 44th street. The group that came was small, it was no more than twelve people. The drummers and musicians used to come up to the dance studio because they could hear the drumming from classes and rehearsal. So finally, they started bringing their instruments to class. Ladji Camara was in the first group that came so he was with them. All of the members of the Ballets left and Ladji stayed. He used to come up often and drum because he needed a job."

Ladji Camara had already caught the attention of Katherine Dunham in Paris. So, when he performed with Les Ballets in America for the first time, he also grabbed the attention of high-profile jazz musicians, dancers, and legends like Chief Bey and Babatunde Olatunji. Ladji's friendship and collaboration with Chief and Olatunji would help to feed the jembe to culturally-starved artists, promoters, and activists who would subsequently spread the jembe fever through the 1960s into the 1970s.

Chapter 7

Drums of Passion

"Tunji wasn't a drummer. He was a singer and a political activist."
Baba David Coleman
~

I grew up thinking that Babatunde Olatunji was a legendary drummer who came to America to perform with his drums, train other drummers, and teach drumming. Those first albums, Drums of Passion and More Drums of Passion, that Tunji recorded are classics and earned a place in recording music history. However, once I started interviewing elders for this project, I learned that Olatunji was a singer, not a drummer and had excellent timing. Record labels, radio, and music fans were ready to embrace world music, specifically African music during the late 1950s and early 1960s. Babatunde Olatunji, with the assistance of Taiwo DuVall, hired African American drummers to record his first album "Drums of Passion" in 1959; it was released by Columbia Records in 1960. This album moved African drums into the mainstream by selling over five million copies. Although, it was Olatunji singing some of his traditional Yoruba songs, it was also African Americans playing the rhythms they had learned from teachers along their own musical journeys.

Taiwo DuVall: "Columbia Records wanted Olatunji to produce an album and they wanted him to do it alone. Tunji asked me if I would help him with this album. At the end of the first session Tunji said, "Taiwo, I want to add a few more drummers. Can you help me with this?" I said, "Sure, I have some drummer friends who I am sure will be interested in doing something like this." I called Montego Joe and Chief Bey, two drummers I had worked and studied with before I met Tunji. Next, he added the female voices: Akwasiba and Afida Derby, Barbara Gordon, Peggy Kirkpatrick, Beebee Capps, Helen Haynes, Delores Parker, Ruby Pryor, Louise Young, and Helena Walker. The rest is history. We produced the Drums of Passion album. The drummers got a one-time payment of $300 per session and there were about two or three sessions. The singers got less than the drummers. The next step was to produce the album More Drums of Passion. For the album I got Olatunji to hire a few more of my friends to help him, like Chief Bey, Montego Joe, Ray Barreto, Robert (Beans)Whitley, Sabu Caldwell, and Roland DuVall."[1]

Baba David Coleman: "Tunji wasn't a drummer. He was a singer and a political activist. It was Chief Bey, Taiwo DuVall, and Montego Joe who created his sound on the Drums of Passion album. That was our shit; African Americans."

Bradley Simmons: "The jembe was there but we still didn't catch on until Olatunji's second album called More Drums of Passion in 1966. Drums of Passion was the first one. The second one was More Drums of Passion. On the first album he only had Chief Bey, Montego Joe and Taiwo DuVall."

Babatunde Olatunji: "Drums of Passion played a significant role in all the social change taking place around that time. It was the first percussion album to be recognized as an African contribution to the music of African Americans. It also came right at the beginning of the Civil Rights Movement. This meant that we were recognized as pioneers in the 'Black is Beautiful' movement. The whole idea of 'black power' came along at this time too. And so did the wearing of the dashiki and natural hair. We found ourselves right in the middle of this, going from one rally to another, sponsored by different organizations fighting for freedom: from the NAACP to CORE to SNCC to the Black Muslims."2

More Drums of Passion was the album where drummers paused and wanted to know more about the new drum that drummers were calling the "Guinea Drum." Olatunji hired a host of African American drummers and singers again for his More Drums of Passion album, only this time he also hired Ladji Camara to play jembe for the recording in 1966. That's when many drummers decided to put the congas away and find a way to get one of those "Guinea drums" (jembe).

More Drums of Passion front album cover Released: 1966
Source: Bradley Simmons

More Drums of Passion front album cover Released: 1966
Source: Bradley Simmons

Bradley Simmons: "The second one (album) he had Chief Bey, Pablo Landrum, Sonny Morgan, Stacy Edwards, Babafemi, Ladji Camara, Ralph A. Dorsey, Baba Ishangi Hassan Razak. Tunji gave Ladji a solo on one of the cuts called "Wasalu". THAT'S when the jembe started to catch. Everyone started paying attention to what Ladji was playing at that time. The only Africans were Tunji and Ladji and he was playing a drum no one heard before. We were trying to figure out what drum he was playing because the sounds were completely different from the sounds of the drums the other drummers were playing. They were using congas and ashikos and here Ladji had this high pitched drum cracking through the entire piece. That's the only piece he played on. He only played on "Wasalu" and he was featured on that. So now we were like what is he playing and how can we get one?"

By the early to mid 1960s, Ladji Camara had relocated to New York and was creating a name for himself while shining much light on the jembe: the drum, the music, and Manding culture.

Baba Billy Bungo: "Babatunde Olatunji unified the Africans and Americans, the Olatunji family and the original Drums of Passion drummers. All of those cats I sat down and learned from each one of them. Bobby Crowder, Babafemi, Chief Bey, Lawrence Tweet, Pablo Landrum, Ladji Camara, Baba Ishangi, and most important was a cat named Baba Delhi. These cats were masters and wizards on anything they touched. Anything that they said they were going to do they did. So that was the lifestyle that I wanted to live."

Another pivotal jembe moment in America that featured Papa Ladji was the 1964-1965 World's Fair in New York.

Chapter 8

The World's Fair of 1964-1965

"The audience at the African pavilion was the most popular one at the Fair."
Babatunde Olatunji

The 1964 -1965 World's Fair was the second World's Fair to be held at Flushing Meadows Park in the borough of Queens, New York. It was the largest World's Fair ever to be held in the United States and occupied nearly a square mile of land. By the time the gates closed, more than fifty-one million people had attended the exposition. The fair's theme was "Peace Through Understanding," and dedicated to "Man's Achievements on a Shrinking Globe in an Expanding Universe." It was often referred to as an "Olympics of Progress."

One of the highlights of the 1964-1965 World's Fair was the African Pavilion. Many remember the huge cage near that pavilion that housed a big gorilla. Others remember seeing Les Ballets Africains for the first time. Some remember seeing, hearing, and even purchasing a jembe at this historic World's Fair. Many of the drummers and dancers whom I interviewed were in their early teens and even younger during the 1964-65 World's Fair. There were some who were already involved in African drumming and dance and were able to recall their experiences at this historic event.

* * *

Yoruba Priest and Drummer, Michael Norwood, speaks about his experience at the 1964-65 World's Fair.

Baba Michael Norwood: "I was eleven years old. I remember hanging out at the African pavilion and feeling like I was 'home'. They had a gorilla in a cage at the African pavilion. As a child of Elegba I always had some candy on me. I gave one of my starburst candies to the gorilla. They had a lot going on there. I was stunned being that close to a gorilla. I had been drumming to Olatunji records at this time on a conga. I remember the Watusi dancers and drummers. Ladji was performing with Babatunde Olatunji each night out there. At that time, Ladji was the only one with a jembe. If anyone else had one, they would have gotten it from Ladji. Everyone else was carving out their own to look like a jembe."

Baba Walter Ince: "The Guinea company was there and that was my first time seeing them. I didn't know anything about African culture like that. It was overwhelming. Seeing dancers leap in the air and landing on the one. And as the ancestors would have it in a few years I would be up on stage doing the same thing. The very first time I saw a jembe was at the 1964/65 World's Fair. I remember thinking to myself that I have to get me one of those eventually. At this time I was following around after Joe Commodore and everyone was playing conga, conga, conga."

Babatunde Olatunji: "We performed at the World's Fair, 1964 and 1965. We were the first African group in this country to perform at the World's Fair. The audience at the African pavilion was the most popular one at the Fair. The money I made there, I used to open the Olatunji Center in Harlem in 1967."1

The New York World's Fair Globe Flushing Meadows-Corona Park, Queens, NY
Source: Library of Congress

Babatunde Olatunji group at The African Pavilion at The 1964/65 World's Fair
(Dancers: Chuck Davis, Afida Derby, Akwasiba Derby, Ijalu, Peggy, Freddie
Musicians: Ralph Dorsey, Al Perryman, Pat Patrick (playing flute), Chief Bey, Ladji
Camara, Olatunji and others)
1964/65 World's Fair, Flushing Meadows-Corona Park, Queens, NY
Source: Jean Lee

Kehinde Donaldson: "I saw them (Les Ballets Africains) again in 1964 when I saw the Ballets at the World's Fair, then again in 1968 at the Apollo Theater in Harlem."

Ayishah Vivian Lewis Shabazz: "Charles Moore, Chuck Davis, Freddie, Noble, and Bobo all danced with Olatunji. They were all at the 1964-65 World's Fair in New York."

Amaniyea Payne: "I remember the year 1964, my Mother (bless her soul) took me to the World's Fair held in New York. There were so many aspects of African dance that I had never seen before, the Watusi dancers from Rwanda, the Burundi drummers, Baba Olatunji Drums of Fire and the Guinea Ballet from West Africa. This experience never left me."

Iya Darcel Abel: "I started dancing a year after watching the Olatunji African Dance Company perform at the New York World's Fair in 1964. A friend of my Father danced in that company, and after hearing the drums and seeing their performance I expressed my desire to dance."

Jalal Sharriff: "I remember in 1963 I was ten years old and my family took me to see Olatunji at City Center. That was amazing. It touched me in a way that I always remembered. The following year in 1964, the World's Fair opened up. Between my aunt and father, I went twenty something times. Guinea Ballets was there at the Fair."

Baba Richard Byrd: "In 1964 I was 10 years old and my father took me to see the World's Fair in Flushing Meadows, NY. We went to the African pavilion. The African pavilion was where Olatunji's group performed. In the middle of the African pavilion there was a cage with a big African gorilla, you could smell the gorilla for miles around. All of the sudden Olatunji comes out on the stage. This group consisted of Babafemi, Sonny Morgan, Charles Moore, Chuck Davis, Akwasiba Derby, Stacy Edwards, Richie Pablo Landrum and this guy climbs up a ladder to this big black drum with these big sticks and it was Chief Bey. I'm blown away."

Baba Yomi Yomi Awolowo: "I got a jembe in 1964 at The World's Fair in New York."

Bradley Simmons: "I remember when the jembe was impossible to get - literally! Les Ballets came to New York at the World's Fair in 1964/65. They had some jembes at the 1964/65 World's Fair but they wasn't selling them. They were just there. There were only a few people who got a hold of jembes at the World's Fair. Nat Bettis, Olukose Wiles, Wendell Hayes, and Sonny Morgan. They were actually locked in a crate and the guy who was running the Guinea pavilion wouldn't open up the crate. Nat Bettis' Sister was working at the Guinea pavilion. So Nat asked his Sister to talk to the guy to open up the crates so that they could buy the jembes. They were able to buy those jembes for like $20-$40 for each one. These guys got these jembes and kept going. We were all younger so we still didn't really know much about the jembes until 1966 when that More Drums of Passion album came out. We saw it at the World's Fair but we didn't know what we were looking at. Had I known what I know now, I would have had about 3 or 4 of them back then. So whatever jembes you could find or whatever jembes came through from shows or in stores, you grabbed one. But for the most part it was the conga drums."

Sam Watson: "I was there at the 1964/65 World's Fair in New York when I was 15/16. I saw Miriam Makeba. I saw the Tutsis from Rwanda. I saw the group from Guinea. I went about five or six times. I was unaware at this time about African tradition. That was a wakeup call for me. That was the first time I saw traditional African music and dance. I was there opening day. I was a junior in high school somewhat aware of Cuba, Brazil and Trinidad jazz. The first thing I saw was Miriam Makeba. I'm looking at what black people are supposed to be. I'm looking at black people who have no white culture in them. They're not educated by whites. They did not go through slavery. This spirit is free. That's the first time we saw the pure stuff since we were abducted when we saw the groups that were at the World's Fair. I saw South Africa Zulu. The Tutsis from Rwanda. Then I saw Guinea. I kept going to those three groups. Those three were dominant in me. They seemed to be the most complete and the most powerful to me. I did everything I could to get as close to the stages as possible because we were far away. I looked at the men and I looked at the woman. I'm looking at African men that are not influenced or exposed to white culture. I'm looking at that and looking at the women and I can see that difference. I could see what we lost in many cases forever; we're not able to get it back. When I saw the Tutsis I was crying like a baby. People were looking and they were in awe because I was standing there crying. Tears coming down my face and then after the show was over I managed to get around security, and I went up close to the Tutsis. I looked at them and I reached out to the men and one of these guys, these 6 foot 9 guys, looked down at me in full costume. He was a massive man. He was a magnificent man. I'm talking about twenty to thirty 6 foot 9 Michael Jordans in full costume looking down at you man!"

Sam Watson took a moment to compose himself from the emotions he had conjured up. This World's Fair memory had brought Mr. Watson to tears.

Sam Watson: "The guy looked down at me and he just grabbed my hand and looked at me and I could feel his spirit coming into me and he's really powerful. I looked at that guy and he was TALKING to me man. He was TALKING to me just LOOKING at me. He said, "Do you hear me?" And I said, Yes. I could hear without words. Then he walked back and looked at me like, you got it now man, you got it.

I had to go back several times to get the sense of it because it was something I had never seen before. It was no interruptions. Pure direct contact with the home (Africa) after 500 years of no contact at all. It occurred to me, Oh my goodness, I'm standing in the continent (Africa) with these people. I'm going back 500 years. This is what we were? This is what we're supposed to be? After that, it never left me. It never left me. And the people that saw that, were different people."

Chapter 9

Papa Ladji

"Today when you see whites and other people all over the world playing jembe it is because of Papa Ladji." Bolokada Conde

The 1960s in America has often been referred to as a "tumultuous decade." The 1960s were definitely driven by counterculture protests and the civil rights movement. There was the emergence of organizations like The Black Panthers and their Black Power movement, the Nation of Islam (NOI), and the Student Nonviolent Coordinating Committee (SNCC). The 1960s was host to major events that further divided an already tense and segregated country such as the Vietnam War, the assassinations of Dr. Martin Luther King, Jr and President Kennedy, and the Cuban missile crisis. Great strides in science, such as the first man landing on the moon also occurred in the 1960s. This decade birthed Woodstock, The Beatles' arrival in America, Jimi Hendrix, and Les Ballet Africains' performance at the UN in New York led by Famoudou Konate on the jembe. Katherine Dunham traveled to Senegal as an Ambassador for the World Festival of Negro Arts in 1967-1968 and brought Mor Thiam to America in 1968 to play and teach jembe with her and her touring group. It was during the early part of this "tumultuous decade" that Ladji Camara made his decision to stay in America to live, perform, and teach about his Manding culture, Islam, and the jembe. This decision brought shade and shame upon his name in his native land [Guinea] but conversely brought him living legend status in his new land – America.

Famoudou Konate: "Ladji Camara went to America first with the Ballets. We went two to three times to America in the early days of the Ballets. We were performing in California when they killed President Kennedy. We went to perform at the United Nations in 1968; they killed Dr. Martin Luther King while we were there. We got a lot of experience while we were in America. We went to New York, San Francisco, Los Angeles, Las Vegas, Cleveland, and Detroit. We visited museums to learn about slavery: when it started and things like that. We learned about the music coming out of slavery. When I saw things like that I got very angry and sad."

Ladji Camara: "The first time I came to this country was January 22, 1959. Broadway and 46th street. That was with the number one African Dance company. Keita Fodeba's group."

Mor Thiam: "The first jembe player from Africa was Ladji Camara then it was me. We were the first two jembe players to bring the jembe and that's it. Ladji went to New York to live in 1960 and I went to the U.S. with Katherine Dunham in 1968."

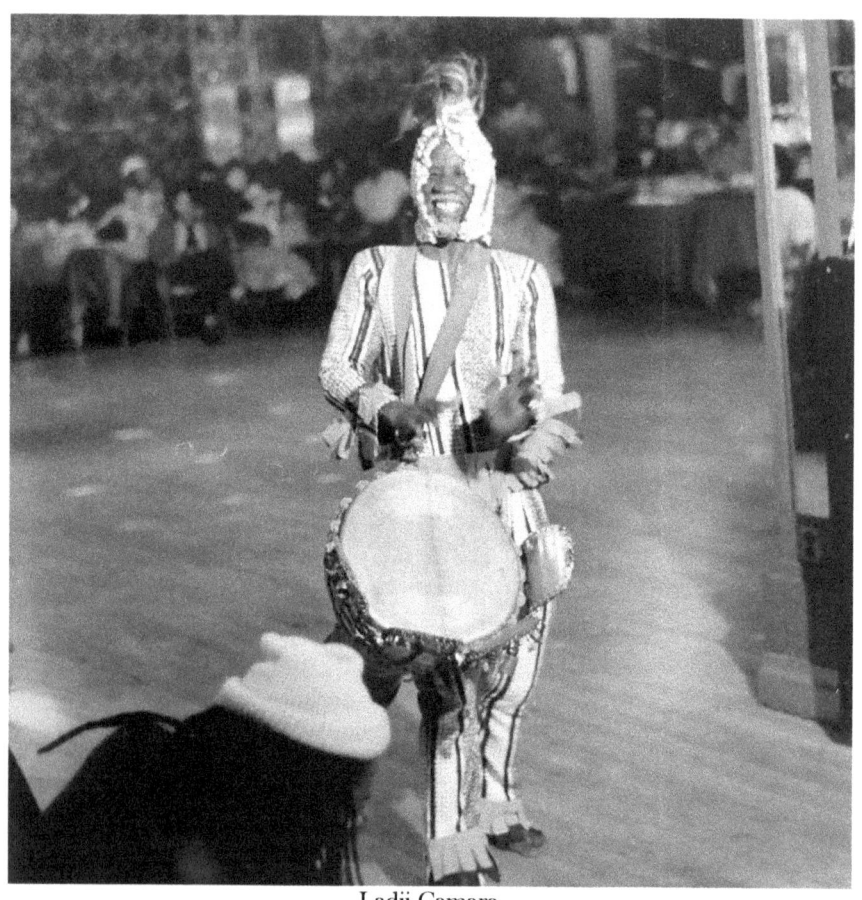

Ladji Camara
Source: Kehinde Donaldson
~

When I interviewed Ladji Camara twenty years ago, I was not fully aware that he was THE conduit responsible for sparking the jembe movement in America. I conducted interview after interview, did research and more research, and reviewed archived videos and films. Everyone and everything pointed to the same source. Papa Ladji was the first to bring the jembe to the people of America. Once I fully wrapped my head around that reality, I then became intrigued with the who, what, when, why, and how. I traveled to Ladji Camara's birthplace, Siguiri, Guinea and also spoke with many artists in America who had experienced Papa Ladji in some shape or form.

Eugene Osborne Smith("Oz" or "Osborne"): "Ladji Camara was a very sensitive guy. I met him in Paris in the 1950s. We worked together a little bit. Ladji was a very good drummer on the jembe."

Bolokada Conde: "Papa Ladji was the first lead Jembefola to tour with Les Ballets Africains. For me the most important thing with jembe is the love and Papa Ladji was in love with jembe. That's why he becomes Jembefola because of that love. Anyone knows Papa Ladji says he was in love with jembe. He was born in Siguiri and I was born in Sankara, very far away. If you go to Siguiri and talk to the people, they will tell you that he was in love with jembe. Today when you see whites and other people all over the world playing jembe it is because of Papa Ladji. Papa Ladji, Famoudou, and Mamady are so special."

Bradley Simmons: "Listen to Famoudou Konate, Fadouba Oulare, Papa Ladji and then Mamady Keita to learn how to master your drum. I studied with Ladji. Right in his house with Richard Byrd and James Cherry. So I learned how to get the correct sounds out of that drum."

Sam Watson: "Ladji saw me play in the Ballets at the repetitions (rehearsals). I studied with Koungbana and Djoliba like I studied with the Ballets. When Ladji saw that I could play sangban, he said "Now I can form my group." And he formed the group around me. He said, now I have somebody who could back me up. So I played sangban and Ladji played jembe and sang. It was Ladji, me, a gentleman named Ali Abdullah (Oliver Jones from Harlem). He danced with the Senegal Ballets and speaks pure Wolof and French and he lived in Senegal for like 15-20 years. There was a girl named Peggy who was a dancer with Katherine Dunham. These people are all older than me. So there was Peggy, Ali, Ladji and me. That's it. Two dancers and two drummers. That's it.

Something about Ladji Camara which was unique was his costumes. He had the best costumes of any performer I have ever seen. His costumes must have cost a fortune. They were heavily embroidered with colorful sequences. His costumes were amazing. When I got with him and I brought what I had, he said yeah ok that's cute; THIS is what you're going to wear. And we had costumes made for us that were unbelievable.

His sense of performance, costume, choreography, and song was at a very high level.

When he left the Ballets he played with Katherine Dunham in E. Saint Louis and California for about a year. It was Julito Collazo who stepped up for Ladji and brought him in his group where he met Chief Bey. Julito is the one who got Ladji his papers. When I say his papers, brought him in the musicians' union. Got him his actor's equity card. Got him an apartment in the projects. No one else. No American black people. Julito is the guy who secured Ladji Camara in America, fed him and took care of him."

"Nii Ayi" Nana Obrafo Yaw Wofa Asiedu: "I played with Ladji not to learn how to play jembe because I was already playing but I went to learn other things. I was proud to be called one of his students though because Ladji was BAD. I wanted "to be like Mike." I believe Butch Jackson and Charles Payne came before me but they may have come at the same time I started with Ladji. We were Ladji's first students on the jembe."

Kehinde Donaldson: "Papa Ladji said "my father used to beat me to play." His father was the head hunter in the village. They used to use the drum to wake the people up. His father used to wake him up to drum to wake the people up each day.

Ladji was not only my mentor on the drum, he was like a father to me. He would always talk about getting the black people together. He used to say "I don't need a lot of people. All I need is sangban." Out of the eight or nine rhythms that we played, I started the rhythm on the sangban. The third show I did with Ladji at the Audubon Ballroom Ladji ate fire and was blowing fire.

Walter Ince was a good drummer, and he was with Ladji. At that time, Balogun was there. He was a better sangban and jembe player, but Walter had the better stage presence. He looked more authentic. Aziz was a good drummer. He learned to play Ladji's intro almost lick for lick. I was a very slow learner so Ladji had to spend a lot of time with me. Some of the principal drummers resented me because I didn't play as long as them and I was older than them. Ladji would work with me for about an hour before rehearsal to bring me up to speed. A lot of players couldn't take Ladji's discipline. He didn't allow any drinking and smoking. He would say things to us often that stayed with us:

"You not the best drummer but I like your inside."

"Good character"

"Music and the drum is pure, it don't lie."

"There are rhythms for healing and there are sacred rhythms that I would never teach."

Ladji's sense of timing was impeccable, and he would bring the tempo up with a gentleness. Papa Ladji taught us to keep your tongue on the roof of your mouth for continuity of energy. Breathe from your diaphragm. Stay focused on what's in front of you and don't let your mind wander. From slowness comes speed.

Papa Ladji didn't negotiate his business as well as he should have. Ladji was very modest. He wasn't into wearing the latest fashion. He used to wear the same clothes often. He was a messenger in New York. He bought a car and was delivering packages in New York City."

Ladji Camara: "My Grandfather dreamed that the number 1 child will be a girl then number 2 will be a boy and number 3 he said to have a jembe ready for the number 3 child, which was Ladji Camara. At that time my Mother didn't come to my Father yet."

Enoch Williamson: "I met Ladji Camara while in New York attending the BAM festival (Brooklyn Academy of Music) they did an African dance festival there. I was a part of Muntu Dance Theater, and we had been invited there to perform. Katherine Dunham brought Ladji Camara here too. Ladji was one of my heroes I had a couple of albums by him which I listened to religiously to teach myself the jembe. He was teaching so I took a private class. He charged $100 for a 1/2 hour class. He showed me this first rhythm KA NA FENDE MA you would just repeat this pattern so I did it for the entirety of the class. I decided to take another class with him, we did the exact same thing again. I decided to take one last class, when we started the exact same way. I got upset and told him that I had given him $300 dollars and this was not enough. He assured me that this was a very old rhythm with many secrets. So I said SHOW ME! He said play anything and he would play that part as an accompaniment and solo. So I did, I knew a few things so I jumped in with both feet, odd meters, everything. He ate it up like it was nothing. Very sophisticated solos, I couldn't believe it, it was amazing. After that I was quiet as a church mouse."

Jalal Sharriff: "My earliest recollection of Ladji Camara I believe was in 1963. My parents took me to see Olatunji's More Drums of Passion group at the New York City Center. Ladji Camara was a featured musician in that group and on the Olatunji album that had the same name. As a very young teen I would go home from school for lunch and practice Ladji's phrasing and especially his tones. Later on in my life it paid off. The first time I actually met Ladji was in a summer youth program in the mid 60s that was created when many of the inner cities burned down after the assassination of Dr. Martin Luther King, Jr. The program was called WEUSI. Many of More Drums of Passion group members was in residence including Ladji Camara, Ishangi Razak, and Chief Bey.

In 1971 I was formally introduced to Papa Ladji through two great friends, Akin and Obba Babatunde who are both great dancers and acclaimed actors and directors. When Ladji saw my drum he immediately asked "Where did you get that drum?" and after he asked me to play something he said, "where you learn that rhythm?" He didn't know at the time that he was being set up. I specifically chose a rhythm that Famoudou Konate had shown the drummers of the Chuck Davis Dance Co.. At that time, whenever Les Ballets Africains came to New York City, they would work with Chuck's company. For me, this meeting was the beginning of a dream come true and a long friendship.

Akin invited me to Ladji's studio to learn. Ladji Camara wasn't the best of teachers. Not because of anything bad. It just wasn't his skill. You had to come with something to understand what he was passing on. Ladji said, "The jembe is a drum of tone not smack." Ladji taught me how to play a different type of tone.

Ladji the musician was second to NONE! His musical sensibility and technical ability was off the chart. I must not forget his tones. His use and placement of a variety of different tones on the same drum was remarkable. That ability is what attracted me to his playing. He had the ability to play tones in places that felt like it came out of nowhere. This would make many drummers unable to hold their part. He was a musician from another era. He never played his drum with a skin pulled so tight that it may as well have been a conga not a jembe. I understand why many musicians do it because they get the Ohhs and Ahhs! This does not develop musicality or real playing skills. When I met Papa Ladji, that was the first time I met a Muslim drumming.

I remember when Aziz first started coming. When he finally started playing with Ladji, he was ready for what Ladji had for him. He had the ears to hear exactly what Ladji was playing."

Believed to be the foremost expert and skilled African American Afro Cuban drummer, Skip Burney, speaks about his experience with Ladji Camara.

Baba "Skip" Burney: "Ladji had his studio up in the Bronx by the train station. He had a jembe with this long neck and I thought it was so bad. I came off the train one day and saw him in the studio and he was stringing up a jembe. I asked, are you Ladji Camara, he said, "Yes, I am Ladji." (in that high voice). I said I have been in the room with you before and I have seen you play but there were always a lot of people around you. I said I would like to learn how to play jembe. He said, "You want to learn to play jembe?" I said, "Yes, I'd like to play." He said "five dollars." I gave him the five dollars and he said, "First, you must learn how to play 'pan to pan.'" I did it and he said "No whack a whack. 'Pan to pan!'" Then he showed me a type of Guinea Lamban. That was my personal experience with Ladji. He saw me play the Afro Cuban stuff at shows and would give me much respect."

Greg Ince: "We all studied under Papa Ladji. It was amazing to be a part of something that was so new and exciting. And being with Papa Ladji who brought the jembe and this drumming style to the U.S. for the first time. So my brother grabbed me and took me with him when I was a little guy. I was 9 when I started taking dance classes with Papa Ladji. My Brother Walter was a teenager studying drumming with Papa Ladji. Walter was always a perfectionist. Before all of the other indigenous African teachers, I always give it up to my big brother, Walter. For me it's always been trying to live up to what he would always tell me. "Don't ever let anyone dim your light. Always represent the culture to its highest potential."

Papa Ladji used to tell Walter before show, "Uh Walter, Please Walter don't do my thingy. Please my brother don't do my thingy!" Walter learned how to play Papa Ladji's solo introduction, note for note. It was incredible to hear and see. But Papa wasn't very fond of Walter doing his "thingy." Those tones that Papa Ladji was known for, Walter had those tones. His tones would go right through you. He STUDIED!

Ladji was doing things on the floor and drum that I couldn't do at a young age. I remember shaking Ladji's hand for the first time and it was flat like a fish fin. That's why he could do that hand movement on the jembe where he would play a rhythm alternating the back side of his hand to the palm on the right and left while staying on time. I tried that one time

125

and MAN, I was in so much pain. I thought I had it down man. Man you have to know your limits. I said let me give thanks for what the Creator gave me!

We would be in the Bronx in that rehearsal space with Papa Ladji and we would have an audience from people catching the train or getting off. You could see into the space from the stairs of the train.

They did a live radio recording session of Ladji's album "Africa New York" with Lamban and SAA on it. I was home when they aired it. It was Papa Ladji, my brother Walter, Obara Wali, and Olukose Wiles. It was just them and they ROCKED IT. Since then I remember thinking this is the music style I wanted to learn.

Papa Ladji left New York and went home to Senegal and was there 2 weeks then crossed over. He fulfilled his mission in life. His mission was to be here and do what he did. Sekou Toure was upset that he defected. He was supposed to represent Guinea and didn't return.

People to this day don't know how awesome Papa was. He would do things on the jembe that I've seen NONE ever do. One time we were at Leslie's Dance and Skate School. I was always there drumming for classes. Playing for Denise Bey's class. Class was over and Papa comes and sits down to play the jembe alone and it was so exotic and beautiful. I've never heard the jembe quite like that by ANYONE before.

I give thanks for being born at the right time to be able to study with Papa Ladji. I might have been one of the youngest but I was born at the right time to be around him and to be a part of all of that. Papa Ladji was one of the baddest jembe players ever. He is the reason we have that jembe. He is the reason my brother became the great drummer he became. Prior to that we were all on conga, bata, ashikos. I know that's why President Sekou Toure was so pissed. He was one of their TOP artists."

Baba Walter Ince: "The first time I saw Ladji, he was playing with Nina Simone. I was so captured by the jembe, the only thing I could say was that this was controlled frenzy. I loved it from the first time I heard it. It was like a cry to home for me."

Broadway and Hollywood actor, musician, singer, and one of Ladji's first lead dancers, Obba Babatunde, spoke about Ladji Camara.

Obba Babatunde: "I'm doing this show with Lillias White and my brother (Baba Akin Babatunde). Joe Walker wrote it and called it "Adodo." There's a little guy there. Everyone is African American. There's a little African guy there sitting on stage with his drum and a watch on his arm. You don't see a drummer playing jembe with a watch on. One of those silver watch bands and nice face. We're rehearsing now. In rehearsal, everything don't just go like this, you take time, and stop. All of a sudden, the guy is drumming - the piano is playing and I see my man packing up. We're still rehearsing. "Uh Ladji we're not finished." Ladji says, "Time is finished, five o'clock time is finished." This was my first introduction. He packed up his bag and he was gone. We were still rehearsing. That began to frame a little bit about how he saw business. Yes, I am a great artist.

I have this saying, "your do is not necessarily your who." Meaning, that what you do affects change in your life but your who is how you affect change in someone else's life. We are talking about Ladji today because of his who, not just his do because he affected change in my life and all of the others that speak about him. He was a man of principle; some might say a simple man. He was a brilliant man. He came to a world outside of his cultural upbringing and made a real indentation in the culture of black America.

Ladji was prophesized about before he was born. They said a child will be born and he will be the first to take the drum across the water to the western world. His name will be Ladji.

Ladji learned to play the drum in the bush from listening to the sounds around him. Papa Ladji was born to drum.

Papa Ladji was a devout Muslim. It didn't matter what was going on, he would pray every day. Rehearsal would have to stop for him to pray. I spent time with him when it didn't have anything to do with performing.

Papa Ladji was a great dancer. He taught us all of the dances. I was his lead dancer for years. He knew when I started to jump (blap blap blap), he would make me fly! He knew his power, but he was very humble and modest. I have photos of me four feet above the dancers and drummers. That's physically impossible for a human being to jump up in the air come down and back up, unless you have Ladji Camara sending you in the air. The dancers would say that something was wrong with me. They said no one has that much energy. I never got tired. But they didn't understand it wasn't me.

127

I think in a way I was his muse. He could show me a step and he would tell me the story so it became that. I understood that Saa was a dance for kids with polio. They would walk on their elbows and knees. When I went to Senegal I saw it and I understood it.

The speed and accuracy at which he played was unmatchable. His tones, bass and slaps would send you into a frenzy; to another world.

We were blessed to be able to do everything with the authenticity of an ancient culture, and to be taught this is the root. This is the story. It's more than just entertainment for entertainment's sake. For me and the others to have the time to spend and be educated by a man that was prophesized to come to the planet to come and do what he did? He came here to do that. We were all blessed.

I decided that in 1978 on New Year's I wanted to wake up on African soil. Ladji gave me money in 1978 to bring to his wife for bricks for building his house.

Ladji taught the dancers how to make the buba; where to go buy the material and how to tie the galae. Ladji was like a seamstress dude. He taught the women how to sew and how to make the costumes. He would make one, and then show them. (Imitating Ladji's voice) "Makey dat...aw I'm sorry...dis a no good...not right." He would make the drummer's hat with the goat skins. He taught everything. He would teach the drummers exactly the rhythm. If the time was bad, then he would stop.

"Please a my bruda no good." (Imitating Ladji showing a rhythm) "do it...no, please my bruda." Plenty brothers would come to learn, and he would see they were high and tell them "no, sorry...no alcohol...no dopey." You were going to be clean to work with him.

He would say, "Business is a business" He would say that all the time. "Business is a business."

We used to have rehearsals up in the Bronx every Thursday night. Hazel Bryant, Anika, and Rhonda Morman were dancers but the number one dancer was Rosa Connors. When Ladji said rehearsal started at seven, then the door got locked, and you were not getting in.

Chuck Davis, Melvin Deal, and Dinizulu were influences of the African dance. When we got with Ladji, it was the first time we were doing authentic traditional dances and rhythms straight from the Motherland."

Shombe Yimbe dancers (James Kregman Studio, NYC, NY)
Bottom row: Hazel S. Bryant, Rhonda Morman, Darcel Abel, Denise Bey
Top row: Gloria Grayson, DaVivienne Young, unknown, Lynda Noni Moore, unknown
Photo credit: James Kregman Photo Studio

(Obba singing Lamban song and playing rhythm and doing dance movements.) "Man! To see a man do Lamban. You have to see Ladji Camara. He would play around with the rhythm then start dancing with the drum, and he had that big heavy drum."

Baba Akin Babatunde: "Ladji LOVED my brother. He adored my brother, like he could do no wrong. He could do all of those acrobatics and everything. He was the dance captain and would push us. Me, Obba, and John Blanchard were the male dancers of the company. He used to light up whenever Obba danced, or John danced. Ladji became like this conduit of connection to that aspect of our world; the African diaspora in us. Every Tuesday or so, we would go up to the Grand Concourse on Gun Hill Road. We would get off that train and go up those steps to the studio. It was like some kind of a spiritual initiation at those rehearsals of Ladji.

Mind you, I had the Dinizulu experience, The Ladji Experience, The Tito Sampa experience, then Shombe Yembe who used to eat glass. My brother got a gig performing at Jungle Habitat with Shombe Yembe. Ladji was our Papa. The term Papa never meant anything more than when you were in the presence of Ladji. On that level that meant you could just be around him. He would say something or give you a look that made you feel like you could go on. He imparted a lot of wisdom because he saw something special in all of us. It was like sitting at the feet of a Great-grandfather. He would LAUGH. He used to love to laugh with me. I would sometimes struggle. "Come on Akin we got to do it again!" We had this support system like a grandfather. Ladji was like an uncle to Walter.

Saa was my dance, and it was hard. When we went around that circle it was like a cleansing. Lamban was my dance too. It was so grand."

One of Ladji's lead jembe drummers and long time student, Aziz speaks on his experience with Ladji Camara.

"Papa" Aziz Ahmed: "I was eighteen when I started drumming. My grandfather was a Garveyite. My brother was in the Black Panther Party and was involved with African cultural programs and activities at New York University (NYU). He told me to go with him to this workshop that was happening at NYU and it was a drumming workshop led by Tony Robinson, a member of the Olatunji group. I was learning ashiko with him with the Afro Caribbean and Haitian music. One day I saw a drum in a duffle bag and I asked what's this drum Tony? He said, "jembe drum." He told me a little something about the jembe and spoke a little something about Ladji Camara. That was the first time I actually saw a jembe.

In 1970-71 my mother took me to see a show. It was Ladji, Balogun, and one other person I can't remember at this time. Ladji picked up a daba and was dancing. He played a little balafon. He played a little ngoni. AND THEN...LOL...He played the jembe! Here's this one man playing this one drum.

The first time I heard jembe was more about how that man got that sound out of that drum. I have seen and heard a lot of Jembefolas. But seeing him for the first time was like the high the drug addict chases for years. The purity of the sound. It wasn't pulled up high - the sound you hear today. It was heated. You had to play. The variation of the sounds and clarity was still intact. Balogun was playing a sangban and Ladji was playing his jembe and he had a scarf throwing it up from hand to hand while playing the rhythm and never lost the rhythm or time. At this time it was only Ladji and Mor Thiam that had that tradition here in the United States. My mom brought me up to meet Ladji and Balogun after the show was done. I shook their hands and told them that I was learning from Tony Robinson. Balogun said I want you to go to his (Ladji's) studio and take his class. I ended up being in the third wave of Ladji's training.

There were waves of Ladji students. The first wave was people like Nii Ayi and Chief Bey that was the first wave; Walter and Greg Ince, Olukose Wiles, Balogun Love, Obara Wali on flute became the second wave. They ultimately became The International Afrikan American Ballet. The third wave was "Papa" Aziz Ahmed, Byrd, and Kehinde Donaldson.

The first time I went to the studio, I was knocking and no one opened the door. Ladji's studio was by the train station up in the Bronx. You can stand on the platform of the stairs and hear and kind of see inside the studio where they were playing and dancing. I did this for about two months. The second month Ladji came to the window and pulled up the blinds and saw me staring in and let the blinds back down. I stayed and later he rolled them up again and saw I was still there. Another two weeks later I was out there. Olukose came out and said, "Oh this is a closed rehearsal so it's not really open for classes." I stayed on that platform to continue to listen. I could hear the bell, Wali's flute, and I could always hear Ladji's drum. Then there was a rainy day where Ladji rolled up the blinds and saw me and rolled them down again. I was now ready to give up on my chances of getting up into the studio. That day I heard the door open and Ladji came out and said, "Come here come here. Sit here." I went up into the studio and everyone shook my hand except for Olukose. I felt like he was testing me, and teaching about not taking on energy from people you don't really know. It was a good lesson for me. He would end up being the first one to help me with the mask dance. I love and respect that brother. It was only about one month later before that group left. Denise Bey stayed so she was in both waves. I came during the transition from the second wave to the third wave. I was going down with the crew with Chuck Davis but Balogun kept pushing me to stay with Ladji. He had learned from Ladji as well and there was something he knew that I didn't know back then as to why I needed to stay with Ladji. Ladji taught me something about intent. "You can play one thing, just one thing and if you play it right and you have the right intent and spirit, you can make someone smile." Basically you can evoke emotion but you had to understand the true nature of this jembe. You don't have to play a lot. I was with Ladji for seven years and I still didn't think I could play.

So now the second wave left and now I get Richard Byrd to come in with Ladji. Yomi Yomi carved Byrd a jembe out of white ash or something; so he had this drum. I told Ladji about my friend Byrd and he could do this thing with us. Ladji said, "Sure bring him." So, this was going to be Byrd's first up in your face experience with Ladji. I don't really remember the accompaniment that we did but when it was over Byrd felt embarrassed because of the sound of Ladji's drum-the clarity. Byrd said to Ladji, "Oh my drum...it don't sound.." and Ladji didn't say anything. He took Byrd's drum. He played that MF drum at another level. After he played it, he looked at Byrd and said, "Richie, it issa not your drum issa you hands."

After everyone would leave, he would keep a sangban and have a jembe for me and he would have me sit for an hour to play Pat Do Pat. He wanted my left hand to sound exactly like my right hand. He would leave and go to another room and I would have to sit there alone and play that part for an hour. After I was there for a little while learning the Pat Do Pat from Ladji, then Balogun and them would allow me to play at the classes. The young people like me could only play for the warm ups. The warm ups morphed into the steps in place then across the floor. But we would have to get off the floor by then. They would transition drummers for that. By the end, Balogun, Yomi Yomi, Kwayao, Spanky, and others would be on then. But certain days Balogun would come in while I was playing the warm ups and he would say I knew you were playing because I could hear your drum from outside. So, I was known to have my sound together. That was probably the discipline of why I had to do that with Ladji. So, I used to put Byrd on what Ladji had me doing and by the time we were the leads, we were a serious duo.

Me, Akin, and Denise were headed somewhere and Kehinde Donaldson was driving and we got in a bad car accident. Car was spinning around and was out of control. After the accident, we felt like we still needed to get back to the studio. We were all F'd up and Ladji told us to sit down. He went and brought out something like a ngoni, some string instrument and said everything will be alright and sat and started playing. I instantly fell asleep. I woke up and others started waking up as well. At least two hours had gone by. Ladji had some healing powers.

The way Ladji taught was he would come out of the room and start singing a song and he would play that break and the sangban would start then the dundun would start then another break and THEN the accompaniment would come in. We just had to know what to play after hearing what he was singing.

The jembe that Ladji gave me was the drum that was made for Ladji in the village before he went to the Ballets. He played that in the Ballets. Walter, Gregory and Olukose and the others had exposure to the Afro Cuban thing and other stuff. I didn't have any of the exposure they had. I was nineteen years old. I was coming and doing these little things with Ladji. One day he brought that drum to the studio and put it by the fire. It was a little cleaner and of course he saw me looking at it. He said, "Oh, let me hear you play your accompaniment." So, I took it, played my Pat Do Pat and then I put it back. And then one day he put it down there and told me to say something on the drum. He never showed me any soloing. I played some rudiments. He listened to that and said, "This is for you." I said, "oh thank you." I didn't really know what I had. I didn't know what he did with his drummers at this time. I was still new.

So, I had this drum, and we had the ritual before drumming for class including prayer, libations, and heat. So, I put my drum down. I was always arriving early to places; that was just always my thing. So, no one was around when I put the drum down. So, when the drummers started coming in, they saw the drum and was saying "Oh, Ladji is here." Now this is back then you didn't touch anyone's drum without permission. You hardly even looked too hard at anyone's drum. So now it's time to play the warm up and I went over to get the drum because I was one of the young ones. When I went to pick up the drum the voices came at me strong like "HEY WHAT ARE YOU DOING??? You can't touch Ladji's drum!" I was like, no no, Ladji gave me this drum. They looked at me up and down with these questions in their eyes; that changed shit for me at that moment. Balogun, Yao, Yomi Yomi and others were there. Balogun was in the corner looking at it and said "Yea that's Ladji's student. Go ahead and get that drum."

There are a bunch of people that said they studied with Ladji. I can tell you who actually studied with him. The ones that he sprinkled the juju dust on them. Those are the ones that studied with Ladji.

There was no road map for Ladji because he was the first. He came to the United States with his drum, gift, and enthusiasm. He started in St.

Louis (working with Katherine Dunham), then went into New York and with what he came with.

How did I know I had the accompaniment right? It was when Ladji would play different shit on his drum. That let me know that I really had the accompaniment. The way Ladji watched the drummers drum and body movement when the drummers would play to make him feel it. Ladji taught me about "nyama"; you could liken it to chi. He talked to me about how you can use the drum to move people called nyama. It is the spiritual energy that exist in all living things."

One of Ladji's early dancers from his group, Rhonda Morman, speaks about Ladji Camara.

Rhonda Morman: "Ladji was tribal like other continental brothers and sisters. We might learn a dance or rhythm from another West African country but we would not perform any of those because Ladji was from Guinea. Ladji was going to perform dances from Guinea. I don't want to come off like this is negative it's just the way it was with these artists from Africa."

One of Ladji's dance students, Darcel Abel, speaks about her studies with Ladji Camara.

Iya Darcel Abel: "What caused African folklore to skyrocket for me was the famous Ladji Camara, drumming on the jembe. There was no drummer that could drum like Ladji. When you heard him playing, you knew it was Ladji Camara.

He had a style that most drummers wanted to learn or imitate. Ladji was my favorite drummer. The sound that came from the jembe with his hands was definitely "The Drum Call." Ladji took African drumming and dancing to a different level when he played the jembe. Brothers and sisters were learning how to drum on and string up jembe drums. He taught dancing and drumming from Guinea, Senegal and Mali, West Africa. He not only played the jembe, he played the tama, dundun, sangban, the kora, balafon and other African instruments. But that jembe! OMG! It was exhilarating! It sang to my SOUL and still to this day CALLS for my feet and body to move. My favorite West African dances were Funga, Patakato, Saa, Lamban, Lendjen, and Mandiani. I've learned many dance styles, my favorite being West African folklore, and how to hear the different rhythms of each drum. More importantly, I'd learned from Ladji Camara how to dance to the drum.

I had the opportunity and pleasure to dance and perform with them all. I met many African folklore dance and drum artists because of Ladji Camara. All had studied with Ladji at some point such as Ronald "Balogun" Love (Ibae), Wali Rahman, Kehinde (Stewart) O'Uhuru, Paul "Ade" Harris, Bradley Simmons, Walter Ince, Wilhelmena Taylor, Hazel S. Bryant, Rhonda Morman, and a few others I performed with. West African folklore took off like a shooting star in NYC during the 1970s and 1980s."

Denise Bey: "I got to see Ladji Camara on the Ed Sullivan show. Then I got to see him with Les Ballets Africains. My Father's (Chief Bey) legacy is in my heart. I considered Ladji as my African godfather or African Santa Claus. When I was 6 or 7 years old Papa Ladji defected from the Ballets and his first home was our house. When I was about 11 or 12 I was one of his first dance students.

Butch Jackson was my first boyfriend. Butch and Charles Payne were drumming for Ladji. Dancers when I was with Ladji were Hazel Bryant, Vivian Young, Gloria Black, Darcel, Rhonda Morman, Baba Akin Babatunde, Obba Babatunde, Gregory Ince. I was the youngest out of the female dancers.

We rehearsed about 3 times a week and it was medicine. It never felt like work. It was like our hangout. The stuff that I got from Ladji wasn't all about movement. I received spiritual blessings from Ladji every time I danced and he would drum. I actually considered Ladji to be a medicine man. He was very good at healing people. He was very good at picking up on your vibe. He would know if something was wrong with your spirit. There were moments when we wouldn't rehearse he would just have us all lay on the floor and he would drum. Then we would be done and we would just go home and we would feel better. It was an unspoken thing when this happened."

Ladji playing balafon with dancers
Photo credit: Hakim Mutlaq

Baba Yomi Yomi Awolowo: "For jembe, Ladji was the Master before anybody. He really was the jembe Master. He was teaching Balogun and Kwayao and those guys. I was a late bloomer because I always had a 9-5. Those guys were fully committed to the drums, I chose to work my 9-5 and studied drumming on the side."

Baba Billy Bungo: "There was a time when I was out in Coney Island eating fire: "Side show by the Seashore." I did that for twenty years. Every Saturday night, people would come see Bungo High Life Band, fire-eater, and the sword swallower. Ladji was a fire-eater too. A lot of people didn't know that because of the Muslim stuff."

One of the premier drummers for the revolutionary group of poets from the 1960s and 1970s, The Last Poets, Baba Don Eaton speaks on his experience with Papa Ladji.

Baba Don Eaton (Babatunde): "Ladji's drum wasn't strung up high like other drummers' jembes. But the SOUNDS that he brought out of that drum. MAN! He was the best. And Ladji didn't have those caked up hands. No callouses like other drummers. He knew how to play up off of that skin whereas most drummers were playing down into the skin, which caused the pain and callouses."

Baba David Coleman: "There was a big heavy set guy named George that was the first American that I saw play the jembe. George was one of Ladji's first students. Sam was another black man that was studying jembe with Ladji. Sam developed Hazel and Wilhelmena. Butch and Charles came next with Ladji. Butch was pure jembe. Walter Ince was next; pure jembe. Ladji had Walter as his accompaniment for years. Then Aziz came in; another pure jembe player. Olukose was taught about sixty something dundun parts by Ladji. He wasn't really jembe. Olukose was a drummer; mostly Congo style. Balogun was the most natural drummer you ever heard. He was a big guy and had more spirit than all those guys before him. Whatever he touched turned to gold. He got a little from Ladji but not like the earlier drummers.

Ladji came to a show that we did with Chuck Davis at the Lafayette theatre and he saw me playing. He said to me "Brotha Brotha, you coming with me!" Now naturally I'm scared of change. I'm with Yomi. I finally made it with Yomi and Chuck and all them; the Bronx crew. Ladji telling me I'm coming with him. I said, "oh no." He said, "I have a brother in Guinea that looks just like you." That's nice Ladji but I'm tucked in right here with Yomi and them. Now had I went with Ladji I would have developed some other things, but I didn't go with him. I stayed with Yomi and I never made it to the top jembe players. I made it to accompaniment player, cuz I'm a natural born rhythm player. Solo lead dancer drummer? That's not for me. I can't remember SHIT. When it comes to sequence of dance, that's not for me. But I learned to be a seriously powerful accompaniment drummer. Make the drummer who's playing the lead sound even better than they are. I benefitted from Ladji just from watching him and his group because I'm one of those type of people that watches people and can absorb the essence.

Ladji made a profound effect on Chief Bey as well. Chief was very observant. He saw Ladji and he knew what was going on. He played with Ladji and Olatunji on "More Drums of Passion."

Baba Richard Byrd: "No one (in America) would know the jembe without Ladji Camara. After Ladji it was Mor Thiam.

Balogun had me, Aziz and Craig play in this concert with him, Yomi Yomi and all of them in front of Lincoln Center. Balogun had me playing balafon. I had never played balafon in my life. Balogun said, "come on man you play drums with 2 sticks - here are 2 sticks man, do your thing." LOL. He had me and Aziz playing all of these smaller percussions and some jembe as well. Olukose came up to us after the show was finished and he started scoffing us, "oh master drummers master drummers." Balogun came over and had to get in his face and they were about to throw down for real. Balogun made him leave. After that Aziz said screw this man we don't have to take this. I got something better. I'm going to introduce you to Chief's daughter, Denise Bey. She's one of Ladji Camara's dancers. That was 1972. He took me up to 174th St. and Boston Road and I never looked back.

Ladji had this couch in the studio. He said "What you name? Richie you sit down there." I sat down there like 3 months. I had already been playing jembe with Balogun and them. Spanky was the only one playing sangban. After 3 months one day Ladji said "Richie you play the sangban." I had been listening to the rhythm and dance Lamban many times. I strapped that drum on and couldn't remember my first name. I played 2 notes and Ladji came over and said "Richie! I thought you were ready. You not ready! You sit back down!" So I sat down for more weeks of study. Kehinde Donaldson had to leave the group because of his work with MTA transit. So I became the permanent sangban player. I remember doing a show with Ladji and Chief was in the audience and I was playing so intense and hard I put a hole in the head. I was so upset. My hand was bleeding . LOL. That was the best thing Ladji did for me. If you don't know sangban then you will never know how to play the jembe.

"Sound, Attitude, and Repetition" was one of Papa Ladji's mottos. You have to have the sound to make language, to talk, to share your feeling. You have to have attitude to give the presentation of what you are playing and saying, and you have to have repetition to sustain the conversation and make music proficiently.

Ladji's Dancers when I joined were Hazel Bryant, Wilhelmena Taylor, Rhonda Morman, and Denise Bey.

Ladji was one of the first Jembefolas that taught us that women drummed on the jembe drum. We knew a woman named Edwina and she would strap up the drum and hold it between her legs like a man. Many drummers had an issue with that. I didn't because I had already seen strong women drumming. Ladji made it clear for us that this was just as much a part of the culture as men playing jembe, only women didn't hold the drum between their legs.

One day after rehearsal, Ladji had Me and Aziz stay and he cooked for us. He cooked up some rice and shredded beef. He showed us how HE cooked. This happened a couple of times. He began to reveal slowly how he got into drumming and how he became to be. This information was very spiritual and sacred. He didn't think we had the capacity to embody the information. The way Ladji taught, you had to become like family. Ladji healed my brother. My brother had sickle cell and he helped him to live hospital and drug free for 2 years. Ladji went into the hospital asked me, my mother and father to leave the room where my brother was. He played music, sang and whatever Ladji did for my brother that day. My brother lived hospital and drug free for 2 years after that."

Chapter 10

Jembe In New York

"What New York had we didn't get in Washington, DC until about fifteen years later." Baba Baile McKnight

The jembe revolution in America began in New York. The major events that brought the jembe to the forefront all took place in New York. As previously mentioned, Les Ballets Africains first performed in America in New York in 1959. Fodeba Keita's production was a hit and the jembe appeared on the American stage for the first time. Ladji Camara stayed in America, specifically in New York, after his group went back to Guinea. He stayed to perform and teach the jembe and Manding music. His base was the Bronx, New York.

The 1964 - 65 World's Fair was where so many drummers and dancers experienced the jembe for the first time. That particular World's Fair was held in Flushing Meadows, New York. Les Ballets Africains' historic performance led by Famoudou Konate on lead jembe in 1968 took place at the United Nations in New York. The first jembe African drum and dance classes were all set up in New York. The first drummers who were making jembes from logs and skins were all doing this in New York. There were a great many people and organizations which contributed to the early jembe music and dance scene in America. While some of these important names originated in Chicago, Philadelphia, Washington D.C., Ohio, Missouri, California, and other locations, they were all somehow linked to New York when it came to jembe music and dance. If you were from New York, then you were affected somehow by the jembe revolution as it spread like wildfire and touched all aspects of life throughout New York City as well as other cities and towns.

My father, Abishai Ben Reuben, was already into African drumming and culture by the time I was born in 1968. He recalls learning how to make a jembe the year I was born. It appears the drumming seed was planted in me very early.

* * *

Abishai Ben Reuben drumming with Akosua Dance and Drum Troupe
Source: Abdur Rahman Wheeler
~

One of the original Akosua dance and drum troupe drummers from Mount Vernon, New York, Abishai Ben Reuben, recalls his transition from the conga to the jembe.

Abishai Ben Reuben: "Elder Puerto Rican Brother Raphael shared with me when I was nine years old, "The drum and heart are one. You have to have a love of self." Respect for drumming is an extension of the sound that God put in the human body. When the drum was made, it was an extension of the energy of the heart in the body. Elder Raphael told me to stay with 'mommy daddy,' like the child that first learns how to speak by calling out 'mama and dada.' The drum is a basic form to summons the people and deity.

The conga spirit connected me to the family in the islands, especially Puerto Rico and Cuba. I was connected to the history and cultural lessons of African and the African diaspora through the spirit of the conga. Conga felt like we were getting prepared to go home and take a journey. Conga felt like a festive, up, happy, and carnival feel for me. The jembe made me feel like I was directly connected to Africa. Once I strapped on the jembe, I felt like I was being transported back to Alkebulan [Africa]. The jembe gave me a wider range to opening me up. There was a certain mystical feeling that I tapped into with jembe that didn't happen for me with conga. Conga feels more grounded but jembe feels like you are moving, traveling, flying.

In 1968-1969, Kofi Kuma (priest, drummer and dancer from Dinizulu Institute) brought me from Mount Vernon, NY to IS 201 school by the train station in New York City. We went to Pablo Landrum, to a drum making series to learn how to make a jembe. I ended up passing that drum off on to Abdur Rahman. Pablo Landrum was really good with multi rhythms on top of rhythms. He said don't worry so much about soloing. Learn the patterns and accompaniment first. He had a lot of people from the Yoruba circle. He had a lot of young women playing. Some of those women were really throwing down on the congas. Playing quinto as well. Kofi and I used to go down together. We didn't get in too close with them because they were into the get high. We weren't down with that. So, we didn't really get in tight with the crew."

* * *

There have been plenty of highlights throughout this interview process. I have been inspired by the various drummers and dancers speaking so highly of each other. I have learned from these artists that this was not necessarily the case when they were all busy performing and rehearsing with each other during their prime. Tension was abundant/high, and compliments were rare/few. I witnessed a couple of the drummers go silent and tear up during my interviews following my sharing of compliments offered by other drummers and dancers directed towards them and their talents and influence.

Baba David Coleman is someone I have known for years, so he was my first advisor on this project. He is known for his extensive knowledge of the African drum and dance history as he had been in it for so many years. It was Bradley Simmons, however, whom Baba David highly recommended for his knowledge of this history. According to him, Bradley Simmons is the number one scholar on this topic. I was obedient and solicited Baba Bradley as another advisor on the project. He accepted the role and gifted me countless contacts to locate and interview and names of organizations to research, and opened his archives for me to study. He and Baba David served as more than a blessing to me and this project.

There were so many of my elders who were responsible for introducing these drums to their respective communities; for being the first to make and tune these drums in their respective locations. There were groups who set the stage for how African drum and dance groups would present themselves and the art going forward. There were those who traveled to West Africa early in the game to learn the dances, rhythms, songs, costumes, and culture to bring back and teach others. There were individuals who established a way to contract with community centers, prisons, schools, and parks enabling them to be paid as artists. If you are currently in America making a living off or benefiting from jembe music and dance in any way, you need to give thanks to these people and organizations who paved the road. These include, but are in no way limited to, individuals such as Papa Ladji Camara, Babatunde Olatunji, Moses Miannes, Saka Acquaye, Katherine Dunham, Mor Thiam, Asadata Dafora, Pearl Primus, LaRocque Bey, Nana Yao Opare Dinizulu, Kamati Dinizulu, Chief Bey, Taiwo DuVall, Montego Joe, Sam Watson, Chuck Davis, Arthur Hall, Sonny Morgan, Bobby Crowder, Garvin Masseaux, Ione Nash, Doc Gibbs, Nii Ayi, The Derby Sisters, Mamady Keita, Famoudou Konate, Yomi Yomi, Balogun Love, Olukose Wiles, Kehinde O'Uhuru, Walter Ince, Greg Ince, Neil Clarke, Amaniyea Payne, Denise Bey, Hazel Bryant, Rhonda Morman, Obara Wali, Obba Babatunde, Baba Akin Babatunde, Bradley Simmons, Shombe Yembe, "Papa" Aziz Ahmed, Baba Billy Bungo, Baba Richard Byrd, Kehinde Donaldson, Eugene Osborne Smith, Harry Belafonte, Melvin Deal, Baba Baile McKnight, Baba Aidoo, Baba David Coleman, Ajaibo Waldrond, Jalal Sharriff, and Akosua Panyin and organizations such as International Afrikan American Ballet, The Katherine Dunham School, Dinizulu Drum and Dance Troupe, The Sun Drummer, Kulu Mele African Dance and Drum Ensemble, Les Ballets Africains, Ballets De Senegal, Ballets De Djoliba, Muntu Dance Theatre, and Dance Africa.

Sam Watson: "These are Americans, West Indians, Cubans, Trinidadians and some Brazilian people born here that were the backbone of African culture in the 1960s. Chief Bey was alone. Chief Bey is very important. There would be no American black men playing a drum with their hands if it wasn't for Chief Bey. That's all I got to tell you. Chief Bey was first! He was the very first. He endured the ridicule from the average black person. "What do you mean some old bongo bongo African bull." Chief Bey endured all of that. Chief would call me to play at his jobs and I would just come in and show the guys what to do. Without Chief Bey there would be none of this stuff man. Chief Bey and Katherine Dunham, they were first. Without Katherine, there would be none of this."

The 1950s and 1960s marked a time when black identity and nationalism were at an all-time high. In this political climate, African Americans were embracing many symbols of power, culture, and self-determination. This flame burned well into the 1970s. Thus, the jembe appeared right on time.

Unlike drumming styles from Ghana such as kpanlogo, which came to the United States via the academy, or from Nigeria, such as Yoruban dùndún and bàtá, which have appeared among the growing number of American followers of Santería and Candomblé (diasporic versions of Yoruban Orisha practices), as previously referenced, the jembe came to the United States as part of Les Ballets Africains de la République de Guinée representing Guinea's revolution and independence from France. From the beginning, African American exposure to and interest in the jembe was not only academic and/or religious, but also political. The introduction of the jembe in the United States was politically potent as it brought together two important moments in black history: the emancipation of Guinea (followed by the rest of Francophone West Africa) from French colonial rule and the emergence of Black Nationalism in America.1

With its prominent position within Les Ballets Africains productions, the jembe became a symbol for revolution for conscious African Americans when it arrived in America. Whereas the conga connected the African American community to its African roots, the jembe became symbolic within Black Power. I feel extremely honored by the generous sharing of stories by the various African Americans who I interviewed regarding their early experiences with the jembe and African drumming and dance.

* * *

Abiodun Oyewole, one of the founding members of the revolutionary poetry group of the 1960s and 1970s, The Last Poets, spoke about the importance of the drum and how the jembe played an important role in the beginning of their career.

Abiodun Oyewole: "It was Divine Order. The first time the Last Poets were on stage was on May 19, 1968 (Malcolm X's birthday) in a park in Harlem called Mount Morris Park...at the time. That name of the park now is Marcus Garvey Park. That was a moment when David Nelson had the idea. He shared the idea of poets coming together as a group because poets for the most part ride solo. They don't hang out with other folks. They are reclusive. They hang out with trees and flowers in the woods some place. That's understandable. That's the life of a poet. David wanted to present all of us working together from three different walks of life to show black people how desperately we needed to have unity no matter what our differences were. So, the idea was sound, I liked the idea. I knew we needed unity, and Black Power had hit the scene because they had just killed Dr. Martin Luther King. So, I was gung ho for doing something. We were at David's apartment which was across the street from the park. David had just met Gylan Kane who he had met at a poetry reading at Columbia University. I didn't know Kane at all. I only knew David. David and I had been sharing poetry. I had been writing a little poetry, just exercising my creative gene. When he mentioned about getting this collective of men doing poetry, we didn't have a name for the group. After they killed Dr. King, I called David and told him that he had to get that group together soon. He put our name on the list to read poetry at Mount Morris Park on May 19, 1968. We were at his apartment trying to work out a way to appear as a group and not individuals. I thought maybe we could sing behind his poetry. David and Kane couldn't sing so that wasn't going to work. I heard and seen a chant done by some Howard University students because they were trying to get rid of an oppressor in the Howard administration. They didn't like him and they were going around a tree chanting "are you ready Niggas you got to be ready. Are you ready Niggas..." and that blew me away cause this is 1968 and I'm listening to some students. I never heard the word "Niggas" on TV before. This freaked me out. So, I told David and Kane. David had a poem entitled

Are you ready Black People, I had a poem entitled What is your thing Brother, and Kane had a poem entitled Niggas are Untogether People. So, I told them let's go up on stage chanting "Are you ready Niggas?" When they called us on stage, we weren't called The Last Poets yet. That didn't come until later. Before we went on stage, we ran into a Brother Hakim. He was one of our excellent jembe drum players in the community. Hakim was on stage playing with his crew. They were getting down. They finished and were shutting down when we were about to go on. Something told me that this was in Divine Order. I waved at Hakim to stay there. I felt that having that African beat behind what we were saying would highlight what we were saying and give it more juice. I just felt the drums would be a great background. So, he stayed on the stage and played in the rhythm of what we were chanting. We walked on stage chanting, "Are you ready Niggas? You gotta be ready!" By the time we made it to the middle of the stage, the entire park had joined the stage performance. They said it was like 5,000 people in the park that day. Everybody was chanting, "Are you ready Niggas? You gotta be ready!" We were affirmed at that moment. So, Hakim was the first person to play the drum behind us. He played the JEMBE. The first time we ever got together the chemistry was right and everything was right. We were such a big hit that we got a gig at New York University the next Friday. We didn't even have a name yet."

Interesting enough, when The Last Poets established themselves, they rented a loft which, as it turns out, was right next door to Babatunde Olatunji's center. Olatunji had been able to gain the support of prominent jazz musicians and others to establish his center.

Abiodun Oyewole: "The Last Poets' loft was called the "East Wind", 9 East 125th Street right next door to Olatunji's Place. Whenever we did events we would have to go to Olatunji's place to get chairs. Amy Olatunji would rent me the chairs for $1 per chair and we had to get about 70-80 chairs. That was a lot back then."

Babatunde Olatunji: "I couldn't buy a building though, so I had to pay $15,000 a year to rent a loft space. Coltrane was one person who was sending $250 every month to help. Then, later on, he did not perform for two years and the last performance he gave was where? At my center. He was very concerned about the way that promoters were cheating the musicians. They go and borrow money from their cousins. They would play at Carnegie Hall and make $50,000 for the show and then they pay them (musicians) scale wages. It was unequal distribution of wealth.

So, he (Coltrane) said, "I want to deal with this and do some research and see where I am, learn what I can learn about Western music and jazz." He was following me at that time. He came to me and said, "You and me and several other people like ourselves should come together. We know how to promote shows. How about three groups? You want to have a concert in every center in America? We can do that? Your group, my group and Yusef's (Lateef) group can start with Lincoln Center and we'll raise enough money." I was appointed Secretary treasurer. I went and booked the first concert for January 1968. Trane passed in 1967 though."2

Greg Ince: "Tunji was sponsored by Coltrane and Art Blakey. The jazz cats loved Tunji because he was working with them."

Ayishah Vivian Lewis Shabazz: "My first time dancing to the jembe drum was when I danced with Olatunji. The jembe drumming gave us a break to change our movements where we didn't do that with the congas and Haitian drums. A major difference with jembe from conga was the tempo. It was the jembe drums, but the jembe had to play for the dances that came with the music. They were very up tempo. The rhythms were always so upbeat. The energy was different with jembe drumming."

Sam Watson: "Babatunde Olatunji had a free jazz program at his studio on 125th St. and 5th Ave. It was held in the afternoon for kids for three or four years. Nobody did that in America. Who did he have? Miles Davis, John Coltrane, Max Roach, and others. Olatunji had a positive effect on culture in America at that time. He was a Nigerian - Yoruba. He understood song and dance so he used it and made a lot of money with that popularity. From a Columbia record company contract as a matter of fact. But he contributed to culture in America because he got the purest jazz giants at his studio in the afternoon. Sunday afternoons for free. Nobody did that.

Babatunde Olatunji was like a Walmart of Afrocentric activities in New York for about 15-20 years. Everyone passed through Olatunji. He was a Nigerian Engineer not a drummer from Columbia University. He wasn't a drummer. He happened to be a good dancer and a singer. He pursued that on the side; interestingly enough, he made money... a lot of money. Olatunji was important. People would be critical of him because he wasn't traditional. But Olatunji and Chief Bey are important because

147

that's where if you didn't know anything, you'll get something from Olatunji and Chief Bey, then you could pursue. I was a purist traditionalist to the extreme. They respected that and I was not critical of them. They were shocked at that because the few people who were around that were traditional, were critical of them. I wasn't critical of anyone who is sincere in the Afrocentric cultural activity. I support them. I didn't have arrogance when it came out that I played in the Ballets. Everyone expected me to be arrogant. No, I did the reverse and I went down to the ground. When I went to Olatunji's place AFTER the Ballets, he made a joke and he got down on his knees and he bowed and I said, please stop it stop it. He said, "We are honored to have his excellency from Les Ballets, Samuel." Everyone fell out laughing. I said, stop it stop it. Olatunji said, "Man do you know what you did?? Do you know what you did??" And I said, I have to respect what I'm told. He said, "Man, Guinea is the Cuba of Africa. It is the most extreme militant pro African nation. And that dance company is their pride and joy. And you played with them! You PLAYED with THEM! And EVERYBODY saw it. Do you know what you did?? Man you brought tears to my eyes! Ask my wife." She said, "Yea, he was crying." He said, "Because this black American did what no other has done. And you played with them, I saw you you!" Then he said, "Are you still going to come here your Excellency?" And we laughed and I said, I will always come here because you represent the community Olatunji. Nobody in Harlem now, represents the whole community like you. Everybody comes here. People come here on Sunday afternoons with their families and children to see John Coltrane, Freddie Hubbard, Mongo Santamaria, Art Blakey...Free. If you have a child, come in with the child and you pay. He said, "Thank you very much."

One of the original Drummers from Westchester, New York's Akosua Drum and Dance Troupe, Abdur Rahman Wheeler recalls his experience with Babatunde Olatunji.

Abdur Rahman Wheeler: "My mother brought me and my brother Rashee up. She separated from my father when I was one year old. We were in Queens. I was sixteen when my mother moved us to Mount Vernon, New York. When I was nine years old, I had an uncle in Harlem who was a Navy man. He played drums in the street with the Spanish brothers. He started me playing drums. He had an old conga. He would go to Park Ave/124th Street under the Conrail. They would be playing congas and tapping on the side. He started me out the way he started out. He played bass with thumbs. I used to play upstairs in the apartment with him, but I wouldn't go downstairs outside with him because that was his thing. They were drinking beer and stuff. After some time of drumming with my uncle, I found myself playing on everything, especially on desks and stuff at school. One time, I got in trouble for playing the desk and they called my mother to the school. My mother was angry but she ended up buying me a drum; that was my first drum. She used the drum like a threat. "If you don't do something I'm going to take that drum." I started playing drums with my father Baba Obafemi Wheeler in Harlem. He was fortunate enough in the 1960s to travel over to Nigeria with Babatunde Olatunji. He didn't go as a tourist. He went with Olatunji. Once a year after that he would take off a month and go with Olatunji to Nigeria. Olatunji had a studio on 125th street on the top floor. My father and his wife were involved with Olatunji's classes and the center. Tunji didn't have jembes; he had the large drums that he played with curved sticks. My father played some talking drums and other smaller percussions. A lot of people were going through Tunji's center. My father jumped into the Yoruba culture through Tunji, and eventually we found out he had another family in Nigeria. We found out about the other family after he passed away. My sisters Christin and Shani were also part of Olatunji's dance troupe. I never went up there to play.

I remember Kehinde O'Uhuru from way back in Harlem. He was a true performer. He used to be about acrobatics along with drumming. He was with Tunji early on."

Kehinde O'Uhuru: "I carried Olatunji's big heavy drums since a teenager for years and developed a hernia. I was there from age thirteen to twenty-one. By the age of eighteen, I was showing new drummers what to do. I started with Tunji in 1969. He got the grant money from Kennedy's assassination and set the center up. I lived about ten blocks from the place. So, I was there all the time. I was the custodian of the center as well. The Derby sisters and Taiwo DuVall were there when I arrived. Akwasiba (Joan) Derby was the one who taught me how to play for dancers. She used to stand right in front of me and dance; play what you see. She used to drum as well.

After Tunji, the authority was Taiwo. I got two paintings painted by Taiwo DuVall that was originally Tunji's. Tunji owed me money for gigs, so I said I'm keeping these paintings. Taiwo was my first and only drum teacher. He taught me on conga and whatever drum we had. He taught me how to even out my hands. He told me to play whatever I wanted, then he smiled. I thought I was doing well. Then Taiwo said, "Everything is on your left hand. We have to even out that hand." Taiwo was the only one to break down things for me."

Front: Kehinde O'Uhuru and Sule O'Uhuru
Back: Jalal Sharriff and "Spanky" Williamson
Photo credit: Hakim Mutlaq
Source: Iya Darcel Abel
~

Iya Darcel Abel: "I was taught Nigerian folklore by Mr. Olatunji and two of the elder performers in the Olatunji Institute, Akwasiba and Afiba Derby from Suriname. It was at this Institute where I also met Chief Bey, Ladji Camara, Titos Sompa, Shombe Yembe, and many other African drum and dance artists that were here in New York city."

Baba David Coleman: "In 1975-1976, I was twenty-eight. Kehinde O'Uhuru was working with Olatunji. I was a gangsta orisha dance and drummer in the hood. Kehinde was a cultural entertainer. I wasn't an entertainer. Olatunji had two gigs; he needed drummers for the Smithsonian in Washington D.C. and one to play at 113th in a public school. Kehinde said, "Being that you are a family guy with Olu, Olori, Oni and Debbie, why don't you take the stationary gig in the public school on 113th Street." That was my first teaching job. Working from nine in the morning to three in the afternoon, then from three to four in the afternoon in an afterschool program; had my own classroom and everything. Public School (PS) 113, Kehinde got me that job. It was his job, but then the other job came to go to the Smithsonian. Kehinde was already with Olatunji [and] I wouldn't go nowhere near Olatunji cause I heard the stories from Chief Bey and Babafemi. Why would I want to go there and get that kind of treatment for? He said, "You stay at the 113th street job, and I'll take the gig in Washington." Olatunji was too big to do a gig like that at the 113th Street job. I used to take Olu and Olori AND Oni to that school with me every day on my bicycle; on my bicycle all of three of them. Oni on my shoulders, Olori on the front standing on the things on the wheel, and Olu on the back seat. That's how my teaching career got started; had my own classroom and everything. Kehinde worked that out for me.

Taiwo DuVall...please come on. Smooth Cooly; barely spoke over a whisper but so dedicated to ashiko drumming with Moses Miannes. He was the first to bring Olatunji up to Harlem to find the drummers that made his 'Drums of Passion.' He was the one to bring Tunji to the drummers or the people to Olatunji; him and Montego Joe. Then Chief Bey, then Babafemi, and Papa Ladji came later."

Baba Walter Ince: "Chief Bey was such a mentor and beacon of light for so many brothers. He had gone through the front lines."

Baba Billy Bungo: "Chief Bey told me that there are only twenty-one different rhythms in the world. Everything else is improvisation. There wasn't a time when I would go to Chief Bey's house and not eat food. He was a very nice human being; very knowledgeable."

Eugene Osborne Smith ("Oz" or "Osborne): "Chief Bey fixed my drums. I knew him before he was initiated and became Chief."

Bradley Simmons: "I met Chief Bey when I was 14. I started playing and studying with him from that point on. We stayed connected because he was a great teacher. A lot of times those older drummers if they liked you they would pull you in. Especially if you are young with ambition and good hands they would pull you in. I hung out with him for years and then I started doing gigs with Chief Bey in Hartford, Connecticut. We did those gigs for a while. I followed in his footsteps. He went into Broadway and I followed him. We ended up working together on Broadway with "Timbuktu."

Chief Bey helped Ladji get his green card to stay and work in the US. Chief was singing opera when he was in Porgy and Bess. Most people don't know that Chief was an opera singer. Chief Bey was the best on ashiko. Taiwo DuVall, Moses Miannes and Babafemi (Samuel Humphries) were the pioneers on that ashiko."

Chief Bey playing the ashiko drum
Source: Denise Bey

Baba Richard Byrd: "When you walked into Chief's house he had a picture on his wall with him sitting at Ismay Andrew's feet. She was Chief's first drum teacher, she taught him dance first, then the bell."

Baba David Coleman: "Do you know patakato rhythm? Aw man. This is OURS (African American). Chief, Montego Joe, and Taiwo taught Tunji (Babatunde Olatunji) rhythms and came up with patakato rhythm during those sessions."

I spoke at length with Baba David Coleman about my own first experience with the jembe. It was a woman, Abayomi "Sista Yomi" Goodall, who put the jembe in my hands for the first time. We co-founded Nevada's first African drum and dance group together. I had known congas and had purchased a few Ghanaian drums while living in Las Vegas. Sista Yomi asked me about my favorite type of drum. I said, "quinto." She said, "That's cool; my favorite is the jembe." Since I was around my father and aunt's troupe when I was young, I had seen the jembe. However, I had never played one. I didn't even know how to spell "jembe." On one occasion, Sister Yomi traveled to Florida and returned to Vegas with a small jembe. She put that drum in my hands and I was hooked right away. It was very interesting to learn that a number of other drummers were brought to the drum by women.

Baba David Coleman: "It was Olu's Aunt Bambi, who turned me onto jembe. Just like Chief Bey was brought to the drum by a woman (Ismay Andrews), I was brought to the drums by women too. My sisters started me on the drum. Three of my sisters were married to legendary drummers, Babafemi Akinlana, Chief Bey, and Nana Yao Opare Dinizulu. I didn't start playing jembe until my Sister Bambi turned me on."

Baba Richard Byrd: "I had a friend that had a conga and used to tell me to do something with this. He just gave me the drum. I used to play in college with the skills I knew from my step and drum days and High School band. I started traveling to NY city to play drums and be around other drummers. I used to go to Olatunji's during 1969/1970. The first time I went in no one was in the room. So I was seeing drums and stuff around so I was playing drums and messing with stuff and soon the Ladies of Olatunji came in and Akwasiba Derby came in and she was Olatunji's everything. She could play, dance, sing and do anything. She said "WTF are you doing?" I said, I'm looking for Chief Bey. She said, "Chief is not here. She said, "Look over there." I looked and saw a hole in the wall with a bell still stuck in the hole in the wall. She said, "That's the last of Chief Bey." I heard the story about that bell in the wall. There was a guy that Chief was teaching how to play one of these rhythms and he came back and Chief expected the guy to have this rhythm down and the guy kind of shrugged him off. Chief took the bell and threw it. So Akwasiba said, "Oh you want to play and you want to do this??" She said, "Gang gang gigang gang gang". I said it with my mouth and then she gives me the bell and said play it. I went home and LOST the rhythm that fast. On my way back the next week I started remembering it. I go in and nobody was in there again and I see the drums again and I wanted to play drums. So I sit down at the drums and start playing. This Lady walks in AGAIN. And said "I'm going to kick your ass! Get up from there! What did you learn?" Because of that sternness I couldn't remember it. And now the beautiful young women are walking in to dance and you know my manhood was at stake. I relaxed and the rhythm came back and I played it. She said, "Now let's see you march, dance and play so we know that you have the timing." I was playing but I had 2 left feet. The girls start laughing. Then I start to calm down and I got it. She then had the dancers dance around me and gave me a choreographed piece. I didn't have it. She said, "You want to be a drummer? This is what you have to do. If you can't dance then you can't play the drum." And that was my beginning."

Kehinde O'Uhuru: "I asked Yaya Diallo about women drumming, and he said those restrictions were put on women from the spread of Christianity, Islam, and Judaism. All of those systems were patriarchic. Diallo said, "We learned that it was the women that made the first jembes."

Baba "Skip" Burney: "I'm sixty-five and for damn near forty years out of my serious drumming buddies maybe eight have been African American. Baba David Coleman was one."

Baba David Coleman: "Yomi was the one who really showed me how to open up and swing with the shekere. Teddy Holiday showed me finesse on the shekere. Babafemi taught me cool in the shekere. Chief Bey showed me the strength in the shekere. Yomi taught me the swing in the shekere. You see finesse is different from swing. Teddy played cool close tuck knit precise; that's finesse. Babafemi, cool ha; he don't sweat. He play with a big sweater or coat on. He played his ass off with no sweat. He showed you how to pace yourself and be cool. Chief Bey showed you the strength. Don't ever get tired. Never give up. Don't go slow, always keep moving forward. Yomi; swish, ah, up hand, up hand, click click, back hand circles, yaa yaa yaa yaa, talk, ah ah ah ah; all the slick talk. I got all that from Yomi. Ishangi was an entertainer. When I seen him and his wife, that was it. I seen Ishangi and his wife way before I saw Yomi, Teddy and all of them, but I was still too tight. I didn't know how to open up. Yomi showed me how to open up. I had years of observation but I didn't know how to apply it until I met Yomi. That's a cool brother right there. Boy he is laid back. Coooool; cool like that."

Yoruba Priest and Drummer, Baba Doc Gibbs, speaks on Philadelphia's influence on New York's African music scene.

Baba Doc Gibbs: "So Sonny, Bobby, Garvin, and Baba Daly had learned the shekere from Saka Acquaye when he came through Philly from Ghana. Those brothers went to the Yoruba temple that Baba Oseijamen had in New York around 1966-1967 playing the shekere. That was the first time New York saw the shekere. The temple didn't last long because they closed it and moved down to South Carolina and set up Oyotunji village."

Abdur Rahman Wheeler: "Around 1970, I started with congas in Mount Vernon; two congas in duffle bags. I used to walk across town from the Heights in Mount Vernon to the South side at the park. I used to play the Afro Cuban music. My man was Mongo Santamaria. He played melodic rhythms and roots music and played multiple drums. I had all of his albums and tried to emulate him. I was playing with a group called Innercity Funk and they played more like Earth, Wind, and Fire music.

At this time, I also started going down to Chuck Davis' dance classes in Harlem. Chuck was in a church in the basement. He was dancing at this time, leading the dancers in movements. He brought a lot of people along. At that time, I was introduced to jembe, but the jembe wasn't that big yet.

When Ballets Africains came, they brought the jembe, sangban, dununba, and playing off the ground. That was another level there. I started strapping that conga between my legs. That's where I got it from, and I brought that to Mount Vernon.

I was scared to drum with Chuck Davis. Those cats were too strong and fierce. I was scared of messing up. But what I did was take photos of people and the classes, developed them, and sold them to the people in the classes. That's how I started getting close to the people. I got into a friendship with Chuck. I got close to Yomi Yomi. I will never forget Balogun. They were trying to pull me in. They heard my hands and said oh this brother got some hands. Since I was playing with the bands, I was hitting the drums much different, and I couldn't remember those rhythms and change overs like they could so I was scared to jump in there. I psyched myself out from going where I could have gone with my drumming. After some time of going there, I finally got me a jembe and started studying with Yomi Yomi. I never joined Chuck's group. I just continued going back and forth from Mount Vernon, learning.

When the Ballets came, they changed everything. They were selling drums. The dancers were showing us a totally different way of relating to the drum. They really showed us the true connection between the dancer and the drummer.

That jembe drum is a superb tool. At this time, I really started becoming a man. I was around a lot of real men. These men were culturally connected and sincere. There were a lot of relationships going on."

Baba Don Eaton speaks about his experience with Chuck Davis.

Baba Don Eaton (Babatunde): "I went to The Church of the Mass to Chuck Davis' class and OH WOW...that's when I was introduced to jembe music. I met Yomi Yomi, Balogun, and Kwayao. Those were the guys right there."

Baba David Coleman: "Yomi went with Chuck; and Aziz and Walter went with Ladji, others with Chief Bey in Brooklyn, and others in Queens with Dinizulu. Kehinde went with Olatunji in Harlem. The rest of the drummers were renegade drummers. They play from the heart. Harlem was where everyone went to get the roots, but they are renegade because they had no rules. Abdul Rahman was a renegade drummer but highly spirited. I worshipped the ground he walked on. When that man took a step, I would say let me dust the ground so you could put your foot there. Brother would just carry himself a certain kind of way. Once you have seen that then some of that had to rub off onto you. That's why people came to Harlem - to see that.

Chief Bey's babies ran the Prospect Park drumming. If it wasn't for the Prospect Park drumming, then the drumming would have died in Brooklyn. The Yoruba culture and Prospect Park kept the drumming alive in Brooklyn."

Baba Yomi Yomi Awolowo: "I grew up in Harlem. I went to visit my friend in Queens and when I got to his house and he had drummers there, Wendel Hayes, Tony Robinson, Nathaniel Bettis, Chief Bey, Lawrence Tweet, Olukose, Clarence (Nii Ayi) - Egbe Ife, Chief Beys organization."

Baba Yomi Yomi with Egbe Ife
Source: Baba Yomi Yomi Awolowo

Obba Babatunde: "In 1977, Geoffrey Holder was directing The "Timbuktu" show on Broadway. He casted me to dance and asked if I walked on stilts because he wanted me to open the entire show on stilts. I told him," YES", but had never walked a day in my life on stilts. I asked Olukose Wiles if he would teach me stilt walking. Olukose told me that "You have to bring back the balls of a lion, then I will teach you." He didn't teach me. Ishangi taught Olukose stilt walking. I went to the stilt walker (Chakaba) in The Ballet De Senegal and I asked him if I could learn and he embraced me.

There was a percussionist that was in the Timbuktu cast and then he got called out on the road for a better gig so I called Bradley Simmons to come in and get in the audition. He came and got the gig. Bradley Simmons was always drumming wherever we danced. Wherever African drumming and dance was going on and you needed a good drummer, you got Bradley Simmons. I opened up the Timbuktu Broadway production on stilts each show with my brother (Bradley Simmons) playing the jembe."

Bradley Simmons: "In 1960 I was at the Gloria Jackson school of dance in Queens on Merrick Blvd. When I first got there, I was in the tap dancing class. That's what most drummers did first, tap dance. I was 8 years old at the time. I did tap dance for 10 years nonstop. The year after

I started in 1960, they brought in a drummer teacher named Pablo Landrum. When they brought him in that's when we all joined the class. We started out on congas. I studied with Pablo for a good 10 years. The congas was the first instrument along with the ashiko. Jembe was here but no one was playing it but Ladji Camara because he was the one who brought it over here. The jembe didn't really hit until the mid 60s around the time of the 64/65 World's Fair. Ladji was playing there with Olatunji and Les Ballets Africains performed there as well.

I played with Shombe Yimbe with Akin and Obba Babatunde, Jalal Sharriff, Hazel Bryant, Rhonda Morman, Darcel Davis (Davis back then but became Abel), Linda Moore. The Drummers were Warren Smith, Me, Spanky, and Jalal. We played at Jungle Habitat. We were working for Warner Brothers in NJ at that time. We did that for 6 months. Shombe was the glass and fire eater. I had never seen anyone do anything like that. That knocked me over when I saw that happening. His father taught him how to eat glass. His father was a Witchdoctor. He was from Cameroon. He was the only one I knew from Cameroon. That was a good gig.

Then I started drumming with Chuck's company in NY shortly after that. The drummers were Me, Kwayao Agyapon, Jalal Sharriff, Spanky (Phillip Williamson), Khalid Saleem. Balogun (Ronald Love) and Yomi Yomi (John Robinson) were there before us. They were our mentors in all aspects. Balogun and Yomi Yomi were Chuck Davis' original drummers for his company back then. And then I moved to NC and started playing with Chuck's company in NC. In between that I was playing with Ladji Camara. It was very interesting playing with Ladji because it was all jembe. The way he played it was much different than how they play today. The drummers back then were, Me, Richard Byrd, James Cherry, Jalal, and Kwayao."

Baba Don Eaton (Babatunde): "When I was a kid before I played with the Last Poets, my uncle had a conga in my dad's apartment. Everybody who was cool had a conga. The conga was your way of saying you cut into Africa. It wasn't the jembe. The jembe wasn't around yet.

I started by taking classes at The Dance Theatre of Harlem. My first teacher was Pablo Landrum. Baba Pablo taught us 5 basic rhythms. Dominican Republic, Haiti, Trinidad, Cuba, and Africa. He said if you learn those 5, then you can work. 5 basic rhythms from 5 different places. All of the lessons were on the conga and ashiko drums. Pablo was making ashiko drums."

Baba David Coleman: "Warner Brothers started the first jungle park in America. Blacks would go in there to play the drums to get the gig; thirty-five dollars a day. All the way from the Harlem projects to West Milford, New Jersey on the bus; thirty-five dollars. Unbelievable. We did it though. 1975 in Jacksonville, New Jersey - Great Adventures; thirty-five dollars. From Port Authority in New York City all the way down to Jacksonville, New Jersey Great Adventures. We were the first jungle park drummers in America. Zak Diouf from Senegal, Sonny Morgan, and fire eater Ali from Trinidad."

Baba Michael Norwood: "Ballets Africains was my motivation for playing jembe. They came to the city and at Town Hall and did a show. Portugal was trying to overthrow Guinea while the Ballets was performing in the U.S. during the early 1970s. The performers really performed that night with passion because of the political climate in Guinea at that time."

Bradley Simmons: "I believe the drums pushed the black power movement because you have to remember that the drum was here already before the movement started."

Jalal Sharriff: "When Ladji came in 1959, no one really wanted to identify with being African. During the 1960s, the black consciousness was up. The mayor of New York City at this time dumped a bunch of money into activities and programs in the black community to offset the unrest from Dr. King's assassination."

Kehinde O'Uhuru: "When I saw Walter Ince you couldn't tell me he wasn't from Africa. After I saw him play, I spoke to him and asked him how long had he been playing. He only played for about five to six years at that time. When I saw Walter, I said that's it, if he can do it born here like me, then I can do this. I don't think I would be here if it wasn't for Walter. There was only one in America in the 1970s that was doing it at that level. Walter was the only one."

Baba Walter Ince: "Montego Joe was an idol to me. Montego Joe and Joe Commodore were my first drum influences. Joe Commodore had done a lot of those early African drum movies. When you looked at the movies, you would say that this guy was clowning us, but he was a serious student of the drum. These guys got whatever jobs they could get when they were available. He had a cleaners business in Queens, and I was always attracted to his drumming. He told me that I needed to go get with another guy; that guy was Sam Watson."

Greg Ince: "When I got started. I was inspired by watching my older brother, Walter, because he was always drumming. I was like 3 and he was 12/13. A teenager, so he had the abilities to drum. He used to go on the roof of our apartment building and practice his drumming for hours. I never knew what he was doing during this time. He told me later what was going on. It was amazing because he wasn't just an icon for me but he was an icon for a lot of other drummers who were his age and older. Some of the master drummers from the continent would look at him like WHOA, you got this."

"Nii Ayi" Nana Obrafo Yaw Wofa Asiedu: "Sam Watson started working with us when I was hired by dancers called Hazel Bryant and Juliet. They formed a company called "Express Yourself Africa". In 1972, we went out and opened up Jungle Habitat in West Milford, New Jersey. I remember one show at Jungle Habitat when Shombe Yembe, the fire and glass eater, didn't go into New York City to see his spiritual medicine lady before the show. We were performing on stage, and he said to me if anything happens don't stop drumming. All of a sudden, he blew the fire and it turned back on him. People thought it was part of the show. He jumped off the stage. I wanted to help him, but he told me to keep drumming, so I did. People tried to help him but he didn't want or need it. He kept dancing and blowing his whistle, and I kept drumming. He finally got the fire under control; burns all over his chest and face. We ended the show; took bows believe it or not. He went into the city that night. The next day, his medicine they gave him made it look like it almost never happened. The show went on. He was an awesome and amazing brother. You can't play around with the juju medicine. They don't like that. He truly ate GLASS. Big medicine from home...AFRIKA."

Sam Watson: "I was with a Cuban Brazilian Haitian group. Those guys taught me how to play Cuban and then I got my own group, "Express Yourself Africa." To the right of the Apollo Theater upstairs is a rehearsal studio. There was a black actor who was in the movie "Nothing but a Man," who owned that studio. My reputation was no drinking booze, no drugs, and no womanizing with the girls in the group. So he trusted me and I was very strict, so he gave me control of that studio and gave it to me for free. He paid the maintenance and electric and all that stuff. I had it for like 7 years. I had a lot of people that came up to my studio. I had Thelonious Monk's daughter for example. And remember, this is like 3 doors away from the Apollo Theater. Right upstairs so people would stand downstairs sometimes and listen to the music. I would look out the window and see police parking cars bouncing their heads to the music. I loved it.

I had classes and I rehearsed groups and we would go on the road. We had a contract with Jungle Habitat in New Jersey for four years, which is where we made our money. Juliet Goosby helped to get that contract. Juliet had no music background at all. She was a little older than me and she was a pioneer amongst the women at that time in Harlem. Juliet designed very expensive clothes, coats, and dresses for rich white women in downtown Manhattan. So she met rich people and high class people. She did their personal tailoring and dresses and all of that. Juliet made a whole lot of money. She had a bald head, was a decent looking woman and dressed very unique. She couldn't dance a LICK. Hazel brought Juliet to me and said, "I know somebody who knows somebody who has a contract and they want to have an African dance group at Warner Brothers Jungle Habitat. We talked money. There was a lot of money. She had no music background and Hazel I had the whole thing and I had theatrical background as an actor so I know how to put together a show way above everybody else. Others come on and they dance and they bang drums and they shake their ass. They don't know how to put on a show. I know how to put on show. James Brown knows how to put on show. He knows it's a performance. Plus my association with the Ballets and theater, I know how to put on a kicking show with six people. Now I have 10 to 15 people with costumes and my approach to the theatrics of putting on a performance? So we discussed money. We got past that. I met the person who was in charge of the contract. We got the contract and I got the people I knew. You need to have three groups because it's seven days a week, three shows a day. I took everybody I knew that was qualified. I got Shombe Yimbe from Cameroon. The fire eater. I got Aero from Antigua. Good Haitian drummer and fire eater. I got Ali. Ali was from Trinidad. Excellent guy. He's a Yogi, a contortionist and fire eater. The fire eating was a big plus for the show. I paid everybody well. I'll give you an example. We're talking about the late 60s early 70s where no dancer on Broadway, not even the Rockettes got over $500 a week. The base salary I paid was over $600 a week. People left their jobs. People left their union jobs with retirement to come and work for me at Jungle Habitat. I put together the show. I got together the choreography. I put together the costumes and everybody made a lot of money. For YEARS! That's when Walter Ince and everybody came together. We made a living man. I had experience on the road as a drummer. I said this is a gig you have to adopt a regiment of being on the road. You have to sleep. You have to eat. You have to have your costumes ready. You can't forget stuff. You have to be together. We have to meet together every day on time. You have to eat healthy. That's when people got into health foods. We were way ahead of other groups. We took vitamins and got into health foods in the late 60s early 70s. I got that concept from the actors and actresses in theater."

"Nii Ayi" and Shombe Yimbe "Glass and Fire eater"
Source: "Nii Ayi" Nana Obrafo Yaw Wofa Asiedu

Shombe Yimbe "Glass and Fire eater"
Source: "Nii Ayi" Nana Obrafo Yaw Wofa Asiedu

Baba Walter Ince: "Sam Watson had studied with Ballets Africains. He was the first African American that I saw playing the jembe in about 1968 when I was about seventeen. I lost contact with him, then I got back with him when I was 22. When I saw him, I was mesmerized by his drum, the jembe. He said, "Well you have to get you one of these." They didn't have any jembes around.

The first jembe I bought was at a clothing store where they sold women's clothing. They were using the jembe as a prop like a table or something. I bought it for twenty or thirty dollars. This was obviously a drum that someone had been playing. It had a wooden patch on it, and I feel it had been fed. There's a group in Senegal, and I think some in Mali, and the way in which they feed the drum they make an incision like a mouth. Then they put whatever offerings they have, mostly I was told was yams, and they pound it and put it inside with other medicines. Then they put a metal covering over it. While I thought it was a repair that someone did over a crack, in fact someone had spiritually fed the drum. I believe that things find you."

Bradley Simmons: "Sam Watson was THE guy. Sam studied with Famoudou for years in the late 60s and early 70s when he was in and out of Guinea. He was Famoudou's student. He lived in Guinea for 1 year and studied with Famoudou that whole time. That's how he became the only African American drummer to play with the Les Ballets Africains in concert. He was the first and only. No African American has ever done that since Sam. He never played traditional style he only played Ballets style. That's all he knew because of his training with Famoudou and the Ballets. At that time it was Famoudou, Moriba, Adafont Toure. Adafont would get mad at Famoudou because he brought this African American into the company. He didn't like the idea of bringing in an outsider. But Sam knew the routine from top to bottom. Famoudou was the musical director so he could do whatever he wanted to do. He adopted Sam as one of his child drummers."

Sam Watson: "Fodeba Keita started the Ballets in France in the late 1940s. He devised a technique for performing African culture. He took the village stories and learned choreography and method of dance and method of performance and method of demonstrating traditional culture in the theatrical format and called it "The Ballets Technique." That's what I learned.

If you listen to Dizzy Gillespie in the 1940s, you learn how to make a musical play type. Nobody knows this stuff MAAAAAN! If you watch James Brown you learn that James Brown was an expert at 'The Show.' He knows how to perform. The group, the dances, the costume, the band. He understands performance. The Ballets Technique has that.

Whenever Les Ballets Africains would come to the United states I would go to the Ballets, every day. I quit my job. I jumped out of college. Every day every day. Every performance. Every rehearsal. If they were here for 90 days then I was there 90 days... to attend 90 shows. That's how I am and no less. Every show and I mean every single show. I didn't miss one and they would come every other year or every year at times. Whatever I was doing, I dropped what I was doing and I went to the Ballets' shows. I went to the rehearsals. When they would go on the road or when they came in the US and they went down to Virginia or someplace, I would got on the bus. I slept in the hotel. I learned how to eat traditional food. I picked up language customs. When they went to Montreal I went to Montreal with them.

I used to play off stage in the show. I played a guy named Moriba parts. Moriba taught me his part. He was a monster. He was a muscle dude man and he was powerful. I had to play his part because by playing his part you'd get the stamina and the timing. The tones had to be exact because the guy who played the solo for Foret Sacree (Sacred Forest) was a madman. Arafan Toure. He's dead now. The slightest thing off, he would scream out. So I watched Moriba play. Famoudou, lead drummer said, "Play with Moriba." After a year, I started playing with Moriba on stage during the performance and Arafan didn't know I was playing. He didn't hear the difference. Then Moriba stopped playing. When that point of the show would come I would play and Arafan was picky. No one non-African had played with the Ballets...To this day. He turned around and looked at me and said, "You got this Nigger American guy playing behind ME?!" That was coming out of him, but I played. After a while he didn't say anything anymore. The lead drummer looked at me and said, "Yeah you're doing it." So I was playing accompaniment for Arafan in the show. It's not the solo if you're accompanying the soloist it's called Accompaniment.

I played in the Ballets. I didn't just watch it, I played in the Ballets on the stage; at The Fashion Institute on 28th St. and 8th Ave. in New York City. I was glad because my supposed contemporaries were there. They saw it. I wasn't prepared to play. I had been playing with them for like a couple of years and this particular night the lead drummer said, "Samuel you are going on stage." I said, What? He said, "Take your shirt off. You're going on stage." I said, Oh my goodness Man. This particular segment of the performance was the Foret Sacree (Sacred Forest). It is a long piece. It's 20 minutes long. It's very intricate. It's spiritism...Juju.

When I came out on stage at the Fashion Institute, for some reason that day all the dance schools in Manhattan in the area were there. Chuck Davis, all these people were there! All these people were there. I don't know if Famoudou knew that. I didn't. So I came out and then I heard everybody saying, "Sam Sam Sam!" I was drenched in sweat cause I was scared to death because I'm playing for my own people. That's what did it.

I had some good teachers. Famoudou was first. He is Jembefola. He is from Kouroussa, Guinea. If there was no Famoudou, there would be nothing. Famoudou was EVERYTHING. If it wasn't for Famoudou there would be NOTHING. PERIOD. Famoudou received me the first time I went backstage. He's the drummer for all the ceremonies. He is the let's say, Concertmaster. Then he told me about a guy named Koungbana Conde. He was a sangban master. Koungbana was with Djoliba Ballets. Famoudou told him about me. So when Djoliba came, I ran backstage and Koungbana looked at me and he said, "You must be Samuel." I said, Yes! "Come and I will show you sangban." Sangban is really hard. Guys bang and they call themselves playing sangban. No, sangban is hard. Sangban is like playing bata and abaqua at the same time. When you're playing sangban you're playing two rhythms. You're playing like five/four and six/eight. You're doing two things at the same time. Sangban IS the rhythm not the jembe. Jembe is NOT the rhythm. Sangban is the rhythm. The guy who was playing sangban that's the drummer. That's the cat. I didn't know that. So, before Djoliba came Famoudou said, "You are going to play with Koungbana. He is a sangban master. All of us can play sangban but we are not sangban masters. You will see when you hear him play. Then I heard him play. I said, Oh My God. It isn't that you play a lot but you're on time. So I met with Koungbana and we went to the hotel with his particular drummer which was Bongolo Keita. Bongolo Keita is a dancer drummer. That's another thing. That's not a regular jembe player. He's a dancer player. We went to the hotel for 90 days every day and we did the same thing every day...every show. I watched the show. I would get with Koungbana and Bongolo Keita. I would play what Bongolo would play and then I would play the sangban and Bongolo would play on top of me. 90 days...seven days a week...three to four hours a day, not counting the show. So I got a feel for sangban from Koungbana. Then when the Ballets came back, Famoudou told me Koungbana told me you play sangban now. I played with the Ballet and I played sangban. Then Famoudou said you play for the repetition. Repetition is the rehearsal. So the Ballets would play and they'd have the repetition after the show or before the show. I played for all the repetitions because I played a little bit...I played Ok. I'll say that much. So they could cut loose with just me. The section is you have dundun which is the big drum. You have kenkeni which is the drum in the middle. You have sangban. You have accompaniment jembe and you have solo jembe. Now you could have a another drummer. Two accompaniment jembes and one solo jembe. But if you have a sangban master, all you need is sangban and the group could rehearse. The sangban could play the changes. From what I learned from Koungbana I could play the changes in each song. So they would rehearse freely and they could work out the drum sections because I was holding it down on sangban. Sangban in jazz would be the bass and trap drum combined. The trap drummer would be like Art Blakey and the bass, Mingus. So I'm playing sangban with Ballets Africains.

I eventually went to Africa in 1973. I went for 21 days and stayed 11 months and 15 days. I couldn't leave. The first place I went was Sierra Leone then I went to Liberia. So you know you have music seven days 24 all the time. But you don't have the level of Ballets. It's traditional but it's so refined like Ellington or Basie. I was waiting calmly and just looking. I was waiting for the next day. The next day I asked, could I just like play accompaniment maybe. And they said, "Ok, this American. OK yeah it's OK yeah yeah yeah OK go ahead American." Then I played and they said, "Oh my goodness what the hell is this?" I played some sangban patterns and they were completely shocked! They asked, "How did you learn how to do that? We don't know how to do that! The guys in the national company can BARELY do that." So they took me to the national cats in Freetown, Sierra Leone. They were Mende. When I left Sierra Leone I went to Liberia and the same thing happened there; and I went to Senegal and the same thing. Côte I'voire, same thing. I had a good time. I couldn't leave. When I came back, I came back with Africa in my loins."

Baba Richard Byrd: "While I was in Middle and High school in East Orange from 1964-69 Baba Kwame Ishangi brought his group with his wives. Then Dinizulu came through with his group. Chief had this saying "You have to know the rule to bend the rule."

I started with Olatunji, went to Balogun who was drumming with Chuck Davis, then to Ladji, Chief Bey, then back to Olatunji. When Olatunji called me back to play Chief and Ladji talked me up. I ended up as a lead jembe player for Olatunji. I traveled all over the world touring with Olatunji."

Bradley Simmons: "Olukose Wiles was a great drummer. He knew his stuff. He was a drill sergeant. He would push you to the point where you were either going to like him or you were going to hate him. A lot of people didn't like him because he would push people pretty hard. I wasn't affected in that way. He would stay with you if you showed that commitment to what you were doing."

Baba Billy Bungo: "One time Pablo sent me down to meet Olukose, Obara Wale and Walter Ince and those guys. He sent me down there with some skins and told me to bring my jembe. So, I had my jembe and some skins. They were at the Armory in Brooklyn. They were in there playing some beautiful music. I waited and introduced myself, and they looked me up and down like they wanted to kick my ass. They asked, "Well, who are you?" I said, "I'm Billy Bungo." They said, "You Bungo?" Olukose said, "PLAY!" Those were his first words to me. "PLAY what?," I asked. "Break it out and let's PLAY," he said. I started playing and playing with those cats and I've been down with them ever since. Olukose was the one who taught me how to play Bembe and Orisha music. Olukose introduced me to those Spanish cats."

Jubal Harris: "Baba Olukose Wiles biggest influence on the Ohio African cultural arts scene was as a drummer and stilt walker. He would perform for the Dayton Black Arts Cultural Festival. Ohio's largest Black cultural festival. He established the Chakaba (stilt walking) society in the US along with Baba Ishangi."

Left to Right: Jubal Harris, Soleman Diop, Olukose Wiles
Source: Jubal Harris

Abdur Rahman Wheeler: "Yomi Yomi was strong. One thing I liked about him was he remembered technical stuff. He retained a lot of the lessons. Yomi had a fierce callous on his hand from hitting that rim. He was up front so he had a lot of work to do. He was the lead drum and you could tell from his hands. I remember Spanky as well. He was young and he played the dundun. He was strong too. Abdur Rahman from Harlem played with them too. He was a dark skinned brother."

Baba David Coleman: "Everybody underestimated Yomi Yomi. They underestimated Yomi cause he wasn't trying to break no record. He wasn't trying to be a great jembe player or none of that. Just clean. Straight up clean heart. Right like that. Showed me how to open up and be myself."

Baba Yomi Yomi and "Spanky" Williamson
Source: Baba Yomi Yomi Awolowo

Baba Yomi Yomi Awolowo: "Me and Balogun were very close. We went to Africa together. We got initiated over there together. How I met Balogun was very interesting. One day I'm down at Central Park and I heard this drum way in the distance. Something about the sound. I kept hearing this sound and it was calling me and calling me. I kept going and going until I got to a big crowd. I wiggled my way to the front and I saw it was Balogun playing that drum. Yea man he called me. I said, "Yo man, can I play?" He said, "Yea man come on." After I played we were locked in together. After that I brought him to the company. I brought him to Chuck Davis. He fit right in. People in the company would try to pit me against Balogun because we were both top notch. But they didn't know how tight we were. We went and got initiated in Africa together. Balogun lived across the street from me. Someone broke into Balogun's house and stole his drum. Me and Balogun took our elegbas and fed them all together and 3 days later that drum turned up at my Godmother's house. In fact, there were rumors about his passing. When he passed away they tried to accuse me of having something to do with it. I didn't give any rebuttals or anything. I just kept my distance and stayed away from all of that. But the thing about it was that when he got initiated he was told that he should stop playing and he didn't. He could really play."

Baba Richard Byrd: "When I graduated, we had a lot of black consciousness going on. Everyone I hung with in Newark came through either the Nation of Islam, The Black Panthers, or Amiri Baraka's group. We had James Brown's I'm black and I'm proud. We had dashikis and afros. Balogun was the one that impressed upon me to study deeper into the African music. Ron "Balogun" Love was a camera man for "Like It Is TV show." He was the most natural drummer that there was. All of the guys liked Balogun. Balogun studied. He was into Ethnomusicology. He was studying with an Ethnomusicologist from Long Beach, California. That College had one of the first African Ethnomusicology classes in the country. Balogun studied with a woman from Columbia University. She studied in Senegal. He learned about the intricacies of sabar and the art of stick drumming."

Baba Walter Ince: "Balogun knew his way around sound systems and stage sound. I believe he may have had a sound gig with CBS at the time. Balogun was a big man, and most cats playing jembe were rather thin. Balogun was very special with some of the things he was able to do early on. Some of the speed he was able to engender. At least I know he pushed the envelope for me, and I know that this music really was a lot faster. You had to make your spirit push your hands, mind, and body to go in that direction and yet still keep it within the framework of the music."

Baba Michael Norwood: "Balogun was playing serious conga because he spoke Spanish."

Greg Ince: "Balogun was one of those drummers from back in the day who we saw as a serious drummer and craftsman."

Jalal Sharriff: "Ishangi took me under his wing at this time when I was about thirteen years old. I traveled from Coney Island to Hollis Queens to study with Ishangi.

When I got my first jembe I was about fourteen. I was walking down the street in 1967 and saw a gift shop. They had African artifacts in there and I saw this jembe; they didn't know what it was. When I started studying jembe, I didn't want to sound like an American playing jembe.

We were in Jamaica and had just finished performing. I was playing a jembe I had made and was performing with some Senegalese drummers. Mor Thiam saw me play a jembe that I had made and said "You all are my countrymen, but Jalal outdid you all." Ibrahim said, "You're right." The drumming and dancing helped to fuel people to recognize their Africaness. Many people didn't know about drummers that would urinate blood after playing. I found out for myself how to prevent or else I was going to quit. I didn't go to the doctor because I knew they would tell me to quit drumming. I remember speaking to Balogun because he went to the doctor. The doctor told Balogun that straining, and that where the jembe was strapped on, was putting pressure on the kidneys. So, I learned from studying martial arts that whenever something becomes more stressful, you breathe and relax. It took away my strength initially, but then I learned how to prevent it by breathing."

Kehinde Donaldson: "I bought my first jembe from the Amram brothers. They used to import shells from Haiti to New York and they looked something like a jembe. So, I purchased a shell that looked closest to a jembe. I ran into Chief Bey one day and told him that I bought a shell and needed a head put on it. Chief Bey put the head on for me around 1972-73. He told me that it will look like a jembe but it won't sound like one. Chief said, "You have to clean some of that wood out of the shell." Chief Bey was the first to talk to me about brotherhood.

Yomi Yomi was the one who showed me how to sew the skin on the drum. James Cherry came out with the concept of the three rings on the top of the drum.

Chief Bey, Yomi Yomi, and Balogun were straight up people. We had other brothers that were very good drummers but they didn't want to share. When I was around Balogun, Yomi Yomi, and others they were all into chess, martial arts, and herbal medicine.

I would get with Gene Osborne who was living in Jersey. He told me that we could go to a slaughterhouse in Jersey and get skins for five dollars."

Baba Baile McKnight: "What New York had we didn't get in Washington DC until about fifteen years later. "Papa" Aziz Ahmed became the protégé of Papa Ladji."

Babu Atiba Walker: "My first jembe instructor was a brother I met from Senegal, West Africa, Mor Thiam. I saw Mor Thiam in Chicago perform around 1974. I met him and he told us that he was teaching in East St. Louis. So, a group of us started traveling down to East St. Louis between 1974-1979 learning from Mor Thiam. He always gave positive energy. The most profound thing I learned from learning jembe with Mor Thiam was to be yourself; not to copy anyone or try to be the baddest cat but be the best you can be. Always understand the reflection of our culture and how it relates to all of us and how we are all connected; be authentic. It was really connected to what I got from Sun Drummer. In Sun Drummer, we say it's on the drum that needs playing, it's the drummer that needs development.

I remember when we traveled to New York and International (International Afrikan American Ballet) was killing it. We were vibing with drummers like Balogun, Olukose, Walter Ince, Bradley Simmons, and them. I linked up with another one of Ladji's students named "Papa" Aziz Ahmed. Aziz came to Chicago when I was working with Darlene Blackburn at that time. I got real tight with Aziz. He gave me a lot of insight. He gave me the vibe on Ladji. Ladji was the first to bring the jembe to America. Then Mor Thiam came with the jembe from Senegal in 1968."

Kehinde Donaldson, Abdul "Papa Aziz" Ahmed, Ladji Camara, Richard Byrd, James Cherry
Source: Abdul Aziz Ahmed

"Papa" Aziz Ahmed: "I love Billy Bungo. He was one of the ones that befriended me and took me to some places. He would take me to "The East" and I would meet another set of drummers and artists. He knew so many people so he was able to get into different circles. I was fortunate to go play with Chuck and them and with other circles even though I was really strong with Ladji."

Baba Billy Bungo: "When it comes to jembe, the baddest lead jembe drummer was "Papa" Aziz Ahmed. I was close to all of these cats. Chuck Davis, Charles Miller, Nana Dinizulu, Baba Ishangi, Babafemi, Baba David Coleman, Chief Bey, Olukose Wiles, Olatunji, Yomi Yomi, Bobby Crowder, and Pablo Landrum. I can tell you about these cats that were friends of mine. It's about eat and sleep the African drums. It was about respecting the drum and tradition. My advice is more African dance class and more teachings of African culture to the children; teach the children."

Baba Michael Norwood: "Back in the day, drummers would play jembes, congas, and everything together, but things would get tense and the drumming would go in all different directions.

When we moved to jembe from conga and found out that you could play all of these different sounds on one drum, you felt the power. The jembe is a young man's drum; helps to keep you young."

Baba Walter Ince: "Here, most of our music is predicated on swing; got that down beat going. If you want to understand Lamban, listen to Charlie Parker, because all of that riffing that he did on top was above a basic rhythm. Lamban talks about several passages of life. It gives us an opportunity to see that in life that there are always extensions in life. Life is about a central rhythm that is running through. Many times people are not doing well in life because they don't understand their own One. So, for you to understand someone else's One is impossible, because you don't understand your own One."

Sam Watson: "Walter Ince and Nii Ayi were some great guys. They really put up with a lot with me. I was very strict and hard on those guys. That wasn't easy to get training from me, who spent that focused time training with the Ballets. They had to deal with second hand info from someone intense like me. Nii Ayi is about my age and I really loved that guy. He had a rough life. I took him in to train him. He said, "You are so strict, but I needed you in my life right now. I borrowed your discipline for my life. I was able to do things personally that normally would not do. I figured if you could do it and you are from the hood like me then I could do it too.

With Walter Ince, Nii Ayi, James Cherry and them it wasn't just about the jembe that I taught them. It was a complete African cultural experience. When I was 18/19 John Henrik Clarke taught us African history in a group that I belonged to in Harlem back in the 60s. This is before he had his PhD. Imagine, John Henrik Clarke tutoring me personally. He came to this group and taught us for seven months, two or three times a week. He taught us African American history and he introduced me to this guy named Ivan Van Sertima. I met Dr. Ben Jochannan. When I went to Senegal I met Cheikh Anta Diop. I sat with all those cats. I also sat with Thelonious Monk's saxophonist Charlie Rouse. I got to see Mingus, Max Roach, Monk, Eric Dolphy. My Aunt turned me on to bebop. With Walter and all of them I didn't talk to them about me. I talked to them about THEM. I was only passing on what was given to me. None of it was mine. I talked about Clarke, Van Sertima, Diop, Malcolm. I was part of Adam Clayton Powell's Young Democratic Club at Abyssinia Church. It was Adam Clayton Powell who brought Malcolm out to the world. So whenever I would see Malcolm on the streets in Harlem we would talk and talk and talk because he knew me from the Adam Clayton's group at his church. It was all of these experiences that I shared with Walter and them. THAT'S what I gave them. Not just the jembe."

Kehinde O'Uhuru: "What happens to most brothers and sisters is that they learn enough to have the drum feed them; the drumming makes them feel good spiritually. It winds up turning into the equivalent of like getting high. It makes them feel like they can deal with this shit. The ancestors don't want that. They want to be acknowledged again. They don't want you to continue to be a slave and that's what will end up happening if we continue doing what we're doing."

Kehinde Donaldson: "It was difficult to pick up the dance and drum back in the 1960s and not think political."

Baba Michael Norwood: "During the late 1960s, only drummers that had jembes were drummers that carved them out themselves or was sold or gifted a jembe from drummers from Les Ballets Africains. The early drums they were carving out was not carved out well so they were very heavy. You couldn't strap those on. It was like carrying around a tree trunk they were so heavy. The drum makers were tacking the heads on during that time. The heads had to be heated up before playing. Sometimes you come in late to a gig and the drummers are looking for where to find some heat. The dancers would get to the gigs early and ask people where are the outlets because they knew the drummers would be late and would need to plug their heaters or hot plates in when they arrived. Sometimes there would only be one outlet, so only one hot plate could be plugged in. The drummers would be crowding their drums around the one hot plate, and the hot plate would fall on drums at times and put a hole in the drum. Then that drummer would not have a drum to play for the gig; that meant no pay. They would want to play a shekere or something to still get paid. Once they took their drum away from the heat, they would be ready to play one hundred miles an hour because they knew that the drums would go down."

Chapter 11

African Spirituality

"The drum is the archetypal instrument between chaos and order."
Dr. Phil Valentine
~

In 1959, another major event occurred within the African American cultural community besides Les Ballets Africains making their debut in America. Christopher Oliana and Walter Eugene King (Baba Oseijeman) traveled to Cuba and became the first African Americans to be initiated into the Yoruba tradition as Priests. Baba Chris as a Priest of Aganju and Baba Oseijeman as a Priest of Obatala. Baba Ed James received Palo in Cuba in 1959 and the following year, Baba Ed was initiated as a Priest of Shango. Baba Chris became known for his accurate readings. Baba Oseijeman set up the first Yoruba temple in New York and eventually established the first Yoruba village in America called Oyotunji African Village in South Carolina. Oseijeman had already earned a reputation in the cultural dance world performing with the Katherine Dunham Dancers and serving as Dinizulu's first narrator for their stage productions. Baba Ed would become a scholar in a variety of religious systems and societies within the Yoruba culture. He became known as the "Grand Puba" or "Grand Master." He was both my godfather in Ocha as well as my cousin; as my cousin and godmother, Iya Yvonne Dickerson, was Baba Ed's wife.

When I was in college, Iya told me that I needed to get to her Ile and study with Baba Ed. I was on the West Coast, and the Ile was on the East Coast so that was not geographically possible at the time. When I moved back to the East Coast after graduation, I started visiting the Ile for readings and lessons. I had already been performing and drumming a lot by that time. Baba and Iya shared an abundance of information and wisdom with me during those early years. I gained a new respect for Ifa, Ocha, Lukumi and Santeria. I also learned about Palo while studying with Baba Ed and Iya Yvonne.

These pioneers would be the ones to open the doors for others interested in a religion rooted in African tradition. The African drummers and dancers who were dedicated to their craft and discipline did not have many places to go for African dance and drum classes. Most of these teachers, drummers, and dancers in the late 1960s and 1970s had been exposed to the Yoruba tradition. With each interview, I began to feel as though initiation into the Yoruba tradition was a rite of passage for the African drum and dance community.

The jembe drum and music is no doubt entertaining, but also therapeutic and stimulating on a cellular level. The spiritual nature of the drum and its sounds has remained a mystery for enthusiasts and practitioners for decades now. The physical and mental benefits of experiencing African drumming are innumerable. As for the spiritual nature of the jembe, I believe it must start with the drummer. One can say that holistically working on oneself through character development could position one to experience the plethora of spiritual benefits from drumming. I am immensely thankful for teachers like Abishai Ben Reuben, Baba Ed James, Iya Yvonne Dickerson, Famoudou Konate, Baba David Coleman, Kehinde O'Uhuru, and others who always spent more time talking about spiritual matters and character development as opposed to simply the mechanics of drumming and its physical and mental benefits.

* * *

Baba Ed James: "Too many people feel Palo is a system of quick magic and so forth. Philosophically, Palo is as complex as the Yoruba system, if not more so in some ways. The system of Palo, the actual religion is the exact opposite of the Yoruba tradition. The Yoruba tradition is based upon the idea of devotion. The idea of the individual calling upon orishas to aid in their everyday living - and eventually in their evolution. One translation of the word orisha means those to whom we pray. Yoruba tradition is a devotional system not involved in magic as many people reinterpreted it to mean. On the other hand, the Congo system Palo is based on the individual helping himself. The principle of self-help. Yoruba is other help and the Congo system meaning self-help. This means the individual is responsible for all that he does."

Baba Ed James
Source: Iya Yvonne Dickerson

Iya Yvonne Dickerson: "Baba Ed attained his spiritual knowledge at a time when others who had the knowledge was not willing to share much. Most of the time, he and I learned from watching and observing. Anyone who had the opportunity to attend Baba's lectures, classes, workshops or private instructions was truly blessed. He gave thorough lessons and had a different perspective on many subject matters that was documented by Babalowas, Priests, and Priestesses."

Baba "Skip" Burney: "The Black American Santeros that I respected especially when I was young was Alfred Davis. I respected Ed James. He was very knowledgeable to the point they thought he was insane; especially with that Egyptian stuff. No one read into Odu like Chris Oliana. They said he read so deep into the Odu that he was insane. No one read into the Odu like that; he was albino and Aganju like me."

I can remember Baba Ed teaching me about his view on protocols with regard to my honoring the warriors (Elegba, Ogun, Ochoosi and Osun) during my performances. Baba wanted to assist me with spiritually upgrading my performing troupe's repertoire. He taught that we needed to acknowledge (play and sing to) Ogun first, even though it had always been our way to acknowledge Elegba first. He explained his unconventional approach from a historical perspective:

Baba Ed James: "Since so many of us (African Americans) came over in chains via the trans-Atlantic slave trade, as African Americans we need to acknowledge Ogun first then Elegba. Those that follow protocol in Africa had a completely different experience from us who were born in America."

I received lessons like this from Baba Ed on a regular when I would visit the Ile while he was still alive.

It is no coincidence that so many drummers were initiated into different African spiritual systems during the 1960s and 1970s. Whether it was Akan, Yoruba, or Islam, there was a surge of initiations into these systems during this time, particularly the Yoruba-rooted religions, such as Santeria, Lukumi, and Ifa. The pioneers of African drumming and dance in America had the greatest influence on this movement. The 1960s and 1970s was a time when Africans born in America were striving to align themselves with self-determination. For many, that meant living a more African way of life, changing government names, wearing cultural hairstyles and clothing, speaking African languages, learning African drumming and dance, and practicing traditional African spirituality. Through drumming and dance, one could interact with the invisible world while participating in a cultural movement which was rooted in African pride and resistance.

Reverend, Percussionist, Metaphysical Educator, Writer, Lecturer, Healer, Dr. Phil Valentine, spoke on the nature of the drum:

Dr. Phil Valentine: "The drum is the archetypal instrument between chaos and order. Every drum that is formed has a soul that immediately enters because you are creator. You can't create anything without a soul. The one thing that the soul wants to do is to reach its highest potential.

The drum itself as it represents today first and foremost is continuity. Once your heartbeat stops, there is no life. If anything, it's an archetypal resonator that maintains the heartbeat or soul beat of the ancestral bloodline. When you walk into a circle of drums with a particular rhythm, your energy changes."

Bradley Simmons: "When it comes to Ocha and the Yoruba thing, we drummers all wanted to be into something that was connected to the drum. You couldn't get any more closer to the drum than that. We all came out of Christianity, and said "but this is what we really do." When I started hanging out with drummers and saw everyone beaded up, I started to make inquiries and I was talking mostly to Pablo Landrum because he was the one giving me all the insight.

Then I was hanging out with Olukose. At that time he was Tony Wiles. Then I found out he was in Sunta's house so that's why Pablo wanted me to go there because she had a lot of drummers in her house. Olukose, Yomi Yomi, Nat Bettis, and I believe Balogun too."

Baba "Skip" Burney: "The holy mother that brought Black Americans to the Ocha. A White Puerto Rican woman who brought Cubans the blues because she was making Black Americans - Sunta Osaunko."

Obba Babatunde: "In 1970, my brother and I were introduced to Ocha and Ifa. My brother became a Priest of Shango and a Babalawo. I didn't get initiated. They marked my head though. Obatala has my head."

Jalal Sharriff: "I played conga in the very beginning of my drumming, but I didn't stay long with Afro Cuban because I was Muslim. The drummers that stayed with congas were into the Yoruba religion. Most of the drummers that were around when I came into it were getting into Yoruba, but most of the continental drummers were Muslim."

Baba Doc Gibbs: "Bob (Crowder) was telling me when some of the early Cubans came to Philly, they needed some drummers. They had met a Cuban lady who put some ilekes on them so that they could play the ceremonies; there were no batas then. So, they were playing to whatever they were singing in the ceremonies. When Sonny moved to New York, he and his wife got ilekes from a black Cuban lady named Juana Meringue. She was the one crowning Black Americans. She crowned my godfather and she's my Oyugbona. Sonny's wife and my godfather were the early ones that made Ocha with Juana. Sonny passed young at like thirty-eight years old.

I met Chief Bey at his Ile because my wife and I wanted to be crowned and our godfather took us to Chief's house to talk to him about renting his house to crown us. We went to the crowning of Norman and about a month later, I was crowned. So, that's when I met Chief. Those seven days during my initiation were magical in Chief's house. After a few days, Chief was walking around playing these little instruments and drums. It was ideal. After that, me and Chief became very close friends. We both had Ocha, so he invited me up to help do a lot of crownings and ceremonies. Bobby, Sonny, and Garvin were not crowned but they were all in the religion; playing and being around it all the time."

Yoruba Priest and Drummer, Baba Kenneth Fauntleroy, speaks about New York's Yoruba temple.

Baba Kenneth Fauntleroy: "Most of the early Yoruba priests went up to New York and were initiated through Oseijeman's temple."

Bradley Simmons: "Olukose Wiles and I did a lot of bembes together. I remember he brought me to this bembe and he told me to play the Oro myself. Then we went to another room and I was getting up and he said go play the first part of the ceremony. Then I tried to get off the drum and give it to him. He said, "No you stay on it, you doing good." It was hot that day. I was trying to get up but he kept telling me to stay on it. I ended up playing the entire bembe from top to bottom for 4 hours. He kept me on that drum. After the bembe I said, "yo man what was that about??" He said, "I wanted to make sure you could do bembe without me standing over you. This way if we get a bembe and I can't make it I can have you go and do the gig and I don't have to worry about if it was going to be played correctly." That's the type of teacher he was. We were in a bembe group. Me, Olukose, Neil Clark, Walter Ince, John Blanford, Ama McKin.

We were heavy into the bembe circuit. We were hitting every weekend. Olukose would show you parts on the drums and shekeres. He hung out with Jolito Carlazo, he played with Gene Golden a lot. He played with Wendel a lot. A lot of times we would go to other bembes and stand on the wall and pick up by watching the others play. If you can watch you can learn. He was good. He had a different style of playing. It worked for me. Steve Loyd was another one calling me for bembes. Olukose was playing jembe, sabar, and kutiro with International Afrikan American

Ballet. He hung out with a lot of the guys from Senegal. He was married to Maribass who is Senegalese. So that was his connection to Senegal.

Olukose made ocha with Sunta. He was crowned Yemaya. Sunta was the one who opened up her house to African Americans. Her Ile was 99.9% African Americans. I was initiated there right out of high school in 1970. Olukose and Yomi Yomi were there. She was from Puerto Rico and lived in the Bronx. She was a wonderful person. She didn't need for anything. When I got into the religion I wanted to get into Carmen's house. That's where my teacher Pablo Landrum was from. But he said let me put you over here. I'm going to put you where you need to be. That's when I got into Sunta's house and linked up with Olukose because he gave me my initiation when I went in. Me, him and Sunta. I was real close with Olukose. He was a lot older than I was. He was definitely one of the elders. He came up under Chief and I came up under him and Pablo. Pablo was my first teacher."

Baba Richard Byrd: "Olumide (Phillip Gilbert) took me to my first bembe. I saw all types of fantastic stuff that I never thought I would ever see. To this day that still has been a great influence. Back then orisha was really strict and straight. Back then ladies wore hat pins, and if they said you were possessed by orisha the ladies would stick that person with the pin to see if they were really possessed. There was a Yemoja who got possessed and the curtain opened and there was a big mayonnaise jar filled with those Texas roaches. The orisha ate all of that. I said, "Oh alright, God is here." I went back to Yomi Yomi and told him about my experience, and he said man you need to go see Chief Bey. I wondered why he didn't take me in himself since he had an Ile. I could have been one of his godsons, but he felt I needed to go get with Chief. Chief made ocha in 1976. When I met him he was a Iyawo. I met him in November and he was made in June."

Baba Yomi Yomi Awolowo: "My Wife and I sang and played orisha music with Milton Cardona. We even recorded an album with him."

Jubal Harris: "I had 2 main teachers who introduced me to African spirituality and drumming, Baba Ishangi and Baba Baile McKnight. I learned a lot from Oloye Adeyemo (Priest of Obatala) and later on I was introduced to my grand godfather, Chief Bey."

The Arthur Hall Afro-American Dance Ensemble also became international ambassadors of dance in the 1970s, initiating tours abroad as a result of their elite status. The troupe's first tour took eighteen dancers to

Ghana, Togo, and Nigeria in West Africa in 1974. In Ghana, the High Priestess and President of the Ghana Psychic and Traditional Healers Association, Nana Okomfohene Akua Oparebea, invited the troupe to perform at her compound in Larteh, Ghana. Arthur's association with Nana Okomfohene Akua Oparebea resulted in her initiating him into the Akan priesthood in 1974. He received the name Nana Kwabena Affoh and the title Asonahene, or King - the one responsible for upholding the Asona and Aberade royal family traditions some centuries old.1

Baba Akin Babatunde: "My first introduction to the world of African drumming was through Nana Dinizulu. Every Friday, they had drumming of a sort. With this drumming, they were doing worship of the Akan deities. The people would get possessed and it was very elaborate. I was very fascinated by it, and one time I was possessed by one of those deities. I was told that I would have to become a Priest; the African had been awakened in me. I was about to get it done but my brother had always been my rock and gave me a warning that something wasn't right. The initiation was all done and I never showed up because of the warning that my brother gave me.

My world continued in the world of African dance. I took classes with Tito Sampa. I started dancing a little with Dinizulu, and then I ended up in a place called the National Black Theatre, me and my brother. I played a Yoruba orisha called Shango. I got that role not knowing that was going to be my destiny; that Shango was going to be very close to me in my life. I'm very private about this, but eventually I became initiated where I needed to be initiated. I was initiated a Priest of Shango. I'm celebrating forty years this year. Through it all, I was dancing and performing wherever my brother was performing. We ended up forming the group International Afrikan American Ballet.

There were a lot of us that danced with Ladji Camara. Ama McKin danced with Ladji; she is a well-known Apon, the person who sings at the bembes for the orishas. She was sought after around the world and a Priestess of Yemoja. Fatima Baker, she is an elder in the Lukumi faith. She was a dancer and became a Priestess of Oshun. I became initiated as a Priest of Shango. Walter Ince was initiated as a Priest of Elegba. Olukose was a Priest of Yemoja and Balogun was a Priest of Obatala. Darcel danced with us and she became a Priestess of Yemoja. Rhonda and Hazel were also staple dancers. Rhonda went to Senegal and Gambia and became our choreographer."

Melvin Deal: "I traveled to Calabar, Nigeria in 1970s to study the traditions, rituals of the Kwa and other large river tribes; the Mami Waters legacy."

Baba Walter Ince: "Oya originates from the Mende people. There is an island where they propitiate Oya. Around that island is an enormously rapid river that has seasons. One season, the waters are so high you can't cross it to get to the island. During the dry season, the waters are low enough so that you don't even need a boat to get across; you can walk across. Oya the line I come from, half of the year she has water and the other half of the year she doesn't have water. You ask why is it that happens? They say because IT IS. It's not until you do the research when you find out they are celebrating how the original shrine is kept. You can only get to it when it's the dry season. Now you have a wet season and dry season with your Oya to celebrate the ancestors of this particular orisha. In my itae, Oya asked for me to play drums. I play a lot of drums. I assume you want me to play bata? Answer: "no." You want me to play conga? Answer: "no." Those are the two primary drums you play in orisha ceremonies. You want me to play timbales? (laughter) Answer: "No." I said my favorite drum is jembe. Do you want me to play jembe. Answer: "YES!" Why would Oya want me to play jembe? Well, first of all Mende people play jembe. She's like, "That's what I listen to Negro and you are my son. Can I hear that in my house?" Later on, when I found out that she originated from the Mende nation, the playing of the jembe for Oya made sense to me."

Greg Ince: "When Walter went to be initiated as Priest in Ocha then Ifa, Orisha said that he could only drum in a small family like setting. He is the King so others have to drum for him. Do you know how hard that must be for someone who drummed and studied as long and hard as he did to be told that he must stop performing and drumming in public?"

Baba Walter Ince: "One of the reasons that kings don't drum is because of the close relationship necessary for you to have and play with someone else. Chief Bey used to say, you have to be comfortable enough to be in another man's jock strap. You have to be really close to him. You have to be in his spirit and he has to be in yours for you to be able to gel well enough to make this conglomerate of energy become musical prose and poetry. I try to carry that and I try to remember that. Bey may have been rough but he knew a lot about the essence of music. Olukose studied with him and so did Neil. Despite who we are as individuals, the energy of your teacher it's reflected in what happens and what you do, and I believe Chief Bey reflected in what they did."

One of Arthur Hall's first lead jembe drummers, Daryl Kwasi Burgee, speaks about Dinizulu.

Daryl Kwasi Burgee: "Dinizulu, Baba Ishangi, and Arthur Hall exposed a lot of us to the Akan religion. Our house would go to participate in Dinizulu's festivals from time to time."

"Nii Ayi" Nana Obrafo Yaw Wofa Asiedu: "I hadn't seen my sister for about four or five years. Gustin Zulu "Dinizulu" initiated me with one of the marks on my arm from one of the shrines in Larteh in Aburi, Ghana. When I was talking to Dinizulu, he was saying that my sister may be there by the shrine. I realized that my main mission was not just about doing shows or the tourist thing. I was going HOME. I wanted to go to the shrine and places where drummers would drum somewhere all night.

I went on tour with Arthur Hall's performing group. We traveled to Ghana. I traveled into Accra and rented transport. When I got to the top of the hill, I saw a sign that said, "Priestess Nana Okomfo Oparabea". A greeter came to me and I said, "I'm looking for my sister Makeda," and he said you mean "N'Waba?" He asked me who was I. He went down the hill and I looked down and sure enough it was my sister coming out of the shrine. She had been there for two years. They made her a Queen Mother because come to find out she had brought back to Ghana one of the oldest deities that was sent with the slaves from the castle to the Americas, called Densu Yao shrine. Densu Yao was the deity that cries. When they saw that I was her brother, the whole community woke up and initiated me right there on the spot. They pulled the knife out, and got to cutting and putting all of that medicine in me like nobody's business, and I let them do whatever the hell they needed to do.

One morning for shrine day, everybody is up and I hear this person singing. I knew my sister could sing but this sound was so beautiful. I go up and see my sister fully possessed in all white clay singing and dancing to all of the elders, and they are responding to her calls. They told me who that deity was. They said this is the deity that cries during the time when the slaves were being taken out of the castles. The Priests sent different deities with the enslaved Africans to the different places they were going to. They said, "Your sister brought him back." From then, my named changed from Nii Ayi to Nana Obrafo Yaw Wofa Asiedu. "Wofa" is someone that has been this way before; that made me the uncle of one of the elders in the shrine. "Obrafo" is a warrior society that is responsible for sacrifices and rituals.

So, the next day I knew I had a show. That night they told me I had to wear this white cloth; I had white powder all over my face and they gave me a stool with a pot to put on my head. They told me not to take that stool off of my head. The Ghanaians on the transport saw me and gave me my seat because they knew that I had just come from Larteh and Nana Oparabea was not to be messed with. Plus, they had seen the power of the mark on my arm. Everyone knew what that mark represented. So, when I arrived at the compound where I was staying, Arthur Hall and the rest of the group was pissed because I had not told them where I went, but they were intrigued because I was in all white, with powder on my face, and orisha pot on my head. "Where the hell did you go??" Most of them claimed to be Yorubas, and they all wanted to go see Nana after that.

So, I took them all back to Aburi. From that, there is a term that they gave me for doing that because I did something that someone else did a long time ago. They brought a lot of people to the shrine. I was reenacting that person. The elders made me medicine to protect me from the greatest dangers for me in the United States. I was heightened by my awareness from my surroundings. They told me that I had to go back because my wife was having twins. I told them my wife wasn't having no children. They said we have too much respect for twins to have you stay, because I was going to STAY. Of course, she ended up pregnant with twins.

So when I went back to the United States with the deity, I'm in my home pouring libations, singing my songs, ringing my bells and the deity CAME. I jumped out of the closet and scared the shit out of my wife. She said, "What the hell is going on??" Come to find out that when Brami comes, he likes to dance in a raffia skirt, he likes to be clayed down from head to toe, and he likes to dance with a machete on a roof top! Can you imagine me dancing on a rooftop with a machete in Philly?? They would shoot me dead! I reached out to Nana Oparabea and told her that I have to send this deity back because it's too much for where I am. She said ask him to go back, and he will stay with you but he won't possess you; that's what I did. I had to send him back."

Congas and batas were the drums readily available when these drummers and dancers of the 1960s and 1970s were seeking out their spiritual paths. Congas came before the jembe. Congas were made available via Cubans, Puerto Ricans, Dominicans, and Mexicans. There were plenty of recordings with conga drumming on it to learn from. Many drummers playing congas could be found in the parks in New York.

Baba David Coleman: "In the early 1960s, the premier drummers at that time all came to my house; Dinizulu, Chief Bey, Sonny Morgan, and Babafemi. They came to 134th Street between 7th and 8th Ave. We moved to the Bronx. I wasn't even ten years old when all this started happening. When we moved to the Bronx, that's when I found out about the conga drums and the religion; at 14-15 years old, my sisters brought me to see all of that. There was conga drumming on the roof and the park benches with the Puerto Rican boys, and Dominicans in the Bronx; no Cubans, only Puerto Ricans. I got into the religion and found out that we had to meet a wall of Cubans; Juan Candero and his sons, Dimeciano, and Maximo. This was a wall of Cubans who were making their life off of bembe. It was their secret world, the bembe. Now, here comes these Black American guys. Babafemi through Francis and Barbara led the charge, and we were the drummers. Babafemi, Renard, myself, and Yomi Yomi came later."

Despite their initial popularity, many drummers put their congas in the closet after they experienced the sound of the jembe drum. Some continued to play congas at gigs with bands while others were connected to ocha ceremonial drumming which consisted mainly of congas and bata, but many returned to the jembe as their drum of choice. There were also drummers like Teddy Holliday, Gene Golden, and Skip Burney who remained committed to tambor and Afro Cuban music when the jembe revolution hit New York. Gene Golden, Skip's mentor, told me that there was no African American drummer who knew more about Afro Cuban music than Skip Burney. Similarly, Duke University Professor and African drumming scholar Bradley Simmons told me that if you want to learn anything about Afro Cuban, tambor, and ocha music and drumming, then there is no other African American more knowledgeable and skilled than Skip Burney. With those endorsements, I sought out Baba Oba Ilu "Skip" Burney and was able to get a compelling interview from him in Philadelphia, Pennsylvania.

When I met with him, he immediately told me he had just finished mixing and mastering his newest CD with his engineer. It was an Afro Cuban and ocha combination of tracks. He told me there were only two people in the room when he recorded the music-the engineer and Skip.

Now, I have heard other drummers record solo projects before; however, I cannot tell you how overwhelmed I felt listening to this collaboration. Baba Oba Ilu would not do the interview with me until we had first listened to each track on this CD. At one point, he was playing the bata patterns on my arm while singing the translations of the notes to various orisha songs. I listened to the background voices of the Afro Cuban rumba tracks. Although he had told me a number of times it was only him on the CD, I continued to ask about the identity of those voices. The depth to which this Baba shared his knowledge of this Afro Cuban and ocha music made me feel as though he could not possibly have a life outside of the music; he must always be on the brink of expiring because one body could not possibly house that much information and skill. We went to a Jamaican restaurant and ordered food to go. We then parked in front of the house where he had recorded this CD, and the floodgates opened. There were times when he asked me to turn the recorder off so he could give me background for what he could tell me 'on record.' He has clearly lived a very FULL life.

Greg Ince: "Skip Burney is to the congas and Afro Cuban music who we are to the jembes and West African dance music."

Baba Don Eaton (Babatunde): "Skip Burney is the one who kept me locked in on that Rhumba. He is a phenomenal talent."

Baba "Skip" Burney: "I'm from New York where you had a large contingency of Latino people. New York was drummer's town. It didn't matter what hood you went to, there was always some drums playing; congas, bongos playing. You had a lot of Caribbean people living in New York; a lot of Puerto Ricans, a lot of Cubans, Panamanians, and a lot of Dominicans. In the late 1960s, my mother had me in choirs and I used to cut out and cut school to get to Avenue B and Avenue A to see the Puerto Ricans playing congas. I would get my ass whipped every night from taking the trains from Queens to deep in the city to see the drumming. "Where were you Kenneth?" I was listening to drums. I went down there one time, and I didn't see the Puerto Ricans. Instead, I saw a brother that was real black; he was blue black and had some gold teeth. He was playing one conga; dark brown and light brown slats like one of those old Mexican ones. He was singing in Spanish. I was like WTF is this?? Because that's the first time I ever saw someone blue-black speaking Spanish. I went up to him and asked "Where are you from?" He said, "Afro Cuba." I said, "Africa Cuba? Is that another country in Africa?" He said, "No, Black

Cuban." I said, "Oh, you play different than those other guys." He said, "I'm Cubano." I asked if could I hit his drum? He said "Go ahead." He said "Oh, you play Cuban music." I said, What? He said "You play Cuban music." I said, "I don't know. I'm just playing what I'm feeling." He said, "Come with me." He lived in the projects. He took me up there, and that was the first time I saw ocha. He said, "That's Yemoja, Shango, that's so and so." He had Shango sitting on a bata drum; that was the first time I saw a bata drum. I didn't know what it was. He showed me ocha and rhythms and that was the only time I ever saw him. I left and never seen him again. After that, I started hanging around all of the drumming in the parks.

I moved to California, and that's where I really started learning the drum; with a brother named Tombu and a hippie guy name Conga Mike. They didn't really know that music but they were playing more than the guys I was seeing in the parks in New York. We still didn't know clave or anything yet. Then, I started listening to stuff and studying myself. I was getting recordings and books and really learning about clave. The difference between how Puerto Ricans play salsa compared to real sons of Cuba touched me. I saw that Cuba was black; that's what I saw. That Ricky Ricardo stuff don't fly. I heard the swing in Cuban sons versus Puerto Rican New York salsa; the swing was different. It was like playing the straight ahead; you got a bass player he can play seven steps but can he play through the changes? Their bass players play through the changes. It was different. It was black. It was soulful. By this time, I'm gigging. I'm knowing more of what I'm doing. I was doing some bembes a little. I taught myself bata with albums. My encyclopedia was the record Giraldo Rodriguez los Tambores Bata. Then, there was an album called Santeira that had bata on it. Those were my encyclopedias. From there, God always blessed me with ears, and for some reason, the vibration always pulled me to be around the baddest MFs. My first literal bata teacher was Hector "Flako" Hernandez. Flako was one of the few Cubans who rolled with us; he still rolls with us.

When Puntilla (Orlando 'Puntilla' Rios) came to America from Cuba in 1980, he went to each New York borough and pulled the best drummers from each borough. When he got to AB and Felix, they were playing a little bata that I showed them. Puntilla asked them who taught them that. They said, "Oh this crazy guy named Skip in California." He asked if they had my number and had Felix call me. Felix said, "Yo man, Padrino Puntilla is here and he wants you to come to New York right away." I said, "Go to New York for what?" He said, "He wants to talk to you about Ana and other stuff, it's important." So, I was on the plane the next day to New York. Three days later, I had scratched all three of his tambors and was initiated. Puntilla said "You taught these guys this stuff?" I said, "Yea, but I just heard better than them." He asked, "You play the Iya?" I said, "No, I understand it but I don't know anything." He was checking me out to see if I had a big ego. I was looking for a big man. I walked in the room, and I see this little tiny man in this big Adam's Family chair with Teddy Roosevelt glasses on with platform shoes on; just in from Cuba and this is the baddest MF on the planet. I said, "No Baba, I don't know shit." He said, "Muy inteligente. Tu toco con mio e no yima." He said, "You play with me and no one else." I said, alright and it was like that for the next thirty-five years.

Through Puntilla I have been able to meet and play extensively with the greatest tambors out of Cuba. I am Giovanna Hidalgo's Oyugbona. I scratched him for Puntilla. I played with Tanganyika, El Gordo, Pancho Quinto, Andre Chacon, Amarol, and Philipito Alphonso, the baddest singer out of Cuba as far as ocha is concerned. These were the guys that you listened to on the records wishing you could meet them. I was playing with them all day every day.

For years, Puntilla would never let me get on the box (cajon). He had me on the okonkolo for about five to six years. I had already played all three bata drums when I met him, but he put me on okonkolo for five to six years. Then, he moved me to segundo. He said you are a natural segundero. He was right. I was very comfortable on segundo. He kept me on segundo fifteen, damn near twenty years. One day, we did this really big tambor; about 200-300 people. He looked at me and said "NOW Kickie Ass..Do what you do!" He wouldn't let me touch it before that. He was grilling me; preparing me for when the time was right.

One day, I was in his living room practicing. I was messing up on purpose, and he came out of the room in his draws, big belly little knees with his adenoids voice, and he said, "Oye!" I said, "What Padrino?" He said, "Dat not my shiii. Dat no my shii!" I said,"Well then show it to me again." He said, "Nah, you not slick. You know how to play. You trying to get me out here to show you something."

Puntilla was living in the Bronx; his sister Ramona brought him. When Puntilla came and got his crew, he monopolized the entire east and west coast with tambor. Everyone based what they were doing in Ana with what we did, because Puntilla revolutionized it. A lot of Santeros here were doing stuff but they didn't know all of the rules; not out of breaking them, they weren't taught. So, when Puntilla came here, he straightened out a lot of stuff because he just knew. Babalawos were calling on Puntilla a lot because he was that shrewd. He said, "I don't want to pass Ifa. Shango got a lot. I'm still learning Shango. Ifa is too much. Babalawo is Babalawo. No time for tambor. You have to stay on the floor taking everybody's problems. Do you want everybody's problems? You got you own problem. Fix you own problem first."

My name in ocha is Oba Ilu. All of the drums are mine. The Osain of the drums is mine. All of the secrets of the drums are mine; also means spirit reader. My Ocha is Aganju. Aganju has many secrets. I'm still learning my ocha. I will wait until I can't play then I will pass Ifa and sit on the mat and take on other people's problems.

Chief Bey would say, "I'm mad at you because you roll with those gangstas." He was talking about Puntilla. He would always put my Padrino down because he felt that Puntilla would take his people away. Plenty of Chief's drummers came to Puntilla. Some stayed and plenty didn't. They disrespected me a lot because of my skills. They referred to me as Cuban. The Cubans were hooking up with the jazz artists and brothers in the music game. They didn't give the music to the Puerto Ricans.

You gotta respect Gene Golden and Jose Fernandez because they pioneered this. They are my mentors. Puntilla came specifically for Black Americans. To teach them the truth."

Chapter 12

Dancers

"It was like we were being reconnected to Africa intravenously." Denise Bey

The most popular rhythm among jembe drummers by far is Dundunba. It is typically described as a dance of strong men originating in the Maninka chiefdom of Hamana in the region of Kouroussa in Upper Guinea. Its popularity as a dance spread north to Bamako and south to Conakry where it entered the repertoire of the national ballet troupes. Famoudou Konate, lead jembe player with Les Ballets Africains in the early years of independence, comes from Kouroussa, the Dundunba heartland.

After Dundunba, the next most widespread jembe pieces are probably Mendiani (Manjani or Mandiani), from Upper Guinea, and Soli (called Suka in Mali). The main dance done in all night celebrations (called Soli Si) leading to an actual circumcision and excision surgery. Mendiani is traditionally danced by young girls, but recent descriptions do not detail its significance within the village, perhaps because the tradition no longer exists. A Mendiani is the best young female dancer in a village. Ladji Camara describes Fanta Kamissoko, the lead dancer with the original Ballets Africains in the 1950s, as a Mendiani in Siguiri when she was younger. A Mendiani is a young girl chosen for her ability in a dance competition, a tradition local to Upper Guinea. Every village that can support one has a Mendiani. They were formerly sorceresses.

Famoudou Konate indicates that the Mendiani dances by herself while another young girl dances in a circle around her. She remained a Mendiani until puberty, at which time she returned to the ranks and another was elected in her place.1

When one speaks about African dance in America during the 1960s to the early 1980s, there are certain names that stand out. Chuck Davis, LaRocque Bey, Pearl Primus, Katherine Dunham, Arthur Hall, and Melvin Deal. These dancers carved out their own distinct lanes in the African dance world in America. There were other dancers as well who were instrumental in establishing the model for African dance in America. I have always been fascinated by the similarities in the structure among African dance classes and performances. I have visited African dance classes in Vermont, Connecticut, New York, New Jersey, Washington

D.C., North Carolina, Georgia, California, and Nevada. After interviewing some of the premier African dancers from the 1960s and 1970s, it became apparent that it was they who were responsible for establishing that model which remains as the foundation of African dance classes and performing groups throughout the U.S..

* * *

Denise Bey: "I started dancing because my father (Chief Bey) was drumming at Bernice Johnson's dance class. I was dancing at this time to congas. Sonny Morgan, Olukose Wiles, and Nathaniel Bettis were the drummers.

When I started dancing to the jembe, it was exciting. It was like a firecracker. It was really good. Spectacular. It was amazing to hear what came out of the dundun, jembe, kora, and balafon. It wasn't just about the jembe, it was about the conglomerate of what came out of that sound. It was like we were being reconnected to Africa intravenously. That's how I felt with the jembe and the dances. It allowed me to be in Africa without being in Africa.

My mentor is Sister Amaniyea. She's the one. The cornerstone of someone that has the history and a photographic memory. Between her and Hazel Bryant, they are the keepers of the history. Hazel was fortunate enough to go back and forth to Africa. Because she had that photographic memory, she would remember the songs and dances and share with us. When the Africans would come to the U.S. they would be shocked to see and hear that we had it all right.

Hazel was always a Jehovah witness so in her spiritual journeys she finally after many years of sacrifice for us and the dance community she surrendered to Jehovah completely. But before she continued her spiritual journey, she gave us an immeasurable amount of dance, song and traditional attire with history and vocabulary; we owe her, and Amaniyea a ton of our gratitude."

Amaniyea Payne: "I was born in Baltimore, Maryland in 1954. In the late 1960's early 70's there was the cultural explosion of Black arts (all realms) with dance, music and theatre. There was a program called CETA (Comprehensive Employment and Training Act) which fed into our communities to work, train, and perform with prominent experienced (in our case) artists while receiving a stipend. During this CETA experience I met one of my first African dance teachers, Aissatou Bey Grecia who happened to be studying at Antioch College. She had come from the Olatunji University in New York and we learned dances from his repertoire (Fanga, Patakato, Odunde and others). During that time Baba Chuck Davis also came to Baltimore along with his assistant Marilyn Banks and shared his knowledge with us dancers as he has always done. Baba's workshops gave me much inspiration and fortitude to continue to push forward.

When I lived in New York my first performing gig in 1977 was with a Cameroonian Brother, Shombe Yembe. There I worked with artists like Hazel Starks Bryant, Obba Babatunde, Bradley Simmons, Kehinde (Stewart) O'Uhuru, Jalal Sharriff, Darcel Abel, Walter Ince and more...all I can say is when you are in the midst of the best, The best comes to you.

I lived in New York for 13 years. During that time, I had the opportunity to meet Brother Alyo Tolbert, the first Artistic Director of Muntu Dance Theatre of Chicago. He was such a gentle, kind, and beautiful spirit who worked with all of the African related companies in New York. When he came to visit, we became good friends and from that relationship a bond was formed way before I became the Artistic Director of Muntu. If not mistaken, the longest running African Dance and Drum organization in America is Koi Thi Dance Company from Milwaukee, Wisconsin in existence for fifty-three years and then Muntu Dance Theatre of Chicago in existence for fifty years.

In Baltimore, we danced to the conga and ashiko drums. In DC we danced to the congas, ashiko, duns, talking drums, assimilated sabar and kutiro drums. In New York and Chicago, we danced to the jembe, kutiro, sabar, bata, conga, along with the percussive ensemble of various instruments. It was a different call back then. To me, the major difference between dancing from conga to jembe or any drum for that matter, is understanding how to respond to the language of the drum, each has its own distinct voice. If the spirit is open and ready to receive, then it's going to dance. Spirit sometimes moves even without knowledge or understanding. That's what I mean when I say, now your mind has to catch up to where your body is....STUDY.

There will always be a love of Lamban, and Sunu; it's so slick it has that temptation walk energy all up in it. They both are so spirited, you can see when I dance that it touches my soul. I love Ekonkon, the dance of the Djolla people, it reminds of when we use to play the rhythms and the music gets up underneath of yourself; all you can do is feel free and get down. I love Wolosodon, I love the freedom that it brings to one's soul when you're playing and dancing. This dance made us emote the aspect of internal suffering where you would quiver the body, not for ecstasy but to show the internal strength within that can't be broken regardless of what the situation is, or you can dance for the sheer joy of dancing. I even found the jazz linkage within this rhythm and applied the style of swing dance to show its parallelisms. We called it 'African Swing.' I love all of this. Triba excites me, I love the aggressive and the sultry energy that can be projected and it's dynamically funky. I love the sensuality of Sinte or at least how you can project it especially when the rhythm is in the pocket.

It's not about being a Diva, it's about showing the Divinity inside of oneself; sometimes we have the tendency to put things in the wrong context. Of course I love Mendiani, Soli and Dongba where you can bust out and just be yourself.

You see, dance really deals with how the spirit moves and as the spirit moves, yet it is important to understand foundation."

Baba Walter Ince: "The very beginning International (International Afrikan American Ballet) Dancers: Denise Bey, Obba, Akin, Judy, Joanne, Rhonda, and Greg"

Greg Ince: "Makeda Myorba was my first dance teacher. After Makeda Myorba I started studying with Baba Ali Abdullah when I was 4. He was one of the first African American men to study dance in Senegal for 16 years. He studied with the Senegal Ballet with Abdoulaye Camara. Spoke Wolof like we speak English. He's from South Carolina but his passion to be a part of the arts was like he wasn't born in this country. We always looked at Baba Chuck Davis as the Baba of African dance here. But Chuck Davis called Baba Ali "Baba" and wasn't into African dance until he learned from Baba Ali. Chuck was doing modern dance when he met Baba Ali.

I danced with Brother John Blandford for years in International and didn't know his first dance teacher was Baba Ali. It should have hit me like a lightbulb because John Blandford danced more like Baba Ali than I did. He had the same flow as Baba Ali."

Rhonda Morman: "I went to National Black Theater on 125th street in Harlem, New York. I was visiting and next thing I know I was IN IT. It was there where I got into the arts. Olatunji's place was close by so that's how I got to see him and others who were studying with him. I was going to school to become a teacher. There were some guy dancers at the National Black Theater who I heard danced with Ladji Camara. Hazel Starks-Bryant was the one who got me into the African dance. She invited me to dance sessions. I went to what I thought was a dance class with Ladji and then I found myself in a dance group. Sam Watson was part of Ladji's group at that time. Sam Watson is pure of heart. I never said that to him. I never described anyone else like that. He is one of those people that doesn't deal with Ra Ra. He was always true to the culture. I have so much respect for him."

Sam Watson: "Hazel Bryant was my student and I could say she was the closest to me out of everybody. I took her under my wing and I showed her everything. She was with Chuck Davis. I took away from Chuck. And Chuck just sat and watched because remember he SAW me play with the Ballets. I was the only one not from Guinea playing in the Ballets with them. So Hazel was trained in ballet, tap, and modern dance. She saw me in a group and she kept coming. She kept coming to see me and then I showed her moves. She lived around the corner from my son's grandfather around 119th St. and Madison Ave.. I saw her move and I looked at her. There was no flirtation. She was absolutely drop dead gorgeous. I tried to never mix the two. So I took her. She is the only girl I brought to the Ballets with me. Remember I told you I went every day. I took her backstage and I introduced her to everybody. I personally tutored her in a way that I tutored no other. She took in everything. She started wearing traditional clothes from Guinea. Hazel brought Rhonda Morman to me. Rhonda was a shy thin dark girl and bashful as could be. Hazel brought Rhonda upstairs left her at the door and walked away and I had on full costume and we was rehearsing. I looked at Rhonda. I just looked at her and the guys was playing and I went over and grabbed her hand and started dancing with her. I showed her the dance and she picked it up. I knew she would pick it up. And Hazel knew she would pick it up. I didn't say a word to her. I didn't even know her name. I just pulled her out onto the dance floor and started dancing with her. She had on street clothes, a coat and all that stuff. She kept on dancing. We danced for a couple hours. Hazel was on the floor laughing. Rhonda looked at me and she was in tears and she said, "How did you know?" I said, I know my own and that's why Hazel brought you to me.

Rhonda and Hazel were in their early 20s. I was about 35. Then Julia came. Julia was very pretty. Another type of girl. Natural talent. No formal

195

training. And could do anything you showed her. That was my core group. Julia, Rhonda, and Hazel."

One of the Brooklyn-based Calabash troupe lead dancers, Abayomi Goodall, speaks about Arthur Hall.

Renee Abayomi Goodall: "Arthur Hall was the shit because he was the only connection we had to the African culture and dance in Philly. Arthur Hall was IT."

Amaniyea Payne: "At this time on the east coast, there were several major influences in keeping and growing the African dance culture. Melvin Deal, Chuck Davis, Arthur Hall, LaRocque Bey, Nana Dinizulu, Charles Moore, Baba Olatunji, Baba Ishangi and many more. Even the movers and shakers of other forms of dance applied African dance and music to their repertoire. See it was all about being Cultural Ambassadors; representing, that's what we aspired towards."

Rhonda Morman: "DanceAfrica didn't start with Chuck Davis. Chuck Davis took someone else's idea. That concept came from Arthur Hall. I was at the meeting in Philly when it went down. It was me, Olukose, maybe Walter Ince and John Blandford, Nana Dinizulu and one of his Wives, Charles Moore, Arthur Hall, Chuck Davis, and Melvin Deal. For years Charles Moore's wife, Ella, didn't believe him about that meeting and how Arthur Hall came up with that 'DanceAfrica' concept. She told me about what Charles told her and I asked, and you didn't believe him? She said "No!"

Arthur met with American Airlines and Coca Cola. He also met with the city of Memphis, TN for the connection to Memphis, Egypt. Then he called on the premier African drum and dance groups to meet in Philly to talk about a program that would tour major cities. The first part of the program would be each group would perform what they decided was their signature piece. The second part would be all of us wearing the same African clothes and we would perform a piece that was put together with all of the drummers, dancers and all of the choreography then mix the songs. Chuck runs to New York because BAM (Brooklyn Academy of Music) was under fire. My neighbor, Marion Holmes, at the time was a community activist and had been applying pressure to BAM because BAM was not doing anything for the community. They were bussing white people in the neighborhood but not doing anything for the people living in the neighborhood. All around BAM was brown and black people. There were a bunch of community members who had Harvey Lichtenstein, then

President and Executive Producer of BAM, "over a barrel." The lead activist, Marion Holmes, was not happy with Chuck up to the day she died. She said "Chuck was not from Brooklyn and negotiated with BAM to talk about some damn DanceAfrica." And not to mention the community was in protest of Harvey Lichtenstein.

Betty Carter lived across the street from BAM and SHE couldn't get in there to sing. They would not hire her. It wasn't until years later when Betty Carter finally performed at BAM. So Chuck upset the Brooklyn community by bringing DanceAfrica to BAM and not living up to the vision of the community activist Marion Holmes and Arthur Hall's original vision. Arthur Hall envisioned the tour moving around to various cities throughout the year. Starting in Memphis, TN and finishing in New York."

Iya Darcel Abel: "My first dance teacher was LaRocque Bey Wright. I learned Afro-Caribbean dance and started my theatrical training at the LaRocque Bey School of Dance in Harlem, NY. From 1965 – 1970s I was taught dance and songs, how to play the drums, martial arts, and even learned Yoruba language. The LaRocque Bey Dance Company performed and went to see other dance performances in NY and in other states. One performance that was so profound for me, was when Mr. LaRocque took us to see Les Ballets Africains from Guinea, West Africa. Little did I know that I would study and perform in the future with their lead drummer, Ladji Camara.

During those years, most African/Caribbean dance classes were played by drummers who used the conga drum. The sound of the drums always had me feeling more creative. I had ventured into learning other styles of dance. However, what was so profound for me was traditional West African folklore. The rhythm of the drums and the dance teachers I had, placed my senses right into West Africa when I danced."

LaRocque Bey
Source: Photographs and Prints Division, Schomburg Center for Research in Black
Culture
~

Bradley Simmons: "In 1967 I started drumming with LaRocque Bey. Those cats were really good. They were young but they were good. Paul Harris, Michael Goodman, Ike Bryan, Steve Christian, a guy named Larry. There were 5 of them so when I went there that made 6 of us drummers. LaRocque snatched me up from Gloria Jackson's school. He had a vision to build an empire of drummers over at his school. So he was trying to recruit all of the drummers from Gloria Jackson's School of Dance. There were 4 of us there at the time but I was the only one that went. LaRocque Bey had all congas when I joined. Jembes didn't come in until later. We were playing congas standing up strapped to our wastes. We didn't switch over until Sonny Morgan came to a performance and we were playing pretty hard. He told LaRocque that we needed to take those congas off of our backs because it's going to mess up our kidneys. That's when we started putting drums together and strapping them to our shoulders. We were cutting congas in half and making them small congas then tacking straps to the drums then started carrying them that way to ease the pressure on our kidneys. We did that for a while until we got into the jembe. Ladji came by the studio one day. That's when LaRocque introduced everyone to Ladji Camara. He played for us. 3-4 blocks away from where LaRocque's studio was there was a store called Imram's. They

198

had jembe like drums from Haiti there. We bought those and started playing those as our jembes. It wasn't the best made jembes. They had a lot of wood inside. They were light and they worked for the time that we were using them. We didn't string them up; they were tacking the heads on and heating them for tuning. We played those for a while but once we got our hands on the real jembes and they were easier to get, we got into the jembe world and stayed there from then on. LaRocque made us go see the Les Ballets Africains whenever they came around. LaRocque Bey would rehearse us 4-5 hours a day. He used to drill us. We used to play for dance classes for 2-3 hours. We used to rehearse and do dance classes at performance pitch.

LaRocque Bey was a perfectionist. He was not going to have his group go out and not do this thing right. He was an entertainer. He was heavy in the flash. He wasn't the traditional West African dancer. He came out of the Dunham Technique. He came from The Dunham School in Detroit. He performed a lot in nightclubs so that's how we ended up playing in a lot of nightclubs. We would have that high energy and we were playing in front of people drinking and drunk. We had to go through all that. The training was the best thing that any drummer could go through. It was like being in boot camp. I started there in 1967 until I started doing Broadway shows in 1977."

Baba Richard Byrd: "Me, Aziz, and Craig all played with Balogun for Chuck Davis. The three of us were there the year before they were selected to go to the first FESTAC in 1977, held in Nigeria. It was Balogun, Yomi Yomi, Kwayao, and Spanky who went with the Chuck Davis Company. We couldn't go because we were just juniors at that time. They labeled us "The Renegades.""

Renee Abayomi Goodall: "Chuck Davis' top contributions to the African drum and dance world in America would be acceptance of the culture, documentation, and traveling to the Motherland. He used to travel often and documented all of his trips for those of us that could not make those journeys. Chuck would always share with us during classes and workshops. He would play videos for us to observe the culture in action. I loved Chuck and Chuck loved me. He loved Ayanna (Calabash choreographer) so that's how we were able to connect."

Iya Darcel Abel: "I had studied West African dance with Baba Chuck Davis at Minisink Townhouse and with Michael Babatunde Olatunji at the Olatunji African Dance Institute. Both dance classes were held in Harlem,

NY. The traditional African drums that were played were very different in shape, size, and sound than the conga drum used in the African-Caribbean dance classes that I was used to. In traditional African dance you learned the song, the meaning of, the cause, certain rhythms and sometimes that only certain drums played for each dance."

Baba David Coleman: "As far as dancers, Chuck was a baby. You had dancers before him; Phil Stamps, Milo Timmons, Russell Barros, and THEN there was Chuck. Tunji had all of these tall male dancers doing Watusi. Chuck's claim to fame was dancing that Watusi. King Soloman's Mine showed the Watusi dance; that turned the tall male dancers OUT."

Chuck Davis dancing with Olatunji at the 1964/65 World's Fair
Source: Jean Lee

Chuck Davis: "I started my dance career in DC. Three of us started a trio. We called ourselves La Dalemo Trio. We took the first two letters of our last names Da for Davis, Le - Lewis and Mo for Ernestine Morris. We were good. We were performing all over DC. On the night of the March on Washington, we were performing at the Crow's Toe. Olatunji decided to see us perform after he was supporting Dr. Martin Luther King, Jr. At the end of the second show, he told us we were hired. I was in heaven because Olatunji was the tops. For him to say that we were good enough to join them on stage was an honor. I went to New York after that."2

The Chuck Davis Dance Company, based in the Bronx, attracted a large audience to their performances of African dance, even carrying their performances of Yoruba dance ritual to Nigeria during FESTAC, the international festival held there in 1977. Chuck Davis and others initiated "DanceAfrica," a festival of African American dance companies, at the Brooklyn Academy of Music, which became an annual event. The first DanceAfrica in 1978 program featured the following companies:

- Dinizulu and His African Dancers, Drummers and Singers
- Chuck Davis Dance Company
- Arthur Hall Afro American Dance Ensemble
- Charles Moore and Dances and Drums of Africa
- The International Afrikan American Ballet

Jubal Harris: "My first trip to Africa was with Dr. Chuck Davis founder of Chuck Davis African American Dance company."

Baba Yomi Yomi Awolowo: "I was lead jembe drummer with Chuck Davis Dance Company from when they started in 1974 until I left. Chuck used to live with us on Davidson Ave. I had a Brownstone. Every weekend we had dance class and artists used to be there all the time. We were all living in my house. Chuck was living upstairs. Chuck was like my brother. We were family.

International and Chuck's company were the hottest African drum and dance groups of the time. International had the sabar thing with Obara Wali. We were strictly jembe and dundun and bells."

Baba Yomi Yomi's wife, dancer, and costume maker, Carole Robinson, recalls her experiences with the Chuck Davis Dance Company as a dancer.

Carole Robinson: "Yomi Yomi and I met each other in Jamaica, Queens at Bernice Johnson's class. We met Chuck Davis there as well. He was teaching dance there at that time. When Chuck left and started his dance company, we were all in it. Then the Ballets came and taught us their stuff since we were established. Itolo Zombo was the main dancer from the Ballets. Itolo was the main one working with us at Chuck's company. Chuck's company started DanceAfrica. DanceAfrica brought out jembe playing more than any other festival or concert."

Baba Yomi Yomi Awolowo: "Famoudou Konate and I had a close relationship. He used to come to my house and stay when he was in town. When they came with the Ballets they got stranded by their manager and was here for 6 months. So we used to bring them to our dance studio and they taught us a lot of songs, rhythms, dances, costumes. It was a beautiful thing. So when we saw Famoudou in FESTAC we were like here we go again, family."

Jalal Sharriff: "The drummers around 1966 with Chuck Davis were Balogun, Me, and Spanky Williamson. Around 1978, I went with Chuck Davis fulltime. The reason Chuck stayed in business so long was because he had the most structured business plan. He tapped into the National Endowment of the Arts (NEA), education division. He toured around the country. We were the ones that traveled all over the country with the dance and drum group."

Kobla Mensa Dente: "When DanceAfrica first started, it was all of the big dance companies cooperating with Chuck to bring that production."

Obba Babatunde: "I have a very strong dance background because I had worked with all of these dancers that were on the major scene teaching classes. Teachers like Bernice Johnson, Pepsi Bethel, Frank Hatchett, Luigi, Phil Black, Thelma Hill, Charles Moore, Shombe Yembe, and Ladji Camara. I worked with Babatunde Olatunji in 1970. He was playing with Baba Chief Bey, Sam Watson, and Delhi.

Chuck Davis, Melvin Deal, and Dinizulu were influences of the African dance. When we got with Ladji, it was the first time we were doing authentic traditional dances and rhythms straight from the Motherland."

Shombe Yimbe drummers and dancers
Top: Bradley Simmons Dundun, Jalal Sharriff, Walter Ince
Middle: James Cherry
Leaning Back: Akin Babatunde and John Blanford
Kneeling: Obba Babatunde and Shombe Yimbe
Photo credit: James Kregman Photo Studio

~

Baba Akin Babatunde: "I loved a woman named Sevilla Ford. She was Katherine Dunham's right-hand lady. Sevilla Ford took me under her wing and taught me the Dunham technique when I was nineteen/twenty [years old]. Sevilla Ford's significance and role as the one who was integral in teaching Dunham technique in America. Joan Peters was another one of Katherine Dunham's dancers that taught the Dunham technique.

Ladji Camara's Saa was my dance, and it was hard. When we went around that circle, it was like a cleansing. Lamban was my dance too. It was so grand."

Ajaibo Waldrond: "Charles Moore and I danced together in "Destine. Akosua Panyin and I danced together in Katherine Dunham's group "Caribeana"."

Akosua Drum and Dance Troupe's first dance student and lead dancer, Basimatah Muhammad, speaks about her experience with her teacher Akosua Panyin.

Basimatah Muhammad: "I was 11 in 1966 and Akosua moved next door to me in Mount Vernon, NY. I used to go over and talk to her. We became friends as a child and an adult could be. She talked to me about having a son and expecting another child. I learned a lot from her. More than just dance. My mom was a single mom and worked a lot. So she really filled a void.

She used to talk to me about the Kathrine Dunham Technique and African dance and music. When I was 12 in 1967 she asked me if I would be interested in joining her African dance class. She proposed to the Principal of Graham school to teach an African dance class after school at Graham school. I was her first student. I spoke to my friends Evelina and Denise, Rhonda Moore, Donna Robinson to join the class. At that time we used records like Babatunde Olatunji and Miriam Makeba. We would learn the songs and Akosua would choreograph movements to go along with the songs. We grew out of the afterschool program and went to the Macedonia center to do more of a community class. Here we stopped with the records and now we had drummers coming. We still did the songs but no records. Welcome dance was a big thing for us then. Akosua learned the Welcome dance from LaRocque Bey.

Once we became a community class then we had different teachers come through to teach us. We then started to develop our own repertoire. We did Welcome dance, Congolese Lament (Miriam Makeba song Dance by Akosua), Boot Dance was from a South Africa teacher but she changed it a bit. Kings Rhythm was fully Akosua and rhythm from Kofi and Abishai Ben Reuben. Nago (choreographed by Akosua but rhythm was from Olatunji). In 1969 other dancers started coming in. Yeboah, Akuba, and Afiba.

When we moved from Graham School to Macedonia School we stopped with records and went to live drums, congas. When the jembe came it felt more African and rootsy. The actual movements began to hit home more as if I had never seen African dance before. The jembe brought more of the African feeling. Before that I felt like I was learning the step before the rhythm. As more African drums came in we seemed to start moving from the Caribbean sound to more of an African sound and look. Abdur Rahman started attending Chuck Davis' classes and was introduced to jembe there. Abdur Rahman played congas with different groups and was playing conga with Akosua. When he got with Chuck Davis, they were only playing jembe there. It was Abishai and Abdur Rahman that brought the jembe in first to Akosua's class. After dancing to the jembe I remember feeling like how did I ever dance to the conga drum.

I felt that the Katherine Dunham's technique was Caribbean to me. Welcome Dance and Congolese Lament would be the defining dances for Akosua. Even though Akosua was an Akan Priestess from Dinizulu's order and a very close friend to Nana Dinizulu, she didn't dance and perform with Dinizulu's troupe to my knowledge."

Akosua Dance and Drum Troupe Mount Vernon, NY
Source: Abdur Rahman Wheeler

Yaa Serwaa Oparebeah Pintora (Janet Rush): "Floretta Donald (Akan Name: Akosua Nsia Oparebeah Panyin) was from Nevis. She was born on January 7, 1928 in New York and at two years old was brought to Nevis to be raised by her maternal grandmother. She came back to the United States at nine years old.

I remember her having to go down to class or rehearsal before she started her group in Westchester. She used to play recordings all the time

205

in the house. Papa Augustine was a Haitian drummer who she mentioned often; he drummed at the Katherine Dunham School. She learned Haitian, Brazilian, and Caribbean dance.

Syvilla Fort was managing the Dunham School in New York. I remember sitting on the floor after classes and rehearsals, and she would go to lunch with Syvilla Fort.

There are two dances that stand out when I think about my mother; Welcome Dance and Congolese Lament. Welcome Dance because it depicts her character; community, welcoming, and love. My mother began dancing in the church in Nevis. When we were in the spirit of the Welcome Dance and performed it, there was no stopping us. I think that my mother's classes were filled with her passion. It was the love. You were required to do your very best for the mission; all of your energy with no reservation. It was Dunham Technique, but the love, energy, spirit and passion was my mother.

In the very beginning, we had congas, bongos, and timbales. The first drummer to bring the jembe was Abdur Rahman. In 1970, we added Henry P. Warner, Awusa, Rahman on jembe, and Zeleka with the different African percussions like kalimbas. We had keyboards and guitar. Rashee picked up the jembe and he and Rahman would stand back to back playing jembes at shows. Kofi was a Priest at Dinizulu, and he joined during this time."

Abdur Rahman Wheeler: "Abishai was the spokesman of the group (Akosua African Dance and Drum Troupe). He introduced the artists and the different songs. He used to dance around and get the audience going and participating with us. We had congas, timbales, and sax. I brought the jembe up to Mount Vernon after hanging out at Chuck's when I was sixteen/seventeen around 1970-1974. My brother Rashee played dundun; Abishai got him a jembe. We rehearsed three times a week, and we all made it. Our lives were centered around the group.

I was one of the first drummers with Akosua's group. Basimatah was the first dancer. They used Olatunji's record at first. Me, my brother Rashee, and Abishai were the beginning drummers. Akosua didn't want to change her style. The group wanted to learn some of the Senegalese and Guinea style, but Akosua didn't want to change. So, we kind of got stifled. I wanted the drummers to go downtown with me to learn about the new jembe music, but they were set in their ways in Mount Vernon."

Rhonda Morman: "I never took any dance classes from Chuck Davis. There was no drama. I just didn't feel I needed to because of the way I studied. I wrote songs and ballets. John Blandford and I wrote ballets."

Calabash Troupe's Dance Choreographer, Dancer, Singer and Musician, Ayanna Fredreck McCray, speaks about Calabash.

Ayanna Fredreck McCray: "I started with a group called "The Creations." It was children. We worked for The Department of Parks and Recreation. Then I met Brother Abiodun in 1974 - 75 when I was twenty, and he told me about African dance because I was doing ballet, tap, jazz and modern. He told me about a calabash. I didn't know what a calabash was. I was in college and asked people, and they told me. So, I went to a bodega and bought a real calabash and brought it back to him, and they were all laughing at me. He said the calabash is a shekere. He showed me, and I told him that I didn't know.

We got together, and he told me let's change the name of the company from "The Creators" to "Calabash." We went to get Chief Bey and Barbara's blessings, and they gave me lessons on the cow bell. Everything was falling in place. I met Rose Marie Giroux. I met Yomi Goodall there at a Rose Marie Giroux production, and we brought her to Brooklyn with us to be a part of Calabash.

Abiodun had a dance company called the "House of Elijah." One of the dancers was a good friend of mine and she taught me Zulu dance. I took that and performed it with my group. I took classes with Chuck Davis. I learned with Rose Marie. I was a quick learner. I could dance, but I was more of a choreographer.

International was very good. I used to love that group. Me and Amaniyea used to bump heads.

Abiodun was in prison one year. When he was released, he played ashiko drum but the drummers were only playing jembe. So, there was some conflicts because Abiodun didn't play jembe, so it took him a while to get with that sound."

Renee Abayomi Goodall: "At 20 years old, I saw Arthur Mitchell and the Dance Theatre of Harlem. It was the first time I had ever seen black dancers on point. When I moved to Harlem, I applied and was granted a scholarship, thanks to my training at The Philadelphia School of Dance (Philadanco). Being on scholarship at DTH, I was not only studying

Ballet, I trained in Tap, Jazz and Interpretive Dance which much later known as African Dance.

My "Interpretive Dance" instructor was a powerful woman named Edwina Tyler. Unlike all the other genres, in this class we wore no shoes. We were instructed to take off our shoes, bend our knees and stick out our butts. I remember thinking, this can't be right, what kind of dance is this? All other styles of dance that I was familiar with up to this point had taught me to pull up and elongate my body and tuck in my butt. It felt awkward at first yet, it felt very freeing. I felt grounded and connected to the earth, I felt free without shoes.

I was coming out of class one day and saw a flyer posted by this woman from the Ivory Coast who had written an African Dance drama called "Vengeance of Mommy Wata." Rose Marie Giroux was holding auditions for actors, African dancers and musicians. I auditioned for the lead character of Mommy Wata; the role called for an actor/African dancer. I was strong as an actor but was still young in African dance training and experience. Rose Marie took me to her home in The Village in NYC and strengthen me by sharing African culture. She told me that for us African people dance was a way of life not just entertainment. She cooked traditional African cuisine and fed me. She braided my hair and adorned them with beads and shells. She put beads on my waist. She put the culture inside of me. I stayed with Rose Marie for days at a time, she re-birthed me, she Africanized me then she took me back into the studio privately and taught me Ivorian dances for the production. When she assembled the entire cast, I was ready and had a lot more confidence in my African dance skills. Judith Jamison was my classical dance idol and now Rose Marie Giroux was my African dance mama.

The entire Calabash Dance Company auditioned for Rose Marie's production and became the village people, village dancers and musicians, this is how I met Abiodun McCray and Ayanna Fredricks back in 1981. When Rose Marie's production ended, Ayanna said you need to come with us. I didn't know about a place called Brooklyn. I went with them across the bridge and that was another rebirthing for me. Brooklyn was a whole new world to me. I begin going to Brooklyn a couple of days a week training and eventually lead dancing with the Calabash Dance Company. Ayanna told me I was to her what Judith Jamison was to Alvin Ailey and she choreographed dances just for me. Ayanna also took me to see The National Ballet of Senegal. It was the first time I ever saw a traditional

African group with all their aura, energy, drums, singers with voices like I've never heard before, acrobats, stilt walkers, balafons, mbiras and more.

While at Calabash, I was exposed to and took classes with many other great artist like Charles Moore, Chuck Davis, Pearl Primus, Levinia Williams, Nana Dinizulu, Baba Ishangi, Baba Bey, Sister Hazel and other members of International as well as studying footage of late artists like Asadata Dafora."

Considered/Regarded/Revered by many as the Godfather of African dance in Washington D.C., Melvin Deal, speaks about his New York studies.

Melvin Deal: "I studied with my brother Chuck Davis and the Olatunji School in New York. During the summer months, I would go there to study with them. I studied with Arthur Hall in Philadelphia. Those of us that were serious about the African culture were connected."

Arthur Hall: "Most of my experiences in African dance has been in West Africa. The more I learn, the more I will use, but most of the dances I have learned have been from West Africa. I think that is significant because in facing our history, those cultures would be a part of Black America. When you trace the roots, the West Coast of Africa is mostly where they took the slaves."3

Arthur Hall's primary choreography included Obatala which came to him in a dream and was performed originally as his own dance solo in 1958, ultimately evolving over the years into one of his finest major productions. Obatala became known as the signature dance of the Arthur Hall Afro American Dance Ensemble. On December 12, 1973, Obatala was performed with the accompaniment of the Philadelphia Symphony Orchestra at the Academy of Music. Obatala's origin in a dream forebode Arthur's career-long spiritual service as one destined to bring forth art forms capable of changing a world through quiet revolution and cultural renaissance. Obatala represents that divinity of created forms, the patron saint of artists, the patron of all created form, the king whose every day becomes a feast, and who as the Lord of the White Cloth is one of the principal orisha of the Yoruba people of Nigeria. To the Yoruba, Obatala is the embodiment of the creative spirit who represents cosmic consciousness and the manifestation of purity and righteousness. In Arthur Hall's production of Obatala, this king teaches his children the lessons of compassion, patience and love; approaching each child to answer their requests. The powerful symbolism in Obatala standing as one of his greatest creations and reflecting the purity of his artistic genius rests in the reality of how Arthur served as master teacher who loved his students as children to whom he gave the wisdom of dance and music. As king of his domain, Arthur gave all of his students of dance and music gifts that they could cherish for the rest of their lives, answering the unspoken and spoken requests of students' innermost soul to learn the universal language of dance and music. All were spiritually transformed in the process.4

Chapter 13

Philly Drum and Dance

"Folks get degrees and then they teach drumming and culture without knowing the story and who was here." Baba Doc Gibbs

Philadelphia has a rich history when it comes to African culture, spirituality, and the arts. Philly has Ile Ife (cultural institute), The Annual Odunde Festival, Kulu Mele African Dance & Drum Ensemble, The Philly Sound (Billy Paul, Teddy Pendergrass, The Stylistics, The Spinners, The Jones Girls, McFadden & Whitehead, Harold Melvin and The Bluenotes, Blue Magic) and more. Philly was also home of the great Baba Doc Gibbs. I can still remember seeing the Emeril Live show for the first time – this Chef cooking on television with all this energy and with a band led by a percussionist, Doc Gibbs. The show and its energy were great. Doc always looked like he was having fun. I wondered if that was his stage presence or if he truly enjoyed the music. I finally got the opportunity to meet Doc Gibbs when my godbrother, John McGill, told me that Doc was in the religion and was a good friend. I contacted Doc and we hit it off right away. I got my answer to my earlier question. He wasn't faking it on the Emeril Live show, Doc Gibbs loved percussions, loved life, and loved to have fun.

When I decided to write this book, Doc Gibbs invited me out to his home in California where we took a journey down memory lane to talk about Philly's early contributions to African drum and dance in America. Doc told me about his close associations with legends in Philly like Bobby Crowder, Sonny Morgan, Garvin Masseaux, Baba Ishangi, Baba Dehli, Arthur Hall, and others. He confided in me about the good, the bad, and the ugly during those early days in Philly. Doc introduced Saka Acquaye's music to me which was such a treat because of my love for the country of Ghana. When it came to African dance in America, I always thought about Chuck Davis. At least until I started learning about Arthur Hall, who opened the way before Chuck Davis stepped into the African dance scene. I learned how Arthur Hall inspired many dancers to expand their reach beyond just dance and choreography. Arthur Hall was a pillar in the Philly community. He not only inspired many drummers and dancers to make a living from their art, but he also encouraged many to devote their lives to African spirituality whether it was Akan or Yoruba. Right when I was convinced Arthur Hall was THE man in Philly when you speak about African dance and drumming, here comes Doc Gibbs telling me about this Saka Acquaye who taught Arthur Hall his art. As Doc had been very close with Arthur Hall, I felt extremely blessed for my time with Doc as he recounted his early days drumming in Philly.

* * *

Baba Doc Gibbs: "I met Grover Washington, Jr. while I was playing with George Benson at Carnegie Hall. I talked to Grover and asked if I could sit in with his band when he came to Philly. I did a weekend gig with Grover and he said to me, "Man I like what you do so if you want the gig, it's yours." I asked him, do you mean when you work then I work? He said, "Yeah!" So that's how I got the gig with Grover. About a year later, we were recording a record and he was real sick. I mixed up a bunch of herbs and gave it to him and the next day he felt much better. On the record in 1976, he said there are two doctors in Philly, there's Dr. J and Dr. Gibbs. That's where I got my "Doc" Gibbs.

These are the type of stories that everyone that comes here to America to study or to make a living playing the drums need to know. Every young cat that's playing in a band need to know these stories. These were our stories; African American stories. Most people from outside America that come here don't know that if you were black in the 1800s and caught playing drums, you would get your hands cut off or hung. The white man was afraid of the communications and what was happening with those drums. Most of these folks that come here-Nigerians, Cubans, and others don't know these stories. They have to learn our stories and what we went through to know what we brought to the table. All those cats, Chief Bey, Bobby Crowder, Babafemi, and Sonny Morgan, these were the pioneers of the drum here in Philly.

I went to a club and Bobby Crowder was playing with Sonny Fortune. They were swinging and Bobby Crowder was playing a pandeiro. How the F do you swing with a pandeiro? But he was on that shit, and that's what messed me up man, and then he took a solo with it like the Brazilians, and spinning it and rolling it down his arm and neck. Bobby would cut up with the pandeiro. I was THERE. I was like nineteen. I connected with Bob, and he became like my father. As I got older, I always went back to him.

"Buzzard" Bernard would do dance classes, and I would hang out with him to learn. I started off with the bell and worked my way up to the drum (conga). I learned how to play for dancers and mark the dancers.

We would start off Saturday mornings at dance class in Camden, then hit the bus to New York. With Bernard, I started getting around and seeing other things. We would go up to New York and hit the subway and buy records. We would bring our drums, and he would bring me to Harlem and the Bronx to parties to see some things. Around 1973, I saw a cat named Airto Moreira who was a percussionist for Miles Davis. He was playing all types of percussions around him during his sets. I started going to New York to buy all types of percussions even if I didn't know how to play them. So, when I started sitting in with local bands, I would bring my congas and a bag filled with these different percussion instruments. There were not many percussionists playing anything besides the congas; so that became my thing. Throughout my years sitting with bands, I would still reach out to Bobby Crowder. He was my mentor, and he was my father figure, but where I was going, he hadn't been.

Bobby Crowder, Sonny Morgan, and Garvin Masseaux were the traditional and spiritual cats. Sonny and Bob ended up working with Olatunji with Chief Bey and those cats. They moved up to New York, but Bob came back to Philly and set up his own troupe called Kulu Mele which is probably the oldest operating African American dance and drum company in the United States. Kulu Mele played Broadway; they played on records. They played on Art Blakey records. Back then, Montego Joe, Chief Bey, Bobby Crowder, and them were the hand drummers that the industry called on. Before Chief passed, he was like the elder drummer in the country.

Garvin played congas, vibes, guitar, and piano. He was multi-talented, but Garvin had some mental issues and ended up having a nervous breakdown. Bob studied guitar with a Brazilian cat named Bola Sete. Bola lived in Philly for a while.

Folks get degrees and then they teach drumming and culture without knowing the story and who was here; not knowing who is here and made a way so that you could come here freely and not worry about having your hands chopped off because you are drumming. Someone else paid the dues for you for that. A lot of times I find that people from different cultures don't have a lot of respect for African American drummers here because they assume we don't have "our own". Without understanding that "our own" was the guy coming here from Brazil, from Cuba, from Guinea, from Haiti, and sharing with us.

In 1968-69 when I used to do gigs with my godfather's band, they used to give me about thirty to forty dollars per gig. Then around 1972, when I was playing with another band, they paid about fifty to sixty dollars a gig."

Bradley Simmons: "Sonny Morgan, Ishangi, Bobby Crowder and Garvin Masseaux were the ones that learned the shekere from Saka Acquaye. All in Philadelphia. When they went off from Philly to New York, that's when the shekere made it into the game. Out of the 4, Ishangi was the best shekere player. He was like a magician on that shekere. If he was a basketball player he could've played for the Harlem Globetrotters easily. That's how much control he had with the shekere."

Baba Kenneth Fauntleroy: "In Philly in the 1960s, we were playing congas because we had no jembes. Greg "Peache" Jarman was our teacher. Robert Crowder was his teacher. In 1973, I joined Kulu Mele African Dance and Drum Ensemble fresh out of high school, but it was formed in 1970. While I was going to high school, I took the drum class with "Peache". He advised me to walk this line. The first level was bell, then sticks; then you may go to shekere, then you go to segundo, and then mama. We played and made shekeres all the time.

They also brought pandeiro to New York. Garvin was a genius. He could play any type of instrument that you put in front of him. Bobby Crowder was the leader of Sonny Morgan and Garvin because of his force. The Cubans really didn't want to teach African Americans. Bobby, Sonny, and Garvin were playing with Chief, Babafemi, Olatunji, and the others from Olatunji's group. Bob was very strict when it came to the drum. I remember one time he was teaching shekere; a student told him that he was SICK with this.

Arthur Hall's group played jembe. Arthur Hall influenced many to be initiated as Priests in the Akan faith because he was made a king in Ghana when he visited there. He had an influence over all of us because he was our elder. He studied under Saka Acquaye.

Oba Dehli was an ocha Priest. He used to play with Bob and Chief and Olatunji. He was from Philly, but lived in New York. Sonny Morgan was from Philly, but lived in New York. Baba Ishangi was from Philly, but lived in New York."

Ione Nash (Ione Shirley Osborne Nash): "After Saka Acquaye left, Arthur formed his own group. From there I had a group called

INDE...Ione Nash Dance Ensemble. I didn't join Arthur's group but we partnered on dances. One was called Adam and Eve then we changed the name to Temptation. Any time we partnered on dance we would dance "Temptation." Arthur Hall had a very big influence on African dance in Philly, especially with males. It was good for males to have a man to look up to for dance. He kept me as a partner because I was one of the few dancers he could throw up and twirl around. I started teaching at different centers after Saka left until I opened up my own school. In the late 1960s, I had to go to court because the neighbors were complaining about the drumming. I had to take parents and students to make the judge know that the drumming was for African dance. My husband opened a barbershop in the front of the building to help cut down the sound of the drums."1

Daryl Kwasi Burgee: "I had been playing drums since about four or five years old. I was introduced to the African culture via Arthur Hall's center, Ile Ife. As a child, around 1970, I would pass by the center, and I would hear drumming. I figured I wouldn't really be a drummer if I didn't go in and see what was going on in there. The 1960s was a time when Blacks were beginning to accept our connection with Africa. Ile Ife provided me an outlet to begin to research a lot more about who I was as a person. The drum being the core of who I was, was the natural being bringing me into that entire environment. So, as I went in to Ile Ife in search of understanding the drum, I found another world of history, self-identity, and everything I could be looking for. I became more and more proficient and after a year or so, I was performing with the company, which was the African American Dance Ensemble. Arthur was a dancer and a culturalist. I had different teachers throughout the years like Roy Johnson, James Cory, Bobby Artist, and Bobby Crowder. They all came through that center. The company specialized in different forms of dance; Cuban forms, Haitian forms, and African forms. There was a long period of time when Black folks didn't have access to information about direct cultural dance. There was a period of contemporary dance that they called interpretive. It would interpret what was imagined to be African dance. Arthur took regular people off of the street and turned them into professional dancers. He was able to create ballets like Black Orpheus and tons of productions that gave him the notoriety that he has.

It was through the Ile Ife center where I was introduced to the jembe. The Afro American Dance Ensemble was probably one of the first African American companies to stage jembe dance. New York didn't even have it yet. Arthur had seen Ballets Africains in New York and was naturally enthralled. He took all of the elements and brought it back and recreated what he saw. He featured a piece called Guinea Harvest.

Nii Ayi was the individual who understood jembe drumming and technique. He had moved to Philly to work with the Afro American Dance Ensemble. He was originally from Camden, New Jersey then moved to New York then to Philly. His sister was named Nikita who was married to another pioneer in this thing by the name of Ishangi. She was an incredible jembe player. Ishangi was a stilt walker. She would play for Ishangi while he danced on stilts. Nikita and Nii Ayi had the same mother and father. He moved to New York by way of his sister. He was able to learn a lot of the things that we didn't know as far as technique with the drum. So, he taught myself and a bunch of other drummers here, and we became more proficient at that technique on jembe. Nii Ayi taught about the maintaining of the drum along with learning technique of playing.

The initial person that really introduced jembe to us at the center was a drummer named Bobby Artist. He was Arthur's lead drummer, and he and Arthur went to see the Ballets Africains together in New York. He actually was able to come back and retain the rhythms that was being played for the specific dances, and Arthur retained the choreography and structure of what took place and came back and created a small ballet from that. They developed a piece they called Guinea Harvest which was a dance called Konkoba. Being a part of that gave me a better understanding of production, staging, and preparation; all those things to advance and develop anything you would want if that was your interest. The exposure for me was tremendous all the way around.

When Ile Ife and Afro American Dance Ensemble started to decline, I stepped forward and created an African dance company called Jasu African Ballet which was based on pursuing the technique of jembe dance and drum. At nineteen, I moved to Ghana, West Africa, being exposed to the Akan religion. I immersed myself into the religion, culture, language and all that for two years."

One of the eldest living African American African drummers in Philadelphia, John Wilkie, speaks about his early days of African drumming.

John Wilkie: "I'm seventy-nine years old. The first time I ever seen a jembe played was Papa Ladji. He played jembe with Olatunji in Philadelphia. We had not seen anyone play that type of drum before.

My first encounter with the drums was with William Pal and Charles Brown back in the early 1950s. There were no jembes or batas; just salsa and Afro Cuban/Tito Puente. The first drum I played was the bongos, when I was thirteen/fourteen because that's what Pal played. I followed him around. They had a group called the Afro American Drummers. I used to hear them play on the streets, and I used to go and check them out. After they formed the group, it was just congas and few dancers. They used to rehearse on top of a bar. I was lucky to get up there because they wouldn't let children up there. Pal would get me up there, then me and my friend would be beating on the dining room table at my house what we heard them playing.

When I was in high school in the late 1950s, Rogue and I were in class together playing on desks. We asked who each other were learning from and found out we were learning from drummers from the same group. One of my teachers told me that Bobby Crowder was teaching Pal. Pal let me sit at his house when he was taking a lesson with Bobby. Me, Rogue, and Peache were in the other room. Bobby Crowder started teaching Peache (Greg Jarman) when he was seven. He was a great drummer. He ended up playing with Mongo Santamaria.

Me, Peache, and Kwasi played together in Spoken Hands group that Kwasi put together. Bobby Crowder and Kenny Fauntleroy were in that group together. I started playing in the group with Bobby around 1971. Bobby Crowder was eleven years older than me. He was born in 1930, and I was born in 1941. Bobby had an interest in me after a gig and started teaching me more. The Guinea Ballet came to Philly in early 1970s, and I finally saw jembe in its right perspective. The next time I saw the jembe played was with Steve Jackson, Chucky, and Kwasi with Arthur Hall's group. Nii Ayi taught Kwasi and the other drummers on the jembe when they were with Arthur Hall.

When this group broke up, Arthur started his group Afro American Dance Ensemble and Ile Ife. Bobby was part of Arthur's group but quit and started his own group called Kulu Mele. I would play at Ile Ife but I wouldn't join. Pal didn't join Arthur's group, but he taught for Arthur. Arthur Hall was a genius.

Garvin was playing vibes. He played instruments. Garvin played vibes and drums on Gold Coast Saturday Night. He was a genius too. Stacy Edwards was from Philly and a drummer that played with the Olatunji drummers that people don't talk about.

I first saw Bobby Crowder, Garvin, and Baba Ishangi playing the shekere. They had pillowcases wrapped around them so you couldn't see them. I got shekere playing from Bobby Crowder. He taught us how to play and string them. We got gourds from down south. We had to put the rocks inside of them to roll them around to clean them out then start cleaning them. Bob told me you had to learn how to control the beads."

"Nii Ayi" Nana Obrafo Yaw Wofa Asiedu: "For many years there were no jembes. It was just congas and Haitian drums and stuff like that. I started out in New Jersey playing congas for a dance class in Philly. It wasn't until I moved up to New York when I came in contact with the jembe in the 1960s. After being in New York for some time, I started playing with Chuck Davis, Yomi, and those guys.

Most drummers were learning jembe from albums until Ladji started teaching. No one was getting lessons and getting the jembe in its true sense. Ladji was impressed with what was going on with the drumming and dance scene in New York.

My sister was already playing jembe. I took her to her first dance class in Philly around the mid 1960s. We were the only two in our family that was really connected to the culture. I introduced her to Ishangi, and she started taking classes with him. She ended up marrying him, and he became my brother-in-law. When the Ballets came through, Famoudou wanted to take my sister to his village in Guinea because he was so impressed by her drumming, but Ishangi didn't want her to learn the folklore of the jembe so much. He had another African American take on Africa, so he did things differently. He wasn't doing mendiani, kakilambe, sunnu, walosodon and those kind of rhythms. He wasn't doing those. He created his own. So, she created that sound around his idea of what he wanted; more based on like the Olatunji thing. You get an influx of drummers who know what they are doing, but you want them to play a different way. I left the Jersey/Philly area and moved up to New York. Ishangi and my sister stayed in Philly; that's when my journey really started as far as a jembe was concerned.

When I was still in Philly, I ran across Ibrahim Camara from Senegal. He had a group call "Koumpo". I used to take Tracy, myself, and another drummer up to Boston to have classes with Ibrahim and Yusef. Someone from California was doing scouting from African Dance companies to open up Wild Animal Park. So, we got together Brothers from Senegal and formed a company to go out to California. When we got there, we didn't see anyone playing jembes and definitely not playing folkloric jembe. They just had the drum. So, when we arrived, we gave the jembe purpose. We authenticated the drum. Instead of everything running together, we put the drums in its folkloric place. So actually, we brought the first jembe to Los Angeles in that respect. This was around 1978-79. We opened the park and stayed for about three to four years.

I went to Ghana in 1975. Most Ghanaians thought I was a Ghanaian and was hired by the group from Philly. I went there with Arthur Hall and his group as part of a cultural exchange. In each of the cities, after we performed, people would come up to me speaking Twi. I would only be able to respond with what I learned while there. My normal response was, "Meti Twi Kakra Kakra," (I speak Twi small small).

Famoudou Konate taught me Farekodeba when he came to the United States in 1968. We were very close. We spent a lot of time together. I met Mamady Keita when he was like sixteen. I took him and his drummers to New Jersey and had one of my sister friends to get her girls together and make some African food. They were loving the vibe. They wanted to bring those sistas home. I was that guy after that. Numandy was his second drummer but I kind of liked Numandi's drumming more so than Mamady. Mamady was good, but I thought Numandy was awesome. Numandy's attitude was totally different."

One of the early African drummers and teachers in Philadelphia, Clifford "Peache" Jarman, spoke about his responsibility as a cultural drummer.

Clifford "Peache" Jarman: "Just imagine what we would know if the slave trade or holocaust hadn't happened. You learn about life through the drum, because it takes you places that everybody can't go. Drummers tell me that, in their home places in Puerto Rico and Africa, they can walk where no one is allowed to go, and the same thing happens here in Philadelphia. If a drummer has a drum, he can go to forbidden lands, to places where other people can't go, and nothing will happen to him. I have been able to walk through different doors that were opened by those before me, and I have been able to set up shop. My dream is about keeping those doors open for drummers coming up after me; my dream is to make sure that those doors stay open for drummers after them. I have been privileged by the love, trust and teachings of master drummers: Robert Crowder, Mongo Santamaria, Craig Shinnery and many others. I am honored to work as a drummer, as a teacher, and to contribute my drumming to community festivals, sacred ceremonies, concert stages, family occasions and ceremonies. I will thank the spirit of the drum for my life for the rest of my life."2

Arthur Hall: "I think everything that I'm doing with the dance is about trying to correct some of our social ills.

The beginning of my pioneering was to try to make a place for black dancers to be able to perform. When I was working as a dance instructor, I used my advanced students to begin to build on the company idea. I used the materials from Africa that I learned from my teachers Saka Acquaye and from Katherine Dunham, who I had worshiped; and idolized her ideology in dance. Then there was my own desire to be able to bring forth some positive black images for dance; for black dance anyway, to sort of remove the Tarzan stereotypes from African culture. So with those objectives in mind that was how I started the Afro American Dance Ensemble. To be able to say that I'm proud of who I am. To say that my heritage goes back to Africa and I should have no reason not to be proud of that heritage."3

Saka Acquaye: "We have changed the world through our music and dance. There is no place you go without listening to black music. There is no place now where you go and people are not dancing like black people. We have touched the heart of the world. I call this the quiet revolution. We have changed the world, and we didn't use a gun."4

In 1953, with drummer Bobby Crowder and long-time dance partner Ione Nash, Hall was a principal dancer in the West African Cultural Society, founded by Acquaye.

The quiet revolution began in the year 1958, marking Arthur Hall's service as director and choreographer for the Sidney King Dance Theater. The year 1958 launched the pioneering work of not only Arthur Hall, but also of Martha Graham, Alvin Ailey, and Eleo Pomare, as each established his/her own dance companies at that time. The seeds for a major dance, art, and cultural renaissance in America were thereby planted. As an artistic director, Arthur played his part in the quiet revolution and cultural renaissance by first presenting African Sketches, largely reflecting what he had learned from Saka Acquaye. Arthur had an incredible memory for art forms. People called him a walking encyclopedia, because he could remember all of the dances and stories taught to him by Saka Acquaye and others. Yet Arthur's choreography was original and because of this, Arthur's work represented a link between two cultures - the Africans who were taken away from their tradition and the Africans who still followed it.

Arthur's fulfillment of his vision and the success of the quiet revolution were guided by a philosophy he shared with his students. Arthur believed that the term "Afro-American" made a strong cultural statement and that African Americans had a unique contribution of art to give to the world. Arthur was not implying that the dancers were not African American or descendants of Africans. He instead, chose to emphasize how "Afro-American" meant that the descendants who were taken away from Africa were able to create a unique identity through various cultural expressions. This is why Arthur retained the name Arthur Hall Afro-American Dance Ensemble over the decades. He felt it was important that members of his dance company learned the African traditional dance and music and also follow his direction in fusing it with their own experience to create something through which the troupe could make a unique artistic contribution as African Americans.

In 1969, working with the First Pennsylvania Bank and the Philadelphia National Bank, Arthur established the Ile Ife Black Humanitarian Center in North Philadelphia on Germantown Avenue. Ile Ife, or "House of Love" in Yoruba, was the first community arts center in America to be established by a dance company.

Chapter 14

Sun Drummer

"You don't just learn a song and learn a culture. You have to be the culture."
Atu (Harold) Murray

During one of my interviews with Baba David Coleman, he made it abundantly clear that African Americans have not received proper recognition for our contributions to the discipline of African drumming and dance. He firmly believes that we should have made our own drums to represent our existence in the West. We should have created our own rhythms and dances to represent our unique experiences so that when Continental Africans ask to see African American originality, we could have our own to show them. Baba David taught many people shekere making, drum making, and instrument making. He was always encouraging African Americans to be original and to give the instruments a unique name to leave a legacy. Baba David talked about Chief Bey, Baba Ishangi, Taiwo DuVall, and Sun Drummer as pioneers who lived in the spirit of self-determination and originality. Through Baba David, I was led to the founder and original members of The Sun Drummer. A group of drummers and drum makers from Chicago known for carving out drums and creating their own unique repertoire in the early 1970s. This was not my first time hearing about them. In fact, my godbrother and good friend, John McGill, was part of the Ohio branch of Sun Drummer and was the first to bring Sun Drummer to my consciousness. Like other drumming communities in America, their roots were from New York teachers and artists. Their focus was on drum making and bringing a holistic approach to the art of drumming. I was blessed to locate and interview Atu Harold Murray, the founder of Sun Drummer as well as some of the original Sun Drummer members. Listening to their stories brought the spirit of Nummu to me.

The Sun Drummer story was truly inspiring. To think that these drum makers and drummers in the Midwest built up their presence to the point where they were invited to the 1977 FESTAC in Lagos, Nigeria, Dance Africa in Brooklyn, N.Y., and played a role in starting one of the longest running African drum and dance troupes in America, the Muntu Dance Theatre of Chicago is beyond impressive.

Left to Right: Eli Walker, Babu Atiba Walker, Mosheh Milon Sun Drummer at
FESTAC 1977
Lagos, Nigeria
Source: Mosheh Milon

* * *

Baba Mosheh Milon: "Atu was my first African drum teacher. I was one of the drummers who took off from Chicago to learn and hit with other drummers.

In 1968-1969, we started a group called UHCC - Unified Humanity through Culture and Creativity. We later changed the name to Muntu. Atu had come back to Chicago from New York at this time. He had already started the Sun Drummer. Atiba lived in the projects with me. He had a family at a very young age; he was like nineteen years old. He joined Sun Drummer.

We had UHCC (Later called Muntu) and we wanted to play jembe. We got our jembe playing from New York. We got with drummers like Aziz who was with Ladji, and we became interested in playing jembe. Atu wasn't doing the jembe stuff. There were no jembes around Chicago. You couldn't find a jembe nowhere. Even in New York, if you had one, you probably got it from Ladji or someone that traveled to Guinea and brought some back. Since Atu was a carver, we got with him and a brother named Moussa, who became a big carver in Chicago. So around 1972-1974, we found logs and had Atu and Moussa show us how to carve our first jembes. I played my jembe from Sun Drummer at FESTAC in Nigeria in 1977.

I believe the first generation of jembe drummers around Chief Bey's time was Balogun, Yomi Yomi, and right after then was my time. So, we were the first jembe drummers in this Chicago area. We didn't drum just to get with girls and get into the social thing. We were kicking knowledge as well. In the 1960's and 1970's, we had Last Poets talking about the struggle; that influenced us drummers to be out in the parks and outside drumming. We had James Brown messages; Donny Hathaway and Roberta Flack "Where is the Love?" And the Vietnam War. If you were out, it was based around this stuff. Not the commercial stuff. Atu named it Sun Drummer to say that we were all One, and the Sun would be the root for where our energy base would come from.

UHCC was the beginning of Muntu which became the longest running African drum and dance group in the United States. We started under the tree. Some of those dancers and drummers were the ones that ended up in Muntu Dance Theatre. Muntu was solid West African drum and dance; no improv, jazz or ballet. A lot of the members came in from the Israelite order in the area. Some of the names of the original members were myself, Atiba Walker, Eli, Brother Benyamin, and Sister Yani. A lot of the males from back then are still involved in the culture and drumming somehow. Most of the dancers have moved on to other things. I was the musical director for Muntu from the beginning. Then, I left Muntu and went to Ohio for three years and started Sun Drummer in Ohio. I came back and picked up the musical directorship again, then ended up in California for thirty-five years."

One member of the Ohio chapter of the Sun Drummer, John McGill, spoke about the start of the Sun Drummer in Ohio.

John McGill: "In 1973, while attending college in Cleveland, Ohio, I made the personal decision to study and learn the correct way to play conga drums. I then went to a pawn shop in Cleveland and purchased a Mexican La Playa Conga. I brought it home and, realizing that I did not know the correct way to approach the drum, I spent the night meditating, rubbing my hands on the drumhead and praying but not playing one note. I wanted to learn but I wanted to learn correctly from a competent teacher. The next day, I went to Cleveland State U's Student Union. While sitting there, I see this brother walking by me headed towards the African American Culture Center, dressed in all white African garb with a dundun talking drum under his arm. It was Oloye Adeyemon, a Priest of Obatala, and he was giving a presentation. After his presentation concluded, I walked up to him and introduced myself. As a result, I started studying under him. He introduced me to traditional African and Afro Cuban systems of playing conga drums. Ultimately, we became lifelong friends.

After graduation, I moved to Cincinnati. While there, I took a drive to Eden Park one day and heard some drums playing. Upon investigating, I saw Jubal Harris, Charles Miller, Tony DeMar and a couple of other cats. I saw them and went home and brought back my drum. I returned and asked if I could join them and they said "Yes." I noticed that there was no common training with the drummers. It felt like no one really knew the correct parts to play the rhythms correctly. Everyone was "doing their own thang." So, I talked to them about Oloye in Cleveland. I told them all he needed was bus fare and we started bringing him down to Cincinnati for drum classes on the weekend at my house. Eventually, Oloye moved from Cleveland to Cincinnati and our group interaction increased. That group that was studying with Oloye was the nucleus of those that would become the Sun Drummer in Ohio.

I met Mosheh Milon in Cincinnati after Oloye was working with the drummers. Mosheh, who was living in Chicago at the time, brought the jembe drum and vibe. He also brought the Sun Drummer concept and started the Ohio chapter."

Jubal Harris: "While I was in college in 1968, I saw my first African drum and dance performance by Darlene Blackburn from Chicago. Her group danced with an African centered performance art group called The Pharaohs. Several members of The Pharaohs formed The Art Ensemble of Chicago.

In 1970 at the University of Cincinnati I linked up with a brother named Brett Brown from Harlem. Brett was attending UC on a football scholarship. Brett asked me if I knew how to drum and I told him my story about wanting to learn. He asked if I knew how to play agogo. I said, "No, will you show me?" Brett was an original member of Michael Babatunde Olatunji's Drums of Passion. He appeared on the cover of Babatunde Olatunji's Soul Makossa album playing an agogo bell.

1973/74 Oloye Adeyemon was coming to Cincinnati from Cleveland to teach us Yoruba spirituality and drumming. In 1974, I connected with Mosheh Milon. He was the lead drummer for Chicago Sun Drummer. I began traveling back and forth between Cincinnati and Chicago to study. In 1975, I became an instructor at the Cincinnati Art Consortium teaching students how to play the shekere and agogo bell.

Neil Clark was my first shekere teacher. I met Baba Neil when he performed at the Viking Lounge in Cincinnati with Phillis Hyman, Jean Carn and Norman Connors. Baba Neil taught me the "BOX" technique for playing the shekere. Mosheh showed me how to string the shekere.

During President Jimmy Carter's administration in 1977 I wrote a grant for the Arts Consortium that was funded by the Comprehensive Employment and Training Act. Four jobs were created to teach African music art and dance. I was the program coordinator, Deborah Hardy taught dance, and Johanna Nichols taught art. Moshe was hired to teach African drumming. He also co-founded the Sun Drummer and Dancer company in Cincinnati that became a branch of the Chicago Sun Drummer."

Babu Atiba Walker: "I started drumming in the late 1960's in the projects in Chicago. We were drumming outside in the community and talking that black revolution talk and black consciousness. The drums provided the vehicle drawing people together to get into those conversations. We were playing congas and stuff then, but I didn't get serious about drumming until about 1970. My cousin Michael was my first drum teacher. He gave me my first rudiments. He played for family affairs all of my life. He played congas and bongos and that stuff. From there, I met brother Selah from the Sun Drummer. He taught me how to tack head my conga and how to put the drum skins on. I was introduced to Baba Atu, and he was the senior drummer of Sun Drummer. He asked me to come through to some of the rehearsals; he brought me right in. I was right in with him from there on in. We wanted to do African drumming without mimicking African people.

In 1971, Atu got a jembe from Ladji from working with Chief Bey and them. I was twenty-two/twenty-three at that time. We made up our own songs. We had to make our own drums so we could have that intimate relationship with the instrument. We wrote songs all in English so that we could get across the message to the people what we were conveying. At that time, a lot of dudes were telling us that sisters didn't play hand drums or jembe because of the energy involved. We had a deep thing on that. We were into that for a minute. We continued to study until we understood. When I first went to Africa, I learned that women do drum. So, we had to relate to that and make some adjustments and changes.

We were playing under the sun and got the power of the sun and no matter how many drummers were playing, we were all one; that's why it wasn't plural, it was Sun Drummer.

I was one of the founding members of the Muntu group. We are celebrating our forty-eighth year.

My Israelite cousin who taught me my first fundamentals was directly responsible for pulling me into the UHCC Uniting Humanity through the Cultural Creativity group. Since Mosheh and I were from the same neighborhood, I pulled him in too. UHCC was started by a group of Israelite brothers and sisters. UHCC would change its name to Muntu.

Kathrine Dunham had a student named Lucille Ellis who was deep in the Dunham Technique in Chicago. Me and Mosheh played for Lucille Ellis often; she gave us a lot of insight on Kathrine Dunham."

Enoch Williamson: "I grew up during segregation in Chicago. I had one of those bongos and I played piano. In the 1960's I was a teenager and I was in the Black Panther Party. I was the number 1 BPP paper seller in Chicago. I sold 600 papers a week. Chairman Fred Hampton wanted to meet me because he wanted to meet this guy selling all of these papers. Fred Hampton's principle was he wanted all of the Panthers to live together so that we could better get to know each other. I told him that if we were all living together and the police came then they will get us all. Also, they will know who we all were. I didn't trust any of those people around. We used to have meetings once a month. We had meetings at the office. On one occasion, Chairman said, "Let's hang out at my house after the meeting." Yusef and I were on our way to hang out there and on the way I said, "Nah man I think I'm going to go home, I'm tired." So, we went home. And that night is when they killed Fred Hampton. I know that would have been me too because I didn't have rank. The security guy at the front didn't have rank either and he was one of the first ones shot and killed. So that would have been me had I gone that night. I was 19/20. This was in 1969.

I asked the Most High what is it that you saved me for? A couple of days later an older friend came by my crib and gave me this old conga drum. A day later, my wife's uncle came by and said he knew someone who would teach me how to play that. I said this must be the sign. The following day, I met Atu and he was giving a class on African drumming. I heard Afro Cuban and Caribbean but never African drumming. So, I went in and Brother Atu was teaching at the Moorish spot. Atu was in African garb and sandals on his feet. 2 feet of snow and this cat was walking around in sandals. At first I thought he was off. I thought maybe I'm not reading this right. I kept asking the Most High why did you save me. I asked him why do you have on sandals? He said, I don't want to cover up my UNDERstanding. I said what? He said Pisces rules the feet that's where our UNDERstanding is. He never had on shoes. Atu was about 26/27 years old. He was very muscular from pumping iron and had just come back from New York from studying. We had our first class and he said the drum represents the principles of the Universe. Masculine and feminine principals that are joined when you play the drum. I thought I was coming in to learn rhythms and he's in here talking all of this other stuff. There were 7 of us in the class. I was into numerology so 7 is a divine number. He didn't allow us to play drums, we all played different types of bells. By playing the bell you would learn the ring of the drum. The 7 of us were intrigued by him. He had a bald head and all these rings in his ears and nose. And of course only sandals on his feet. Chief Bey was his teacher. He talked about Chief Bey. Atu came up with "Sun Drummer" meaning 'One Universal Drum.'

In 1985 when I was with Muntu Dance Theatre of Chicago we were invited to Dance Africa. That's where I met Chief Bey. That's when I realized just how much Atu got from Chief Bey's teaching. The original Sun Drummer members were Bro Selah, Bro Sura, Bro Derf, Bro Kewo, Bro Oye, Enoch, Moosa, Atu. Bro Derf was the showman, he played flute, sax, and a hell of hand drummer. Bro Derf did a lot with Ramsey Lewis. Bro Kewo and Bro Oye ended up in the famous horn section of Earth, Wind and Fire.

After I saw the Ballets, I went backstage and brought Famoudou to the hood. We had a Bro bring out his quinto and Famoudou got on the quinto and MAN, I NEVER HEARD A DRUM DO LIKE THAT!! Incredible rolls and slaps. Atu didn't play like that. The other brother could play but nothing like that. I went back to Atu and said these cats are playing their asses off. Maybe we should get them to teach us some stuff to help us come up with our sounds. Atu was very strong willed. He didn't want to copy anyone's style. Atu had this whole philosophy. We would come up with Sun Drummer songs. We would stand in a circle and respect elders. He would always give us high philosophies. Extended the drum past playing so that it was more than a drum. It was a heartbeat of the cosmos. How we had to be a better person to play. Once we became a better person then we could drum. We went on like that for a few years. Muntu Dance Theatre of Chicago grew out of the Sun Drummer. We never wore shoes, no costumes. Pants with no shirts. Atu was muscular so he wanted everyone to see his shit. We were all skinny, but he was like ATLAS. We were all over the place playing. All over Chicago. Anything black or Afrocentric, Sun Drummer was called. We drummed for it. We would play with Darlene Blackburn. She was doing some Egyptian dance. The Sun Drummer was playing for all of these events because we were so Afrocentric.

This brother named Lionel Talburt became the founding Artistic Director for Muntu Dance Theatre of Chicago. Muntu Dance Theatre of Chicago in the early days was called UHCC Uniting Humanity through Cultural Creativity.

We had a jembe that Atu got from Ladji at the 1964/65 World's Fair in New York. Atu didn't really know how to play the jembe. He was making stuff up as we went along.

In 1974/75, after about 4-5 years into Sun Drummer he left and moved to Ghana and just left us there. We felt like we had enough experience to keep things going. When Atu left we felt like we wanted to know more about the jembe. We started learning jembe from the Senegambia drummers. They were part of the Senegalese Ballet that had come through performing. They were very hesitant to teach us because they felt like we looked too much like them and we could take work from them. We learned from the More Drums of Passion album since Ladji was playing jembe on that album.

By 1975 the jembe was hot and everyone wanted to play jembe. We all started bringing heaters everywhere with us. We were blowing out circuits because of these heaters. By this time, Atu returned from Ghana and wanted to take over control again. We were learning new stuff by then. Atu would never play any odd meters. 5, 7, 11, 13. Atu refused to play. He said I don't play any odd meters. I only play 6 and 4. We told him that these are rhythms that we have been learning. We had a drummer named Phil that was with Sun Ra. He made that kalimba that Maurice from Earth Wind and Fire used to play. Phil was teaching us physiology through the music. So Atu was similar but very different. So Phil had his philosophy and Atu had his. Atu thought that these odd meters would not extract the spirituality out of the music that he wanted. I said how do you say that when your whole philosophy was based on the number 7. That's an odd number. You find 7 in nature and all over. He still didn't see it and said I don't want to play. By then Muntu Dance Theatre of Chicago started and a lot of us were in Muntu Dance Theatre of Chicago.

Everything Atu did was a ritual. We would always be in a circle. We would have to pass things to the right in the circle to each other. He told us to learn how to write with your left hand if you were right handed so that you could be more even handed and balanced for drumming.

Adame Drame came to one of our shows and sent a message through one of our dancers that he wanted to meet us. He came back stage and I was taken a back because this is the guy that I had been listening to for some time now. I gave him my jembe to play and he had that thing SINGING! He said you guys play good, you just don't know what you are doing. I told him we needed someone like him to get us right. He went back to Europe where he was based and sent me a letter telling me that he wants to come back to the US to teach us. So we put things together and brought him to Chicago for 2 weeks to train us. He taught us the intricacies of jembe. Taught us rhythms. He got us on the right track. Eventually cats from Sun Drummer started cutting out. Mosheh left and went to Cleveland and was teaching Sun Drummer stuff. Mosheh was a trap drummer in the projects so he had a great sense of timing. Then he had those fat flat fingers; he used to get nice strong sounds out of the drums. So we brought him into the Sun Drummer. He wasn't really with the air drum concept and stuff like that. He said man I'm into jembe, I don't know no air drum man."

Atu (Harold) Murray: "The drum is a sacred instrument. This society makes people conform to non-conformity. Marcus Garvey, One Nation with One Aim, and One Destiny was my inspiration for naming Sun Drummer.

I started drumming at about eighteen/nineteen years old. I was in West Africa from 1969-1974. I played with Fela at the Afrikan Shrine. I was living in Dakar, Freetown, Abidjan, Monrovia, Nigeria, Ghana, and others.

My inspirations from drumming was Baba Chief Bey, and Ladji Camara; but Baba Chief Bey was my main inspiration. I got into drum making in New York with Chief Bey around 1969. When the drum was tuned to sound like a hand bell, then you knew you had the right sound.

The senior Sun Drummer consisted of Enoch, Atu, Atiba, Moussa, and Selah. I never charged any Sun Drummer any money for anything. I taught, but they never offered to pay me anything either. My first drum I ever made was called Mamo, a pickle barrel drum. Baba Chief Bey showed me how to make it with no nails, tar, and bands from the barrel. Chief Bey was my inspiration; anything he said do, I did it.

There was a need for my ancestors to speak through me. When your ancestors tell you hell or high water, you have to do it. You don't just learn a song and learn a culture. You have to be the culture."

Chapter 15

DC Drum and Dance

"The more we respect simplicity, the more we learn." Melvin Deal

One year I received a special call from my cousin Brian who was living in the Washington, D.C. area. He caught me up on his life and the family and wanted to know if I was still involved with my mission work in Ghana and my jembe drumming. Brian had experienced a close bout with death and came through it victorious. I was a bit sad I had not known about his illness while he was fighting the battle. I would have loved to offer up even just a prayer or encouraging words. I was glad to know he had a very strong support system around him.

At the time of this call, he told me he was in D.C. with some family he had wanted me to link up with for some time. Brian and I used to see each other each year at family reunions and when he visited family in my hometown of Mount Vernon, New York. Brian has always been the family guy linking up other family. He said, "We have cousins here in D.C. who have been wanting to talk to you since I told them what you do." I said, "Put them on the phone!"

Diallo was the first to get on the phone. He told me about the years he had been traveling back and forth to Ghana and could not believe we had never bumped into each other. I had been back and forth to Ghana for over two decades. Diallo had even worked with my close elders and the Minister of Tourism in Ghana to come up with a campaign called "The Year of Return." This campaign was one of Ghana's most successful tourism events. Ghana brought in over 1.5 million visitors from the Diaspora to Ghana. Diallo was instrumental in making that happen. He asked if there was anything he could do for me while in Ghana since he was headed there before my next trip. I spoke about the bulk organic moringa from my farm. I needed some brought over along with some drum skins I had waiting for me. He said "We got you, but I have to hand the phone over to my brother who is heavily involved in that stuff." Mahiri Edwards Keita jumped on the phone. "What's up Cuz?," he started off. I replied, "Peace Cuz!" He said, "First let me tell you I don't believe we have met face to face, but I know you because I looked up your group. I looked for the drummer who reminded me of what I would be doing, and it turned out to be you each time." I laughed and remembered a Mahiri

232

who Mamady Keita had adopted and took as his son. He affirmed my inquiry. He said, "Wait, how about this? Brian told me that your group's name is "Sounds Of Afrika?" I said, "Yes." He said, "Mamady named my group Farafina Kan. Do you know what that means in Malinke? SOUNDS OF AFRIKA!" I was blown away. He said, "I heard you telling my brother Diallo that you have a moringa farm in Ghana. I use moringa regularly to make natural products for people here in the D.C. community." I said, "My man, we have been living parallel lives and finally our paths have crossed." Of course, when I told him about the book I was working on, he told me he was working on a similar project on this subject matter. However, he was looking at producing a film rather than a book. Once Mahiri heard how far I had gone with my research, he told me that he would rather study my book when it was completed to know exactly how to put the film together. At that moment, he became a major source of encouragement and support for the book and for getting interviews for me.

Mahiri was blessed to be embraced by the elders and legends in the jembe world as well as the next generation of Jembefolas who established the new direction the jembe would follow. I interviewed Mahiri, and he spoke about his beginnings and identified the elders I needed to speak with for insight on the early jembe days in D.C.. Mahiri also interviewed his father, Mamady Keita, preliminarily to prepare for my personal interview with him. However, not long after Mahiri's interview, Mamady Keita passed away. We were so thankful we got his blessings for the book along with the few jewels he passed on before transitioning.

* * *

Founder of Farafina Kan, Trainer with Tam Tam Mandingue Djembe Academy, Son of Mamady Keita, Mahiri Edwards Keita, spoke about his training in Washington D.C.

Mahiri Edwards Keita: "I sat beneath the feet of the elders and understood the history before the 1980s when the separation of the continental Africans and African Americans really started. My mother understood the places I needed to be and who I needed to be with. I owe all of this to her.

Amadou Kouyate was dominant in my development. Baba Mamady Keita was dominant in my development. I went to Africa at thirteen/fourteen years of age. Baba Michael Norwood and Olukose Wiles were the first to give me structure as to how I was going to drum because I was in the classes with my mother who was a dancer. Baba Jemo really had the group that was family oriented and steeped in folklore; which was a carryover from Baba Michael and Olukose. They stamped in my head what Ladji taught; the jembe has a voice, the jembe talks, and the jembe has certain techniques for different rhythms.

Baba Melvin Deal started D.C.'s first African drum and dance group. If it weren't for Baba Aidoo, we would not have seen the second wave of Guinea drummers coming through the United States. Baba Aidoo brought the first wave of Guinea drummers through D.C.. He was the one that was shaping me to play Percussion De Guinea style.

Normandy Keita was the lead jembe player that Aidoo talked a lot about. His style was like Mamady and Famoudou.

Baba Baile is our Nummu in the D.C. area and taught so many people all over the United States how to carve out jembe.

Mamady Keita, yes he's my father. He gave me his last name and taught me all about the Manding culture, everything I needed to be one with his family. He was really revolutionary; like Sekou Toure was revolutionary."

Melvin Deal: "In 1956, 1957, 1958, 1959, we had the Association of Bongo and Congo Players. In 1958, a white lady went into the Peace Corp in Guinea and brought a jembe back and gave it to Barnett Williams. Prior to Barnett, Francis Leonard had the largest jembe in the area. Francis said it was a secret as to where he got it from. During this era, there were only a few playing jembe, Barnett and Tony Dunkinson.

Trailing in was Baba Aidoo in about 1972-1973. He started growing his company and imparting what they knew onto the artists of the company. When people came together back then, it wasn't about money; it was a pleasure for individuals to learn about African culture.

My group wanted to do Walosodon, and I said no; it's about slavery. They said they wanted to do it because everyone is doing it. So, I put the costume together, and they got attitude with me because the costume was just a piece of fabric in front and piece in the back."

Amaniyea Payne: "In 1974, I started commuting from Baltimore to Washington, D.C., which eventually I moved there and worked with The African Heritage Dancers and Drummers under the direction of Melvin Deal. Melvin was a walking librarian with knowledge of African history, art, music, dance, politics and spiritual sanctions; this cat was deep. In the repertoire of African Heritage we did a lot of Nigerian dances, Ghanian dances and dances from Sene-Gambia, Mali and Guinea. During that time, Melvin would invite all of the cultural groups that came to the D.C. area to present and share. And some of the names of the different styles of dances were different (for instance Ekonkon used to be referred to as Djolla) which wasn't wrong because it is a dance of the Djolla people....just a testament of how things evolve. Moving to D.C. advanced my studies and dwellings in the field. Melvin Deal showed me that he lived his art and that I too would find my niche. He saw I could coordinate the dancers and wardrobe well. He gave me those responsibilities which advanced my growth and knowledge. Mr. Deal was a smart man, he always gave up history and was very creative in managing. He made us deal with precision and exactness."

Baba Baile McKnight: "I first started with African Heritage and Baba Melvin Deal. The first day I went there, the dancers were moving up and down the dance floor. I had no idea that one day I was going to marry one of the women. These beautiful black women were moving up and down the dance floor. It was in the middle of the summer, in July. The studio was steamed up hot with sweat and funk and everything. Those drums were just blaring and the dance, all the dancers with those smiles and laughter on their faces. Talk about infectious. Oh my goodness. So I was back there the next day and eventually I moved away from painting to crafting drums.

Talking with several people who came to Washington D.C. to study dance with Baba Melvin Deal, he's a real task master. I've seen people come off the dance floor with tears in their eyes. I took a number of dance classes. I decided that I could handle the pain in my hands from drumming. But UH! I had pains in muscles in places that I didn't even know it was a muscle. It was just ACHING.

Baba Melvin said to me one day, "I have some drums over in this room. Do you think you can work on some of them?" So we went and looked in that room and there were about 30 drums in there...busted up. So I'm like, I'll put my hands and mind to it. Back then it was difficult to acquire good drums from Africa. We in America, the African American community through the dance companies and the drummers who gathered together on their own were beginning to direct their studies towards the Mande Empire, which consisted of the countries Guinea,

Ivory Coast, Senegal, Gambia, Guinea Bissau, Sierra Leone and Liberia. These are the countries where the culture of jembe is real big. That's the most dynamic of the drums. When the national dance companies from Guinea, Mali and Senegal came, part of their performances representing the Mande or Mandingo culture had jembe as a drum and everybody got addicted to jembe. So the demand was there but there was not a supply. So in 1972 we at African Heritage started to carve jembes.

In 1976, Baba Aidoo brought in Abdu "Abu" Kunta who was the premier jembe drummer with the Ballet of Senegal.

Significant names that were responsible for the jembe coming to America: Kathrine Dunham, Ladji Camara, and Mor Thiam.

Like Cheikh Ante Diop said, "The unification of Black Africa" if we are African Americans, then we are African. We are valid. Our culture is valid; an amalgam. We are valid here. We matter in our position in what we have contributed to the world. We have layers and layers of validity like the cabbage and the rose petal."

Founder of the African drum and dance troupe WO'SE, Baba Aidoo Holmes, spoke about his early drum and dance days in Washington D.C.

Baba Aidoo Holmes: "When I was young Melvin Deal's group was doing all of the African drum and dance stuff. I was also exposed to real African drum and dance at Melvin's studio because they were doing the Akan Akoms there at times.

I came through the 70s with Black Power movement and African awareness and committing to the culture. I was a music education major but then later I changed to a percussions major. The conga and Afro Cuban. But to me that was all Cuban. I went to Howard on a music scholarship. I wasn't feeling the Afro Cuban as much because it didn't give me the authentic African feeling. I started searching and heard some music from Ballets Africains. I was like this is off the chain!

Ballet Djoliba came to Howard University in 1970. Djoliba was President Sekou Toure's private group. Mamady Keita was in Ballet Djoliba. Even though Ballets Africains started in 1957/58, Djoliba became the President's personal group and gave them more resources. When they came and they finished everyone was standing up in that audience. No one had ever seen anything like that. After seeing Djoliba, I had Baba Baile to make me a jembe drum. I went in search to find drummers in the area that were playing jembe. I studied with Taiwo DuVall and his ex-wife

Aisha who had been with Pearl Primus. Taiwo was teaching me the ashiko drum to help me adapt African music to the plays we were doing at Howard. I was still looking for jembe players to learn from and there really wasn't any in my area until Ballet Senegal came to D.C.. They lit the place up. It was around 1978 and I brought Abdou Kunta from that Ballet back to D.C. for a residency. I started my group and had Abdou Kunta teaching the drumming. Abdou ended up bringing one of his partners Assan Kunta in who ended up setting up Kankouran. Assan started working with Melvin Deal initially. Assan Kunta took half of Melvin Deal's group along with Abdou Kunta and started Kankouran.

I went to FESTAC in Nigeria in 1977 and met Famoudou there. I bought my first traditional jembe from Famoudou at FESTAC. They had a big representation from D.C. at FESTAC."

Melvin Deal: I've been dancing in Washington D.C. for well over 50 years. It started in the late 1950s, early 1960s when as far as people would go with African culture was Afro Cuban. So, our first introduction to things African in Washington D.C. was from a Cuban Afro Cuban perspective. It was not from an African perspective which meant that as close as people would get to Africa was by way of Cuba and of course Candomblé, traditional religious shrines and things of that nature were one of the things that brought people together to want to know more about the culture because it was "exotic." I want everyone to know that it was primarily through Afro Cubana that the culture started in the District of Columbia.

It was me and Baba Ngoma, who was called Cal Joyner, who was the originator of the Association of Bongo and Congo Players and Associated Instruments. Associated instruments were the shekeres, the bells, the clave, the wash pan. Whistles, flutes and any instruments that were played with the bongo and congo orchestra that was not necessarily a percussion instrument.

Baba Ngoma the drummer would allow us to come and dance in the corner of their studio on 1407 U Street Northwest and we started coming together to do class. I would invite Africans that I knew who could show us something and then my research and tapes and whatever. My first trip to Africa was 1969. Prior to then, I had established the African Cultural Dancers which matriculated to African Heritage Dancers because there was a split in terms of the mindset of some of the people involved."

Chapter 16

International Afrikan American Ballet (IAAB)

"Folklore is living and breathing. It is the extension of the dynamics of culture."
Baba Walter Ince
~

I spent a considerable amount of time with Kehinde O'Uhuru learning his jembe system and training with him. He was the first drummer I had ever met who had a system in place for training people on the jembe. He was, and still is, a true warrior. I can recall during my early days of drumming with Kehinde in Harlem, many drummers used to battle about who was the better drummer, Kehinde or Walter Ince. The Ince Brothers had Brooklyn on LOCK with the jembe music. I never got the opportunity to get close to Walter or Greg Ince during those days because of how close I was to Kehinde and other drummers. However, when I started interviewing for this book, my relationship with the Ince brothers took flight. First, I interviewed Greg. We ate and laughed, and laughed and ate, and laughed some more. He gave me the lead on his brother's whereabouts, because to so many of us, it seemed like Walter Ince disappeared from the jembe drum and dance world. Walter Ince was one of the first lead jembe players to play that drum at a level where one could not tell if he was born in Africa or not. I found out that when he was initiated and made ocha (initiated as a Yoruba Priest), he was told to stop playing the drums publicly and that people had to drum for him. He was obedient which explained why so many of us had not seen or heard from Walter Ince.

Walter and I exchanged calls a few times before our interview. Then, I didn't hear from him for a month or so. I was concerned and reached out to find that he had been running so hard with his work that he became ill. Walter is Baba Walter, a Priest of Elegba as well as a Babalawo. He spends days and days on the mat with Ifa (Yoruba religion).

He runs hard all over the country performing his duties as a committed and dedicated Babalawo. When I asked what was wrong, he told me about the condition that had had him down for some time. I told him about the roots and herbs I grow on our farm in Ghana. He is a believer in natural medicine, so I sent him a medicine package. He later told me that nothing was working for him except for the medicine I had sent to him. He offered testimonials about each root and herb which let me know that he did indeed take them and had studied their effects in the process. We had previously had great conversations, but our relationship skyrocketed to another level after the roots and herbs. I believe he was appreciative of someone looking out for HIS well-being for a change.

I visited his home where (as I had with his brother, Greg), we laughed, ate, shared stories, and laughed and laughed some more. Baba Walter and Greg Ince have some of the best personalities. I love humor, and those two are walking comedy shows. As I listened to both of them talk about the legendary International Afrikan American Ballet they had founded, it became more and more apparent that they too helped create the model for what an African drum and dance group in America would look and sound like- up to the present day. Many African drum and dance troupes in America are not aware that the structure and functionality of their organizations exist as they do because of the International Afrikan American Ballet model.

* * *

Baba Walter Ince: "The founders of International Afrikan American Ballet were me, Greg Ince, Obara Wali, Denise Bey, Olukose Wiles, Mama Ince, Obba Babatunde, and Rhonda Morman. Olukose was one of the musical directors of International. The other was Obara Wali. We started International before Wali came in, but when he did come we made him musical director with Olukose. We had founding members of which I was one. Wali's discipline, his alignment with the kutiro and sabar, earned him the right to be one of our musical directors. He understood those two instruments really well. He was able to share that entire concept with us in a way that was enormously helpful, and helped us integrate into what we were doing as a whole. Olukose was really the principal person with the orisha music. I was around, but I was still hanging out with Putillo and Julito Picasso. Sometimes nationalism is our biggest enemy because it creates another side of prejudice within us. "Oh, you are not Cuban so you could not possibly know anything." Olukose brought me into the orisha music. He had us go around and check out others who was doing orisha music. He had us go check out Teddy Holiday one time. Olukose said I was to focus on Teddy playing the omile, let Neil focus on the okokalon, and he would focus on the Iya. I was looking at Teddy's hands, and I was like I am NOT going to get this by just watching this guy.

After the bembe was over Olukose asked, "So what did you get?" I said, "I got the fact that he was playing the hell out of that drum." He said,

"You mean you didn't get anything?" I said, "Uhhhh, as a matter of fact...NO! Look, I may not be the fastest learner amongst us. I'll keep at it. I hope he slows down so I can get some of these parts!" LOL. I tell people attitude is the be all and end all of everything. Do you really want to do something? Cause if you really want to do something, an ancestor will come and help you to be successful to do this thing.

The very beginning International Dancers were Denise Bey, Obba Babatunde, Baba Akin Babatunde, Judy, Joanne, Rhonda, and Greg Ince. In the beginning, when we set up International, we had founders, musical directors, and a dance director: male and female. Wali and Mubdi helped to bring the business arm. Wali was a major player in incorporating International. Ma Ince was biologically my mother. I went out to California to visit a brother that used to be like a groupie of International back in the day. He had my mother's photo on his altar. He gave a powerful testimony about the impact my mother had on his life. When International went on the road, my mother went out on the road with us. All of the men used to stay in one room and the ladies in another. On one occasion we were all up late laughing and talking, and my mother came and knocked on the door and said, "Don't you all have to get up early tomorrow? You need to go to sleep." We all went to bed and were still up talking. Olukose had me by about ten years. Olukose said, "Man I'm forty-two years old and somebody just sent me to bed and I WENT!" It was hilarious, but it was true. The costumes that International was known for was done by my mother and Rhonda. International was the company to start the cowrie shell dance tops. One of the things that made International special too was that we rehearsed in the costumes. We wore traditional clothing all the time. So, when we performed it wasn't strange to perform in the costume garments.

"FOLKLORIC ADVANCEMENT." We were doing Walosodon and Rhonda Morman wanted to have this particular step come after this other step. The problem was you had to wait for the break. It looked odd after the break with the dancers' legs still up in the air. They asked what can we do with that? We said what can be done you have to wait for the break to change the movement. Then Olukose Wiles Ibaye said let's just cut the break in half; let's shift the one. We knew what it was. By cutting the break in half, we were able to shift the one, and it worked. It looked real slick. This brother Jabel Gay had a Ballet company in Senegal; Les Ballet de Jabel Gay in Senegal. He saw it, and it blew his mind. He went back to Senegal and used the very same thing in his ballet, but he gave us credit for it. It was reported in Senegal media, and he said that he got this from The Ballet in America; not a ballet in America but THE Ballet, the International Afrikan American Ballet. It was really wonderful; the difference between folklore and absolute tradition. Absolute tradition says you have to do it exactly this way. Folklore is living and breathing; it is the extension of the dynamics of culture. There's that story about the family that always split the turkey and you ask, why it is that? The elders say because that's the way we do it - you don't cook a turkey whole. In this family, we cut the turkey in half and cook them in two different pans. Going back a few generations, the great great great grandmother didn't have a pan that could accommodate the full turkey. So, it was either get a new pan which was not financially feasible, or cut the turkey in half and put one half in one pan and the other half in another pan. It wasn't the ideal situation, but everyone got fed. It worked. After a generation or two, no one knows why this was done. We could afford a full pan, but the elders are saying this is what grandma did so this is what we do. A valid point, but there is also the issue of things moving and advancing predicated upon the necessity of the moment.

Obara Wali is a deep dude man because when we started playing the sabar, he said, "Look, I have some inspirations on how this drum is played." Ain't none of us been over to Senegal, and here is this Negro from the Bronx saying that he got some inspirations. At this point, the only thing we can do is to go with it or not. He said, "I have notation patterns for the drum and music. Here are the rhythms." We studied that on Saturday mornings at six in the morning for about one and a half years at Wali's house in the Bronx; but SIX in the morning on Saturday?? You really have to love what you doing cause otherwise that's a teensy bit early. LOL. Some years later, we are doing some stuff, and here comes the griots that were working with Alex Haley. People think that the griots play only the kora and balafon and that's it, but they don't. They actually have several instruments; one of which is the sabar drum. So, we do a performance, and after, the griots come to us ask us who is our teacher. We point to Wali and say well this brother has taught us pretty much everything we know on the sabar. Then, they ask Wali, who is YOUR teacher? He says I sort of got it from inspiration. They looked at him strangely and said the way you play, people don't play like that anymore; only the oldest people play like that. We showed them the notation that he taught us. Then, they showed us their notations. They had similar notations to the ones we used, and there was one figure that was different from what we used, but you could see how the one we used could have become that one. They were that close in terms of shape and stuff. My take on this is that the ancestors are real. These were dead people that came and gave this to him. They didn't know the new way, they only knew what they knew."

Greg Ince: "All dance and drum groups after International pulled from International's repertoire and choreography. Rhonda was the dance captain and learned all of the songs from her trips to Senegal. Chuck Davis and her would butt heads often because he and other groups would take Rhonda's choreography and songs and not be accurate with it. Hazel was always going to Guinea so we got the Guinea style dance from Hazel and the Senegalese style dance from Rhonda.

International Afrikan American Ballet set the standards. Chuck Davis used to travel around to the different African dance and drum groups when Dance Africa was starting to tape the different dances, songs, and rhythms to come up with his choreography and repertoire."

International African American Ballet
Front Row(Left to Right): LaVerne "LV" Anduze, John Blanford, Akin Babatunde, Hazel Starks Bryant
Back Row (Left to Right): Rosa Conners, Greg Ince, Wali Rahman, Olukose Wiles, Sauti Mills, Walter Ince.
Middle Row (kneeling): Obba Babatunde and Lauren Ince
Source: Obba Babatunde

International African American Ballet
Front Row (Left to Right): Sauti Mills, Hazel Starks Bryant, LaVerne "LV" Anduze, Rosa Conners, Lauren Ince.
Back Row (Left to Right): Walter Ince, Wali Rahman, Olukose Wiles, Greg Ince
Source: Obba Babatunde

Founded in 1977 as a collaborative effort by Obara Wali Rahman, Olukose Wiles, Hazel Starks Bryant, John Blanford, Rhonda Morman, and Walter Ince, International Afrikan American Ballet (IAAB) quickly became legendary in the African dance world. The company was appreciated for the exquisite detail in its music, costumes, choreography, folklore, and movement idioms. The founders of the IAAB studied or performed with Ladji Camara, Olatunji, and their students.1

Rhonda Morman: "We had a meeting at a restaurant in the Bronx and I said there are groups that are like 'super groups'. Next thing I know, this person brought someone in and that person brought someone in and so on. I didn't bring anyone in because I didn't know anyone. My circle was not into what I was into. Denise Bey was the one who gave the group the name "International African American Ballet". Olukose and the men wanted me to be a Director. It was all men that were in Supervisory roles. Olukose and I used to battle but he spoke up to the Directors that I should be a Director as well since I did so much studying and teaching."

Kobla Mensa Dente: "Most people were using congas for African music from the sixties to early 70s to mid 70s until groups like International Afrikan American Ballet as well as many others starting using the jembes. Walter Ince could bring down the walls when he played jembe. It was jaw dropping when you saw those guys play. Olukose and other talented drummers were playing jembe. Obara Wali who mastered the sabar drum orchestra, brought a whole new dimension of African drumming and dance. Back in those days of my youth, we all just thought all this was normal."

Kehinde Donaldson: "When I left Ladji, I played with International Afrikan American Ballet. Some of the drummers that were there when I got there were Joe Barnes and Butch. Rhonda Morman was the Director of International and Joe Barnes was the lead drummer at that time."

Renee Abayomi Goodall: "When I witnessed my first performance of the International Afrikan American Ballet, I was blown away. They looked, sounded and professionally performed just like the National Ballet of Senegal."

Baba Billy Bungo: "I played with a lot of different dance troupes. My favorite group was the International Afrikan American Ballet. It was because of Neil Clarke that I played with the International Afrikan American Ballet. Neil Clarke decided he wanted to go on the road and make some real money. So, I was his replacement."

Amaniyea Payne: "I moved to New York in 1976. Even though I knew Baba Chuck and Baba Ishangi, I resided with the Nago Incense Family; Iya Tima (IAAB dancer) and Baba Delhi Fann and ended up becoming a member of the International Afrikan American Ballet (IAAB) during my stay in New York. Neil Clark (IAAB drummer) was playing with Norman Connors at that time as his percussionist. Norman's former wife (Dr. Rosa Kincaid) was also a dancer with IAAB. I remember Norman Connors performing at Howard University when I lived there (it was Norman Connors and Jon Lucien) and in the show there was a segment called "The Dance of Life". It was powerful, as a matter of fact it reminded me of the Guinea Ballet when I saw them flying in 1972...and all I could say is I WANT TO DO THAT. So the people who performed with The Dance of Life was Obba Babatunde, Baba Akin Babatunde, Hazel Starks Bryant, Denise Bey, Rhonda Morman, John Blandford, Olukose Wiles, Walter Ince, Rosa Connors, Neil Clarke, and Laverne Anduze. I was blown away and again, the search was ON, soon afterwards I moved to New York.

I was blown away when I went to my first International (IAAB) rehearsal. I truly give thanks for being a part of that dynamic company. From my perspective, I think that company served as a catalyst and inspiration for many of the African dance groups in North America and Africa as well. This company made many other companies aspire to be as authentic as possible while presenting dances from the village and bringing it to the western stage while maintaining tradition and keeping the "Africanness" inside. IAAB studied, I mean really studied. We didn't want to deal with the "Bastardization " of the culture. Being in IAAB also ignited another spirit within me. Sometimes dancers can do lots of stuff and do them well but your mind has to catch up to where your body is. We're talking about spirit. Talking about Ancestral Energy. Talking about culturalization. Talking about politics. We had the opportunity to perform all over, as well as working and representing as Cultural Ambassadors with the Senegalese Tourist Bureau; all of this inside of dance and drumming."

Rhonda Morman: "We (International) got hit from the modern dance people. They would say, "Oh International can't be a ballet." I said, Ballet is French for 'dance'. We had prominent modern dancers who wanted to dog us. But we had people like Talley Beatty, who had a signature piece called "Mourner's Bench," and came to everything we did. Talley was one of the Grand Dons of modern dance. He used to come to see us in his tuxedo. He called me in the middle of the night one night. He said, "Rhonda Darling, what they don't realize is that this is an AMERICAN African dance company.

One of the things I noticed was that the so called vanguards of African dance and drumming were not traveling to Africa. Who goes to Africa 17 times. I did. Those of us who were traveling to Africa were inspiring others to travel over to Africa to learn. I couldn't understand why these people never went to Africa and were perpetrating the fraud. It doesn't mean going to a dance class. You have to absorb the history and culture. You have to absorb the culture and what the people are doing. You have to absorb the little girl sitting on the side of the road...that's singing a song. What's that song?

When I was making my mark on the African dance scene I wanted to bring authenticity. I used to see dance companies in New York and dance companies in Africa when I used to go. I can remember performing and a stage hand came to me and said your group doesn't belong here with these other groups. Your group is much different. Your group looks like it came straight from Africa. John Blandford and I used to go see other companies from around the world perform. Everything looked clean and authentic. When we watched the American Ballet Theatre and saw that they didn't look different from the Ballet Theatre from England and this place and that place. Why was it that African dance groups looked different from the groups in Africa? It wasn't clean. When I started teaching African dance, everyone had to wear lapas. We found out what a FULL lapa looked like. No tights underneath a lapa with it cut and your leg hanging out. Hazel and I hated using the word 'costume'. We called our wears 'clothes'. When we learned about various cultures in Africa, people were not wearing costumes. They were wearing clothes. So if we are transplants from Africa and we are displaying our African culture on stage then we should be saying African clothes rather than costumes.

A lot of people copied a lot of things we (International Afrikan American Ballet) did. Cowrie shell bras. We had that. That came from us because Ann bought one of the bras from one of the dancers from Les Ballets Africains, then we redid it. I said why aren't we doing that? So when people stole what we did, which they did; or copied what we did, Olukose would say "Oh no it's Africa." I would say, it's Africa in my HOUSE. Africa in my ROOM. I saw women doing baby naming ceremonies in Africa. Village stuff. I said look at that, it's beautiful. I took that inspiration and went home and started writing stuff and then...I see it. Don't tell me you got it from Africa. African dance is choreography. Someone choreographed that and that was ME."

Author's Epilogue

In order to know where you are going, you must first know where you came from. Today, the jembe appears to be the most popular and most played hand drum on the globe. I am not here to judge or throw shade at any of the self-proclaimed Jembefolas or master jembe players all over the world. I want to encourage jembe drummers and enthusiasts to learn all of the available knowledge and history about this dynamic drum. What a phenomenal privilege during my interview with Nummu Amara Kante to witness him identifying the parts of the jembe in his native tongue, Malinke. I was moved at the many sentiments that Amara gave during his interview about his Manding elder, Famoudou Konate. A defining moment for me came when Amara explained that it was Famoudou Konate who started the "no hole" tuning system on the jembe in West Africa. It made perfect sense given Famoudou's travels and interactions with 'Black American' drummers. After Famoudou successfully copied their tuning system, Amara, other Jembefolas and drum makers in West Africa would come to the conclusion that he started this new tuning system. Even more passionate than I could have dreamed, Famoudou Konate, the Grandmaster, told me during one of his interviews that without a doubt it was Black Americans who invented the "no hole" tuning system for the jembe and dundun drums. That simple statement defined the tone in which I approached this publication. When I think of the millions of people in the world who play jembe, I have to ask how many actually know this jewel? Does anyone know that Black Americans helped to improve the design of the jembe drum? How many know the names of the drummers who engineered the new design of the jembe drum during the 1970s and 1980s? This publication highlighted Chief Bey, Yomi Yomi Awolowo, and Ron "Balogun" Love as the pioneers who channeled the Nummu spirit and collectively gifted the world with a new and improved jembe drum.

Taiwo DuVall gave us insight on Moses "Machine Gun" Miannes and the ashiko drum. We learned that Moses Miannes' teachings set the stage for Taiwo, Chief Bey, Montego Joe, and Babafemi to carry the baton and usher in a new revolutionary drumming era-one that spoke of self-determination and mainstream acceptance. It's no coincidence that these were the drummers who eventually created the sound that made Olatunji's Drums of Passion a global success.

I want the reader to know that there is no dancer without the drummer and no drummer without the dancer. Moses Miannes' drumming was pushed to the higher heights because of dancers like Asadata Dafora, Pearl Primus, and Katherine Dunham. It was Katherine Dunham who encouraged both Ladji Camara and Mor Thiam to bring their jembe drums to America in the 1960s. We must give thanks to Ms. Dunham for her foresight at the time to see that America was ready for the jembe drum.

For years I listened to my grandfather playing Miles Davis, Art Blakey, Dizzy Gillespie and John Coltrane albums when I was young. I eventually inherited those albums and my grandfather's reel to reels with hours of jazz music upon his passing. If I had only known back then how close to the African drums these jazz artists were. How they actually shared their earnings to help sustain Babatunde Olatunji's studio in Harlem.

We learned from Ajaibo Waldrond who danced with Dinizulu for over forty years how important Dinizulu was to the African American community and to the world of African drum and dance. Not only did he live out his Akan Chieftancy right in Queens, New York, but he also started the first African American African drum and dance troupe.

These elders who were so giving of their stories and journeys shared many jewels which I will forever treasure. I think often how my advisors, Bradley Simmons and Baba David Coleman, told me that any African drum and dance troupe formed after the mid 1970s had to have come from one of the major pioneers including Chief Bey, Babatunde Olatunji, Ladji Camara, Saka Acquaye, Katherine Dunham or Dinizulu. These pioneers produced legends like Arthur Hall, LaRocque Bey, Melvin Deal, and Chuck Davis. They all opened the way for African drum and dance groups in America today.

I am taking some quiet time to reflect on the many hours of research I have completed, the miles of traveling, and the many interviews I have conducted with elders and ancestors. We lost legends during my twenty plus years of putting this book together. One ancestor who left a strong impression on my soul was Baba David Coleman. He and I maintained a close relationship for years before this book. I could always count on him to give me positive jewels that would make me proud to be an African born in America. He shared so much with so many. He was a great motivator. Baba David was passionate about African Americans knowing their contributions to the world of African drum and dance. As soon as I approached him about this book, he supported and encouraged me as if it were his own project. He was the first to paint the picture for me about the scene in America when the jembe first arrived. Along with offering to share his treasure chest of knowledge with me, he had me contact Bradley Simmons. As such, I discovered Bradley Simmons is the scholar on the history of African drumming in America. After days of listening to and documenting Baba David Coleman's storytelling, I went to my hotel room and stared at myself for about an hour straight. I was convinced that my research time with Baba David had aged me about ten years. I felt like my vessel could not hold another jewel from Baba. He opened up his vault filled with archives and bathed me with blessing after blessing. The pleasure and the honor was all mine. However, his journey was too vast for me to capture all of what he offered me. I'm sure he had FORGOTTEN way more in his lifetime than all of the knowledge I had gained throughout mine. It was his dream for African Americans to leave our own unique legacy in this world of African drumming and dance. He drummed with the pioneers and the legends in the game. He was and still is respected for his contribution to this art form. He inspired and encouraged me to tell this story.

The last time I was with him face to face, we presented to his Obatala and played shekeres and drums he had created himself. When we finished, he looked at me and said, "People don't know who we are and what we did. You have been chosen as the keeper of our story and the disseminator of our journey. This is a gift for you and no one else. If you go around telling everyone about all of these jewels, then that's just bragging. Package our story for the people to learn and keep the special gifts sacred and just for you. MY MAN!"

Appendix

There were many people who assisted with this publication. The following individuals, who are elders (and some now ancestors), trusted me with their precious stories and experiences. I would like to offer my sincere gratitude to these individuals for their contributions to this publication through their interviews, support, encouragement, gifts from their archives, and spiritual presence.

*Listed in Alphabetical order:

Iya Darcel Abel – Darcel, a Yoruba Priestess, studied African dance with LaRocque Bey and Chuck Davis. She learned Nigerian folklore from Babatunde Olatunji. Darcel performed with Ladji Camara, Shombe Yembe, and LaRocque Bey.

Saka Acquaye – A Ghanaian artist, musician and performing artist who was responsible for bringing traditional African dance and drumming to Philadelphia, PA. He produced an album that was recorded in 1959 with mostly African American artists as the musicians and singers. Saka influenced Arthur Hall in the area of African dance and drumming. His protégé was African American drummer, Bobby Crowder.

Abdul Aziz Ahmed – Abdul Aziz Ahmed a/k/a "Papa Aziz" was a protégé of Ladji Camara. He studied jembe and performed with Ladji in the early 1970s.

Baba Yomi Yomi Awolowo – Baba Yomi Yomi, initiated as a Yoruba Priest in the 1960s is a singer, drummer and is said to be one of the pioneers of the no hole system of making and tuning jembe and dundun drums. He was one of the original drummers with the Chuck Davis Dance Company.

"Nii Ayi" Nana Obrafo Yaw Wofa Asiedu - One of Ladji Camara's first jembe drum students, Nii Ayi was one of Philadelphia's first jembe teachers. His sister was married to Baba Ishangi who taught Nii Ayi how to make drums using the Ghanaian peg system.

Baba Akin Babatunde – Baba Akin was one of Ladji Camara's early principal dancers. He is the brother of Obba Babatunde.

Obba Babatunde – Hollywood/Broadway actor, dancer, singer, and musician; Obba Babatunde was Ladji Camara's first lead dancer. Obba was also one of the original founding members of the International Afrikan American Ballet.

Harry Belafonte - Activist, singer, musician and actor, Harry Belafonte was instrumental in developing Guinea's Ballets Djoliba with then-President Sekou Toure.

Abishai Ben Reuben - Father of the author, Abishai was one of the original drummers for the Akosua African Dance and Drum Troupe.

Mustapha Berete - Malinke translator for interviews conducted in Guinea for this project. Mustapha is one of the top importers of jembes and dunduns from Guinea.

Denise Bey - Denise was Ladji Camara's first dance student and an original member of the International Afrikan American Ballet. Daughter of the legendary "Chief Bey."

James Hawthorne "Chief Bey" - Yoruba Priest, drummer, singer, Broadway performer, and drum maker. Chief is said to be the founder of the 'no hole' tuning system on the ashiko, jembe and dundun drums.

Baba Billy Bungo - Yoruba Priest of Ifa, drummer, singer, and fire eater. Billy Bungo played with many of the early African drum and dance troupes in New York and New Jersey.

Daryl "Kwasi" Burgee - Arthur Hall's first lead jembe drummer in his group, the Afro American Dance Ensemble. Kwasi saw much success as a drummer and percussionist with premier singers and musicians coming out of Philadelphia in the 70s and 80s.

Baba Oba Ilu "Skip" Burney - Long time student of Orlando "Puntilla" Rios, Skip Burney is said to be the most skilled African American Afro Cuban drummer.

Baba Richard Byrd - Yoruba Priest and drummer. Richard Byrd studied and played drums with Babatunde Olatunji, Chuck Davis, and Ladji Camara.

Ladji Camara - The first Jembefola to play and teach jembe in America. He was the lead jembe drummer after Fadouba Oulare for Les Ballets Africains.

Yamoussa Camara - The first lead jembe drummer for Les Merveilles de Guinea.

Baba David Coleman – Yoruba Priest of Obatala, singer, drummer, and drum maker. Baba David Coleman studied and played drums with Chief Bey, Babatunde Olatunji, and Chuck Davis' Drum and Dance Troupe. Baba David was also a scholar of African and Afro Cuban drumming in America.

Bolokada Conde – The lead Jembefola for Les Percussions de Guinea after the great Noumoudy Keita.

Nouma Coulbaly – Manding Elder from Siguiri, Guinea who was related to the original makers of the Bada drum.

Bobby Crowder – One of the pioneers of African drumming in Philadelphia. He was one of Saka Acquaye's first drum students. He was the founder of Kulu Mele African Dance and Drum Ensemble.

Asadata Dafora – A Sierra Leonean multidisciplinary musician and dancer who is credited with forming the first African drum and dance troupe in America in the early 1930s.

Chuck Davis – Baba Chuck Davis was a dancer and choreographer who focused on traditional African dance accompanied by jembe music. Baba Chuck was the founder of DanceAfrica, the Chuck Davis Dance Company, and the African American Dance Ensemble.

Melvin Deal – Founder of the African Heritage Dancers, Baba Melvin was known as the Godfather of African dance in Washington D.C..

Kobla Mensa Dente – A long time member and drummer of The Dinizulu African Dancers and Drummers Troupe.

Iya Yvonne Dickerson – Yoruba Priestess and Wife of Baba Ed James, the first African American initiated as a Priest of Shango.

Gus Solomons Nana Yao Opare Dinizulu I – Founder of the Dinizulu Cultural Arts Institute and The Dinizulu African Dancers and Singers Troupe, the first African American African drum and dance troupe in America.

Akosua Nsia Oparebeah Panyin Floretta Donald – Student of Katherine Dunham. Akan Priestess initiated by Nana Yao Opare Dinizulu I. Founder of Akosua African Dance and Drum Troupe.

Kehinde Donaldson – Student of Ladji Camara and one of his only students who saw Ladji Camara perform with Les Ballets Africains for the first time in America in 1959.

Katherine Dunham – One of the pioneers of African dance in America. Katherine Dunham created her own style called the "Dunham Technique." Dunham was responsible for encouraging Jembefola Ladji Camara to come and stay in America; she also brought jembe drummer Mor Thiam to America from Senegal.

Thomas "Taiwo" DuVall – A student of Moses Miannes, the drummer who brought the ashiko drum to America in the 1930s. Taiwo was responsible for hiring the drummers who played the music on Babatunde Olatunji's highly successful first album, Drums of Passion.

Baba Don Eaton (Babatunde) – One of the premier drummers for the revolutionary group of poets from the 1960s and 1970s, The Last Poets.

Mahiri Edwards Keita – Founder of Farafina Kan African drum and dance orchestra and Son of the legendary Jembefola Mamady Keita.

Baba Kenneth Fauntleroy – Yoruba Priest and Drummer. One of the elder drummers from the Philadelphia African drum and dance community.

Ayanna Fredricks – Choreographer, dancer, singer and musician for Calabash African drum and dance group out of Brooklyn, NY.

Leonard Baba "Doc" Gibbs, Jr. – One of the elder drummers from the Philadelphia African drum and dance community. He is also known for being the musical director for Emeril Live! hosted by chef Emeril Lagasse. Known as "Baba Doc" in the Yoruba/Orisa community, Gibbs was a Priest of Obatala for more than 35 years and was one of the tradition's highly respected and revered sacred bata drummers.

Baba Ralph Ogundare Glover – Yoruba Priest, drummer and singer. One of Baba Ed James' godchildren and students.

Gene Golden – Singer and Afro Cuban percussionist. One of the most knowledgeable African American scholars on Afro Cuban music.

Renee Abayomi Goodall – Dancer, singer, percussionist and choreographer. Lead dancer for Calabash African drum and dance group out of Brooklyn, N.Y. Co-founded Nevada's first African drum and dance groups with the author, CODAME (Children of the Diaspora African Music Ensemble).

Arthur Hall - Akan Priest, Dancer, Choreographer and Teacher. Founder of Arthur Hall Afro American Dance Ensemble. He was known as the Godfather of African dance in Philadelphia.

Jubal Harris - Percussionist, drum maker and teacher. Jubal is one of the Sun Drummer members from the Ohio chapter.

Baba Aidoo Holmes - Yoruba Priest and drummer. Baba Aidoo is the founder of WO'SE African Dance Theatre in Washington D.C..

Eric Sekou Hylton - Drummer and drum maker. Sekou was a member of Calabash African drum and dance group out of Brooklyn, N.Y.

Gregory Ince - Dancer, drummer, singer, choreographer. Greg studied with Ladji Camara and was a founding member of the International Afrikan American Ballet.

Baba Walter Ince - Yoruba Priest, Drummer and Teacher. Walter was one of Ladji Camara's early students of the jembe. He was a founding member of the International Afrikan American Ballet.

Baba Ed James - Baba Ed was the first African American initiated as a Yoruba Priest of Shango in the year 1960 in Cuba. He was considered by most Babalawos as the Grandmaster in America. Baba Ed was a teacher and Godfather of the Author.

Clifford "Peache" Jarman - Yoruba Priest and drummer. "Peache" was Robert Crowder's first student and an early member of Kulu Mele in Philadelphia. Peache was music director and teacher for Arthur Hall's African Dance Ensemble (c. 1968-1979).

Amara Kante - Amara is from a family line of Kante Nummus (Blacksmiths). He trained on the jembe and in the mysteries of Nummu in Guinea, West Africa.

Fodeba Keita - Guinean dancer, musician, writer, playwright, composer, and politician. Founder of the first professional African theatrical troupe, Theatre Africain. Co-founder of the legendary group Les Ballets Africains de Guinea.

Mamady Keita - One of the most popular Jembefolas to date. Original lead drummer for Ballet Djoliba. Founder of Tam Tam Mandingue D'Jembe Academy.

Walter Eugene Oba Efuntola Oseijeman Adelabu Adefunmi King - One of the first African Americans to be initiated as a Yoruba Priest in Cuba in 1959 alongside Chris Oliana. Founder of the Yoruba village in South Carolina called Oyotunji Village. He was a dancer and performing artist with Katherine Dunham and served as Dinizulu's first Narrator for their theatrical productions.

Famoudou Konate - Currently the oldest active Jembefola in Guinea. Known as the Grandmaster of the jembe. Famoudou took over lead jembe and Musical Director for Les Ballets Africains after Ladji Camara left the group.

Ronald Balogun Love - Yoruba Priest, drummer, and drum maker. One of Chuck Davis' first lead jembe players. Balogun had studied with Ladji Camara as well and was very close to Baba Yomi Yomi Awolowo.

Garvin Masseaux - A multi-talented musician. Garvin Masseaux played alongside Sonny Morgan and Bobby Crowder during the early days of African drumming and dance in Philadelphia. Garvin Masseaux was a member of the Saka Acquaye music ensemble.

John McGill - Percussionist and one of the original members of the Ohio chapter of The Sun Drummer.

Baba Baile McKnight - Yoruba Priest, drummer, drum maker, teacher, artist. Baba Baile is the founder of Baile's African Drum Works and was a drummer and drum maker for Melvin Deal's African Heritage Dancers in the early 1970s.

Moses Miannes - Baba Moses was said to have introduced the ashiko drum to America in the 1930s. He was an ashiko drummer from Nigeria who played for the great dancer and choreographer Asadata Dafora for years as his lead drummer. Moses also taught Taiwo DuVall how to play and make ashiko drums.

Mosheh Milon - Mosheh was one of the early members of The Sun Drummer and a founding member of the Muntu Dance Theater of Chicago.

Sonny Morgan - Sonny Morgan played drums alongside Garvin Masseaux and Bobby Crowder during the early days of African drumming and dance in Philadelphia. Sonny Morgan was a member of the Saka Acquaye music ensemble. Sonny also played on Babatunde Olatunji's second album, More Drums of Passion.

Rhonda Morman – One of the founding members and principal dancer, choreographer for International Afrikan American Ballet.

Basimatah Muhammad – Dancer and singer. Basimatah was Akosua Panyin's first dance student when she started classes and her troupe in Mount Vernon, NY in 1967.

Harold Atu Murray – Drummer, drum maker, teacher. Atu is the founder of The Sun Drummer out of Chicago.

Ione Nash – Dancer, Choreographer, Teacher, Martial Arts Instructor. Ione Nash was one of Saka Acquaye's first dancers in his performing group alongside long time dance partner Arthur Hall. Ms. Nash taught dance classes well into her 80s and is a legend in the dance world in Philadelphia.

Baba Michael Norwood – Yoruba Priest and drummer. Baba Michael is one of the elder drummers from the New Jersey African drum and dance community.

Michael Babatunde Olatunji – Nigerian singer, drummer, and activist. Olatunji recorded one of the most successful African music albums in history in 1959 called Drums of Passion. Olatunji was the founder of the Olatunji Center for African Culture in Harlem, NY in the mid-1960s.

Kehinde Stewart O'Uhuru – Played and studied with Babatunde Olatunji since an early teen in Harlem, NY. He learned his drumming from Taiwo DuVall at the Olatunji Center for African Culture. Kehinde is the founder of the El Shabazz D'Jembe Orchestra.

Abiodun Oyewole – Founding member for the revolutionary group of poets from the 1960s and 1970s, The Last Poets.

Amaniyea Payne – One of the dancers for International Afrikan American Ballet. Amaniyea also studied and performed with Babatunde Olatunji, Chuck Davis, and Shombe Yembe. She eventually took over as Artistic Director of Muntu Dance Theatre of Chicago, one of the longest running African drum and dance troupes in America.

Dr. Pearl Primus – Known as the first black modern dancer in America. Dr. Pearl Primus was a dancer, choreographer, actor, and anthropologist. After traveling to Africa in the late 1940s, Pearl Primus dedicated her life to African dance. She depicted the social and political limitations placed on blacks. Dr. Primus was the founder of Primus-Borde School of Primal Dance in New York City.

Carole Robinson - Dancer, singer, costume maker. One of the original dancers for the Chuck Davis Dance Company in New York City. Wife of the elder drummer, Baba Yomi Yomi.

Yaa Serwaa Oparebeah Pinota Janet Rush - Daughter and dance student of the late Akosua Payin, founder of the Akosua African Dance and Drum Troupe.

Ayishah Vivian Lewis Shabazz - Ms. Ayishah Shabazz studied and danced with Dr. Pearl Primus; later she also performed with Babatunde Olatunji. Ms. Lewis Shabazz is the Ex Wife of Thomas "Taiwo" DuVall.

Jalal Sharriff - Drummer and drum maker. Jalal studied and performed with Ladji Camara, Shombe Yembe, and extensively with Chuck Davis.

Bradley Simmons - Bradley Simmons is considered to be one of the foremost scholars on African drumming in America. He is a Drummer, Teacher, and one of LaRocque Bey's first drummers. He studied and performed with Ladji Camara, Olukose Wiles, Chief Bey, Chuck Davis, and Pablo Landrum.

Eugene Osborne Smith - Mr. Osborne Smith was one of the first African drummers featured in Broadway productions. He learned ashiko drumming from Moses Miannes and played with Asadata Dafora, Dr. Pearl Primus, and Katherine Dunham.

Mor Thiam - Mor Thiam is the second drummer from West Africa to bring the jembe to America. He arrived in America in the late 1960s and traveled around the nation with Katherine Dunham and ultimately worldwide drumming, teaching the jembe, and promoting jembe music. Mor Thiam is the Father of the world renowned musician and singer, Akon.

President Ahmed Sekou Toure - President Sekou Toure was the first president of the Republic of Guinea in 1958. He was known for his love of culture and the arts. President Toure orchestrated the development of 2 legendary African drum and dance groups from Guinea, Les Ballets Africains and Ballets Djoliba.

Moussa Traore – Drummer and Teacher. One of Mali's most skilled and popular Jembefolas.

Ajaibo Waldrond – Long-time dancer with Dinizulu dance and drum group and dancer at the Katherine Dunham School. Mr. Waldrond was among the first to dance to the jembe when Les Ballets Africains brought it to America in 1959.

Babu Atiba Walker – Drummer and drum maker. Babu Atiba was one of the early members of The Sun Drummer in Chicago and a founding member of the Muntu Dance Theater of Chicago.

Sam Watson – The first and only African American to perform on stage with Les Ballets Africain De Guinea.

Abdur Rahman Wheeler – Abdur Rahman was the first drummer to play for Akosua African Dance and Drum Troupe. Rahman studied drums with Chuck Davis, Yomi Yomi and Balogun Love.

Baba Tony Olukose Wiles – Yoruba Priest, drummer, and teacher. Baba Olukose was one of Ladji Camara's first drum students. He was a founding member of International Afrikan American Ballet. He was known for his stilt walking and disciplined training with his students.

John Wilkie - Mr. Wilkie met Robert Crowder in Philadelphia and studied batá under him, as well as Garvin Masseaux, master Cuban drummer Kikiyu (Enriqué Adamo Admiral) and a circle of others. At that time, in the 1970s, Mr. Wilkie became a member of the Kulu Mele African American Dance Ensemble. Currently, he is music director of the ensemble.

Enoch Williamson – Drummer and drum maker. One of the first members of The Sun Drummer of Chicago. He was also one of the founding members of Muntu Dance Theater of Chicago.

Glossary of Terms

Aganju (ah-gan-joo) Orisha of volcanos.

Agogo (a-go-go)

A single or a multiple bell now used throughout the world but with origins in traditional Yoruba and Edo music. Also samba music.

Akan (ah-con)

Akan religion is referred to as Akom from the Twi word akom, meaning "prophecy."

Alkebulan (al-ku-boo-lan)

The ancient name for Africa. It means "mother of mankind."

Babalawo (bahbah-lah-wo)

In Yoruba, Babalawo means father or master of mysticism. High priest in the religion called Ifa.

Bada (bah-dah)

A drum that looks like a jembe that has had its stem cut off and only the bowl part remained. The bada drummer would affix five to six seke sekes all around the drum. It was a lead drum and the jembes would accompany the bada back when it was popular.

Badafola (bah-dah-fola)

A bada drum player.

Balafon (bah-lah-fone)

A wooden version of the xylophone with gourds under the keys for the resonance of the sounds.

Balandugu (bah-lon-dugu)

A city in the Kankan Region of Eastern Guinea. The birthplace of the great Jembefola, Mamady Keita.

Bamako (bah-mah-co)

The capital of Mali, located on the Niger river. It's the largest city in the country and one of the largest in West Africa.

Bamana (bah-manah)

The largest ethnic group in Mali. They are part of the Manding culture.

Bembe (bim-bay)

Party for the amusement of the orishas belonging to the Yoruba Patheon gods.

Buba (boo-bah)

Buba is a Yoruba word that means blouse. The buba, iro and gele set is the traditional costume of the Yourubas in South Western Nigeria.

Chakaba (chah-kah-bah)

A West African secret society of stilt-walkers.

Clave (clah-vay)

A percussion instrument consisting of a pair of short, wooden sticks. They are essential in most Latin American music.

Conakry (cah-nakree)

The Capital of Guinea and its largest city.

Conga drums (cone-gah)

Drums staved like barrels and classified into three types: quinto, tres dos, and tumba.

Daba (dah-bah)

African dance and drum pants.

Dundunba (doon-doon-bah)

The dance of the strong men. The dundunba drum is the largest bass drum in the dundun drum set with the lowest bass tone.

D'Jembe (jim-bay)

The spelling the French gave to this drum. Is a rope-tuned, skin-covered, goblet drum played with bare hands, originally from West Africa.

Elegba (e-leg-ba)

One of the Yoruba deities. The guardian of the crossroads and the opener of the way.

Eleke (e-lay-kay)

Orisha beads worn by practitioners of the Yoruba's Ifa religion.

Fanga (Funga) (fun-gah)

A traditional welcome dance which originated in Sierra Leone and is believed to have been performed in America first by Asadata Dafora and his African dance group.

FESTAC '77

World Black and African Festival of Arts and Culture which was held in Nigeria between January 15 – February 12, 1977. African American drummers and dancers had a large presence there.

Fontomfrom (fone-tome-frum)

A type of talking peg drum of Ghana. It is used by drummers in the Ashanti royal family.

Gele (gay-lay)

A headwrap style known and used in and around Nigeria. It typically covers the woman's entire hair and her ears.

Gome (goo-may)

A solo and ensemble drum among the Ga and Ashanti of Ghana. It's a box drum with a skin played with your hands and feet.

Guinea (gi-nee)

A Country of West Africa, located on the Atlantic coast. It was the second African country to gain independence after Ghana. Known to be a true jembe drum country.

Hamanah (ha-mah-nuh)

A region in Guinea in between Kankan and Kouroussa. The birthplace of the dundunba dance (the dance of the strong men).

Ifa (e-fah)

A Yoruba religion and system of divination.

Ile (e-lay)

In Yoruba Ile means 'house.'

Itotele (Segundo) (e-to-tay-lay)

The middle bata drum called "father."

Iya (e-yah)

Yoruba word for Mother.

Iyawo (yah-woa)

The newly initiated in the Yoruba Ifa religion.

Jembe (jim-bay)

A Manding spelling for this drum. A rope-tuned, skin-covered, goblet drum played with bare hands, originally from West Africa.

Jembefola (jim-bey-folah)\

A jembe player. Also said to be the jembe player who can make the drum talk.

Jinn (jin)

A spirit able to appear in human and animal forms and to possess humans.

Kekere (kay-kay-ray)

The smallest size Nigerian ashiko drum called "child drum."

Kenkeni (keen-kinee)

The smallest size bass drum with the highest tone in the dundun drum set.

Kora (kaw-rah)

A stringed instrument used extensively in West Africa. A kora typically has 21 strings, which are played by plucking with the fingers. It combines features of the lute and harp.

Kouroussa (ka-roosah)

A town located in northeastern Guinea in the Kankan Region.

Kpanlogo (pan-lo-go)

A recreation dance and music form originating in Accra, Ghana. The drum is a type of barrel drum and is usually played with two hands. The drum originates with the Ga people of the Greater Accra Region in Ghana.

Kuna (coo-nah)

Wood from the kuna tree that grows in Mali and Guinea. The bada drum was made from kuna wood.

Kutiro (koo-teero)

A drum from the Manding of the Gambia, Guinea Bissau, and Senegal. Kutiro is played with the hand and stick.

Lamban (lom-bah)

A traditional dance of the Manding people of West Africa of the Jeli (griots or storyteller).

Lenke (lin-kay)

Wood from the lenke tree said to have been the original wood that the Nummu used to make jembe drums. Lenke was the most valuable wood for drum making because of its spiritual qualities.

Lukumi (loo-kuh-me)

The Spanish version of the Yoruba's Ifa religion. Practiced in the Caribbean, Latin and South America.

Malinke (muh-leen-kay)

The most widespread language of the Manding people.

Manding (man-deeng)

Another term for Mende. The ethnic group of people indigenous to the countries Sierra Leone, Guinea Bissau, Guinea, Senegal, Gambia, Ivory Coast, Mali.

Mane (mah-nay)

A town located in northeastern Guinea. Birthplace of the great Jembefola, Famoudou Konate.

Mendiani (mon-jon-nee)

A rhythm and a dance for the virgins, the young girls from age six to thirteen.

Ngoni (in-gonee)

A traditional African string instrument which looks similar to a banjo.

No Holes System

A system of tuning the jembe, dundun and ashiko without making holes in the skin and either tacking the skin on the wood or sewing it on. The no holes system used metal rings and strong rope to hold the tune in place instead of needing heat to raise the pitch of the skin.

Nummu (noo-moo)

Blacksmiths in West Africa known to be associated with the origin of jembe making. Responsible for making masks, circumcisions and excisions, hunting and building tools.

Nyama (ny-yamuh)

The Manding force in nature present in rocks, trees, people and animals that inhabit the Earth.

Obatala (o-bah-tala)

The king of the white cloth and the eldest of all orishas. Seen as the quintessential father figure.

Ocha (oh-chah)

The initiation as a full-fledged Priest or Priestess in the Ifa religion.

Ochoosi (oh-cho-see)

A skilled, stealthy hunter orisha who upholds the highest ethical standards and always hit the mark with his arrow.

Odu (oh-doo)

A acred information and secrets of the Ifa religion. Odu contains the knowledge and wisdom that helps realign our ori.

Ogun (oh-goon)

The orisha of iron, tools, and weapons. He is a fierce warrior and protective father.

Okonkolo (oh-cone-ko-low)

The okonkolo, the smallest bata drum called "baby." Traditionally serves as timekeeper.

Omele (O-me-lay)

The middle size Nigerian ashiko drum called "father drum."

Omile (Iya) (oh-mee-lay)

The largest bata drum called "mother drum."

Oro (oh-row)

Usually associated with songs and chants to orishas at bembes in the Yoruba religion Ifa.

Osun (oh-soon)

The warrior orisha who protects the ori (head) of the practitioner.

Oyugbona (oh-yuge-bonah)

Within the Yoruba's Ifa religion, the function of the Oyugbona is to be the second godmother at the initiation of the Iyawo.

Padrino (pah-dree-no)

Godfather in Spanish.

Pandeiro (pan-deh-ro)

A type of hand frame drum popular in Brazil to the point that it has been described as the unofficial instrument of that nation.

Patakato (puh-taka-to)

A rhythm that African American drummers, Chief Bey, Montego Joe and Taiwo DuVall created in the late 1950s.

Quinto (keen-toe)

The lead and highest pitch conga drum.

Sabar (sah-bar)

Sabar is a traditional drum from Senegal that is also played in the Gambia. The drum is generally played with one hand and one stick.

Sangban (sahng-bah)

The middle size bass drum in the dundun drum set with a higher tone than the dundunba.

Santeria (san-tuh-rea)

A religion practiced, originally in Cuba in which Yoruba deities are identified with Roman Catholic saints.

Santeros (son-teros)

A priest of Santeria.

Seke Sekes (shay-kay shay-kays)

Metal accessories with holes around the edges for little rings. The rings rattle against the metal when the drum is played. Typically, jembe players put 2-4 of these seke sekes around the head of the drum.

Shango (shon-go)

One of the most popular orishas and is the king of the religion on earth. Shango is the orisha of drumming, dancing, thunder, and fire.

Shekere (shay-kuh-ray)

The shekere is a West African percussion instrument consisting of a dried gourd with beads or cowries woven into a net covering the gourd.

Siguiri (si-gi-ree)

A city in northeastern Guinea on the River Niger. Siguiri is the birthplace of the great Jembefola Ladji Camara and Fodeba Keita founding Artistic Director for Les Ballets Africains.

Sun Drummer

Harold "Atu" Murray started Sun Drummer. He was inspired by Marcus Garvey's One Nation One Aim concept. The name Sun Drummer meant one drummer under the sun.

Tambor (tom-bore)

Spanish word for drum.

Tumbao (toom-bah-oh)

A repetitive rhythm played on the conga drums.

UNESCO United Nations Educational, Scientific and Cultural Organization.

UNICEF United Nations Children's Fund. An agency of the United Nations responsible for providing humanitarian and developmental aid to children worldwide.

Walosodon (wah-lo-suh-done)

A dance from Mali about slavery.

Yemoja (yay-mo-jah)

The great orisha mother of fish. Known as the goddess of the ocean, the mother of all living things and the guardian of mothers and children.

Yoruba (yo-roo-ba)

Ethnic group of people mainly from Nigeria, Togo, Ghana, and Benin.

Acknowledgments

I want to thank The Most High for life and using me as a conduit to bring forth this project to readers.

Thanks to my ancestors for teaching me and guiding me when they were on the earth plane and from the ancestral realm.

To all those ancestors working for me to assist me in my victories:

My Grandmother, Jewel Jackson, for nurturing me and preparing me for parenthood and healing work. You taught me the meaning of unconditional love and the healing in a loving hug and smile.

My Grandfather, Leonard Jackson, for showing me how to enjoy and love music and the courage to perform.

My Uncle, Skip Jackson, for showing me the importance of fitness and magnetism. You are one of the original Mount Vernon, NY Legends.

My Grandmother, Dorothy Farr, for encouraging me to stay on my path and to be of service to humanity.

My Brotha, Chavez Jordan, for helping me dive deeper into my music. For encouraging me to bring my original music forward.

My Godfather, Baba Ed James ibaye, for giving me new perspectives on my music, performing, teaching, business management and my relationships.

All of my ancestors whose blood runs through my veins known and unknown who have shown up to assist me on my journey.

My Bey Nation:

My Wife and Queen, Franchone Bey, for supporting every aspect of this project including ideas that we used and ideas that we discarded. Thank you for your patience with the bright light and me typing in the middle of the night in the bedroom while you slept and needed to get up early for work.

My Queen, Iya Omi Tola Isis Bey, for lifting up me and my project and promoting it when it was still just a thought. Thank you for all of your prayers for my wellness and Oshun work to move this project to completion.

All of my eleven children, Niaimani, Nile, Khalfani, Rajuma, Kumani, Kayah, Oshanla, Makeda, Shola, Amun, and Nala Bey for your encouragement and giving me a purpose to push through the challenges of this project.

To my inner circle here on the earth plane:

My Mother, Deborah Calhoun, for training me to be prepared for all that life would throw at me. And when I wasn't prepared, you showed me how to formulate a plan to put my best foot forward.

My Father, Abishai Ben Reuben, who showed me how to be confident in my responsibility to the community as a drummer, healer and teacher. Thank you for teaching me the importance of obedience to spiritual matters in all aspects of my life.

My Father, John Calhoun, who showed me courage to stand up and be heard. To speak on truth to power.

My Aunt, Tanya Jackson-Smith for bringing me along with her to her African drum and dance troupe's rehearsals when I was a young boy; igniting that drummer spirit in me early. For raising my consciousness about Africa and my awareness as a young boy that I am an African.

My Aunt, Betsy Summers, for teaching me to be accepting of people of all walks of life.

My Aunt Cynthia for your holistic support of me. . . spirit, mind and body. Thank you for our marathon talks about this project and your encouragement.

My Cousin and Madrina, Iya Yvonne Dickerson, for encouraging me and working for me spiritually around the clock.

My Cousin and Editor, Tareka Allyn Verbal, for always pushing me towards higher heights and refinement since we were teenagers.

My Cousin, Cory Scott, for your encouragement and uplifting conversations about this project.

My Brotha, Aqeel Qadree, for bringing your unconditional love and wisdom always at the right time.

My Brotha, Luis "Jafiyah" Clavell, for your research assistance and support.

To Dr. Ptah Shabazz for the inspiration. Good Looking out Roots.

To Kimberly Wood for your thorough read, feedback and encouragement.

To Erika Szabo for your priceless self publishing guidance and services.

To Kim and Mark Tsocanos for your support of me, this project, and my mission.

To all of my Aunts, Uncles, Brothers, Sisters, Cousins, Elders and extended family for all of your support and encouragement of this project.

Notes

CHAPTER 2

1.Polak, R. (2019). Jembe music.

2.Mamady Keita: A Life for the Djembe-Traditional Rhythms of the Malinke. Uschi Billmeier

CHAPTER 3

1.The Politics of Representation and Transmission in the Globalization of Guinea's D'jembe, Vera H. Flag, University of Michigan, 2010

2.The Politics of Representation and Transmission in the Globalization of Guinea's D'jembe, Vera H. Flag, University of Michigan, 2010

3.Ministère, 1979, pp. 73-74)

4.Mamady Keita: A Life for the Djembe-Traditional Rhythms of the Malinke. Uschi Billmeier (Pgs 17-21;24)

5.quoted in Straker, 2009, p. 86

6.President Sekou Toure 1963: 261, n.d.: 87

7.Charry, Eric.

2000. Mande Music. Traditional and Modern Music of the Maninka and Mandinka of Western Africa. Chicago and London: University of Chicago Press.

8.In D. Horn, J. Shepherd, G. Kielich, & H. C. Feldman (Eds.) Bloomsbury encyclopedia of popular music of the world. Volume XII: Genres: Sub-Saharan Africa (pp. 315–319). London:Bloomsbury Academic.

9.Fodéba 1958: 164

10.Fodéba 1958: 166

11.The Politics of Representation and Transmission in the Globalization of Guinea's D'jembe, Vera H. Flag, University of Michigan, 2010.

12.The Black Tradition in American Dance pgs 105 In 1952

13.Chabasseur, 2008; Diawara, 2003

14.E. Chabasseur, 2008 online article

15.Mamady Keita interview by Mahiri Edwards Keita

CHAPTER 4

1.Mamady Keita: A Life for the Djembe-Traditional Rhythms of the Malinke. Uschi Billmeier

2.In D. Horn, J. Shepherd, G. Kielich, & H. C. Feldman (Eds.) Bloomsbury encyclopedia of popular music of the world. Volume XII: Genres: Sub-Saharan Africa (pp. 315–319). London: Bloomsbury Academic.

3.Sunkett, Mark. 1995

4.The Politics of Representation and Transmission in the Globalization of Guinea's D'jembe, Vera H. Flag, University of Michigan, 2010

5.In D. Horn, J. Shepherd, G. Kielich, & H. C. Feldman (Eds.) Bloomsbury encyclopedia of popular music of the world. Volume XII: Genres: Sub-Saharan Africa (pp. 315–319). London: Bloomsbury Academic.

6.Mamady Keita: A Life for the Djembe-Traditional Rhythms of the Malinke. Uschi Billmeier

CHAPTER 5

1.The Politics of Representation and Transmission in the Globalization of Guinea's D'jembe, Vera H. Flag, University of Michigan, 2010

2.Venial Sins: An Autobiography, Thomas J. DuVall 2014

3.NPR interview 2006 www.npr.org

4.Arthur Hall Interview at Dartmouth, Hanover, NH, ca. 1978. Produced by Amy Wilkinson, class of 1978 and Eddas Bennett, Class of 1979, in the Arthur Hall Collection.

5.Interview with Katherine Dunham, October 26, 1974 in East St. Louis, Illinois. interviewed by Gloria Van Scott at Southern Illinois University. Pacifica Radio Archives

6.Pgs 103, The Black Tradition in American Dance, Richard A. Long

7. Pg 75, The Black Tradition in American Dance, Richard A. Long

8. Daniel Webster, Philadelphia Inquirer, 1968

9. Ile Ife Films as the source of this interview

10. Ile Ife Interview

11. Ile Ife Interview

12. Jason Gross interview for Perfect Sound Forever 2000

13. Thomas "Taiwo" DuVall Venial Sins: An Autobiography Thomas J. DuVall Pages 352-356; 367-373

14. Sherrod, 1997, p. 304

15. Barber, 1984, p. 50

16. Personal interview with Chief Bey, Sherrod, 1997, p. 312

17. Barber, 1984; Creque-Harris, 1991; Sherrod, 1997

18. Dancing Many Drums: Excavations in African American Dance Thomas F. DeFrantz Pg148

CHAPTER 6

1. Miles Davis, on seeing Les Ballets Africains in New York City, 1959 or 1960 (Davis & Troupe, 1989, pp. 225-226)

2. Angela Watson interview (2008)

3. Charry 2000: 252 fn, 15

CHAPTER 7

1. Thomas "Taiwo" DuVall Venial Sins: An Autobiography Thomas J. DuVall Pages 352-356; 367-373

2. Olatunji 2005: 157

CHAPTER 8

1. Jason Gross interview for Perfect Sound Forever 2000

CHAPTER 10

1. The Politics of Representation and Transmission in the Globalization of Guinea's D'jembe, Vera H. Flag, University of Michigan, 2010

2.Jason Gross interview for Perfect Sound Forever 2000

CHAPTER 11

1.Ile Ife Films interview

CHAPTER 12

1.Joyeux 1924:203

2.ERMP interview with Dr. Chuck Davis. 2004.

3.Ile Ife Films interview

4.Arthur Hall Interview at Dartmouth, Hanover, NH, ca. 1978. Produced by Amy Wilkinson, class of 1978 and Eddas Bennett, Class of 1979, in the Arthur Hall Collection.

CHAPTER 13

1.Ile Ife Films interview

2.Interview with Elizabeth Sayre, Philadelphia Folklore Project files. 2000

3.Arthur Hall Interview at Dartmouth, Hanover, NH, ca. 1978. Produced by Amy Wilkinson, class of 1978 and Eddas Bennett, Class of 1979, in the Arthur Hall Collection.

4.Enimil Ashon, The Weekly Spectator, Accra, Ghana, 1/12/91

CHAPTER 16

1.Dancing Many Drums: Excavations in African American Dance Thomas F. DeFrantz Pg150

About The Author

Kojo Bey is a father of eleven, a grandfather, a husband, a son, a brother, an uncle, a cousin, a godfather, a teacher, philanthropist, humanitarian, healer, spiritual life coach, and a student of the jembe. Kojo was introduced to the African drum and dance world as a young child by attending his Aunt's and Father's rehearsals with Akosua Dance and Drum Troupe in Mount Vernon, New York. These encounters sparked a flame for the drum inside of Kojo that would eventually blaze into a lifestyle while attending college in Nevada. Kojo co-founded Nevada's first African performing group, CODAME (Children of the Diaspora African Music Ensemble); co-founded SOUNDS OF AFRIKA African Drum and Dance Troupe (based in the New York Tri-state area); and founded Drums 4 Life (based in Charlotte, North Carolina). Mr. Bey established African drum and dance programs in Accompong Town, a maroon community on the island of Jamaica and in Brenu Akyinim, Ghana. Kojo has fulfilled African drum and dance contracts for various Fortune 500 companies, community-based organizations, and countless schools and universities over the past thirty years. Kojo built, owns, and manages a healing retreat property called Ocean Breeze in Ghana, West Africa. His vision is to host service trips, cultural tours, African drum and dance retreats, and healing retreats at Ocean Breeze on an ongoing basis.